This is a rip-roaring existential picture of the art world that illuminates the energy and vision you brought to the art world.

—Lowery Sims, Former curator at
Metropolitan Museum, New York; former director
Studio Museum of Harlem, and Black Art expert

The Blond with the Balls is a searing and scintillating look into the gritty underbelly of the New York City art scene told by a trailblazer who lived through it all.

—Jonathan Vigliotti, CBS News reporter and
environmental editor, author of *Before It's Gone*,
to be published by Simon & Schuster

A riveting, fascinating, birds eye view of the New York art world from a woman in a what was a man's world.

—Mark Borghi, Director of Gallery in
East Hampton and New York City

The Blonde with the Balls is a terrifically entertaining romp through the art world told as only Hamilton could. Over her long career, she has encountered many characters and experienced several notorious scandals firsthand. Hamilton provides a unique opportunity to go behind the headlines to understand the machinations of the art world. After reading this account, one will come away entertained and better informed.

—Jim Kelly, James Kelly Contemporary,
Art Advisor Los Angeles

Not only did parts take me back to my, our, youth, but I also discovered other aspects of Patricia's personal and professional lives I was not aware of. It is written in a nice, chatty, not boring, indeed entertaining, way which is what we like. Furthermore, she documents a whole side and time of the art world that is at risk to be forgotten, and that is really important. Patricia writes with directness and candor.
—J. Patrice Marandel, former European Curator
at LA County Museum

The BLONDE with the BALLS

AN INSIDER'S VIEW OF THE ART WORLD

PATRICIA HAMILTON

ART WORLD PRESS

Paperback ISBN: 979-8-9900848-1-0
Hardcover ISBN: 979-8-9900848-0-3
Ebook ISBN: 979-8-9900848-2-7

Cover and interior design by Jess LaGreca, Mayfly Design

Cover sculpture credit:
RT Livingston and Nancy Mitchell
Brass Ball Jar. 1991
The Sprockets
5" x 3" x 3"

Library of Congress Catalog Number: 2024902831
First Printing: 2024
Printed in the United States of America

Contents

CHAPTER 1

Chutzpah!

What leads somebody to dive from whatever she thought possible and plunge headfirst into a scene that becomes the center of her life? A scene with as many characters, twists, and unique situations as the different ways one can create a work of art? A scene that fixes itself to your heart and soul—and carries you away for the next 50 years, and counting?

Good question. And I found out early. Right out of college after getting my Master's degree in art history, and after short-term jobs as assistant to the curator at the Whitney Museum and Senior Editor of *Art in America,* I plunged into a project seemingly well above my head: curating "Ten Americans: Masters of Watercolor," an exhibit of the greatest watercolorists in the land.

Not only that, but I curated it in *New York,* the heart and lungs of the art world. The time was heady: the New York art scene was beginning to bust open again after a respite following the abstract expressionism, op art, and Warhol-fueled explosion of the 1960s.

There I was, just 23 years old, standing next to well-known New York art dealer Andrew Crispo as his curator of exhibitions. My job? To present and celebrate the works of Milton Avery, Charles Burchfield, Charles Demuth, Arthur Dove, Winslow Homer, Edward Hopper, John Marin, Maurice Prendergast, John Singer Sargent, and Andrew Wyeth. They were the acknowledged and revered

20th-century masters of watercolor—a medium I always admired. A pretty daunting task, for sure. I needed to look at the watercolors in every major museum collection, then track down and select ten from each of these masters.

My brain tried to bring me back to my rational senses: *Shit, this is the job you want me to do? Really? This is more a job for an experienced curator, like Bernice Rose at the Museum of Modern Art, who's written books on works on paper. Why are you giving it to me?* Why? Because he believed, from my work at the Whitney and my attention to detail and commitment to excellence, that I would get the job done.

That didn't diminish the fact that I was as scared as I was excited.

Andrew wanted me to utilize my existing contacts, which he knew were extensive for such a young art aficionado, to borrow works from the finest museums and private collections. He told me he would offer ten watercolors in the show for sale. This plan was not only incredibly ambitious, but also unheard of: for starters, exhibitions of this kind are very expensive. The shipping and insurance alone cost a fortune. Also, he wanted me to produce an expensive catalogue for an exhibit that, we both knew, held the potential of being a most memorable show.

Did I feel like my existing experience and credentials from the Whitney and *Art in America* were enough? Probably not, but I certainly wasn't going to let Andrew or anyone else know. What I did know is I possessed something deep inside that responded whenever someone challenged me: a relentless drive to get the job done, get it done right, and make it an event people would not soon forget. I *had to succeed.* I could not fail. The size and scope of what Crispo wanted me to do was, well, massive. But massive challenges fueled and drove me, made me feel like everything I was doing was worthwhile.

I was ready to take it on—and by doing so, again send a strong message to my detractors—my family members.

Most of us grew up with a basic level of familiarity in watercolor, since it was featured in school art history books and taught in art classes. Watercolor grasps the essential rhythm and movement of a work of art, but it is loose in construction and pared down to the essentials. The colors bleed one to another. When applied on paper, no mistakes are possible, otherwise the work of art can be ruined. And usually is.

Now, I was dealing with true masters, some of the greatest painters in American history. As my search got underway, my art history expertise kicked in and I thought deeply of the watercolorists I would be curating. I considered how much they brought to the art world, how much joy their works brought to the people who bought and hung them at home, and also how much of an impact they made to the craft itself. I went even further, imagining (or reading) how much the artists themselves enjoyed working with watercolor, sometimes detouring from the medium that made them famous (oils, for example) to paint in the medium they personally preferred. Think of how Dr. Seuss illustrated those beautiful children's books we all grew up on—yet, in his private time, Theodore Geisel sat in his La Jolla, California studio and created intricate, complex, dark, deep and mysterious illustrations and paintings, the subject matter far too mature for schoolkids. Only after he died did the family estate release them to the world.

Some of the people we were featuring painted watercolors for the same reason: as a release, to *have fun* painting in a medium they truly loved.

Winslow Homer, a great American artist from the late 19th century, made glorious watercolors. While his oils are probably his most famous paintings, like "Breezing Up The Wind," scholars felt his greatest gift and talent was in watercolor, not oil. How about John Singer Sargent? The creator of "The Portrait of Madame X," "Claude Monet Painting by the Edge of a Wood" and others thought watercolors were a relief from all of the formal portraits he was commissioned to paint. He carried his watercolors with him at times and would stop and paint spontaneously. It was both his joy and his release.

The watercolorists offered tremendous variety, which afforded me the opportunity to present not only ten historical greats, but also to show the many ways in which you could move and shape scenes, people and images. I loved post-Impressionist Maurice Prendergast, who made very personal paintings with such small brushstrokes they seemed like tapestries. His paintings of scenes in Venice showed both his intricacy and his vision to capture a wide sweep of public life. Arthur Dove, creator of works like "Continuity," "Gale" and "Green," simplified and eliminated landscapes in his work, reducing Impressionism to its bare essentials. Charles Demuth made the most elegant watercolors with eggshell colors that blended one with the next, in paintings like "Twelve Nude Boys at the Beach" and "Two Women Acrobats." And who could ever resist the fantastical, imaginative and whimsical watercolors of Charles Burchfield once they saw them? You couldn't help but feel better about the world and being in nature when viewing pieces "A Walk Through the Oaks" and "Sunrise and Rain."

Then there was visual realist Andrew Wyeth, still very much alive in 1973 and one of the most familiar names to art world patrons and non-patrons alike, owing to works like "Christina's World," which has been all but immortalized in history books. His work was not the strongest among this pantheon of watercolor giants, not by a good stretch to be honest, but his name certainly caught the eye of the press and patrons.

I was inspired, motivated and ready to put on a show that would keep the papers and patrons talking for awhile. I looked over the works of all the artists with white gloves, salivating the whole time. I wanted to expand the exhibit and include them all.

However, it didn't take long to run into challenges, which often seemed to present more like hard brick walls.

After one or two visits to local New York museums, it became apparent that no museum would lend out works for a gallery exhibition—unless it was a benefit event. Andrew Crispo never intended that. I had never curated a benefit, but my job was to do whatever was necessary to make this exhibit happen, and for it to be great. It quickly became my job to find a charity, and I had an idea of just where to turn.

On an ABC News segment, lead investigative reporter Geraldo Rivera (remember Geraldo back when he was a true journalist?) exposed the notorious Willowbrook State School for the mentally ill on Staten Island as the heinous, filthy place it was, filled with patients who were often abused, terribly abused. Geraldo's expose ran for several nights on the evening news, during which he described the place as "a leper colony." How did he come across such startling discoveries at a place that kept the public far from the truth? Well, once upon a time, he was an incredible investigative reporter. Investigative reporters are pit bulls who do not release their jaws until they get what they're looking for. In his case, he took pretty extreme measures: he stole a key and broke into Willowbrook.

I learned that after the segments aired, Geraldo formed a charity called One to One Foundation that set up living arrangements for housed youths. I suggested to Andrew that it would be a great charity for us to select as the beneficiary for the watercolor exhibition. Andrew agreed wholeheartedly, and even gave the charity and its workers a temporary office space.

Now I was off and running. This gave me the cachet I needed to borrow from the museums and galleries. I embarked on separate adventures to collect the works of each of the ten featured artists, Andrew Wyeth being one of them.

Crispo gave me a quick assist, suggesting I have lunch with Andrew Wyeth's son, Nicholas Wyeth. Nicholas worked for the

CoeKerr Gallery and became my direct link to borrow some of his father's works. Unfortunately, he could only give me two watercolors, but he recommended I contact Joseph E. Levine, the celebrated movie mogul and producer of *The Graduate, The Producers* and *A Bridge Too Far,* among hundreds of credits. Apparently, Levine kept a personal collection of Wyeth watercolors that Andrew Wyeth described as 'fabulous." As I learned, this was a fairly common set of events: make an initial contact close to the artist, then invariably, you find out which museums or galleries are willing to lend, and who is holding the best work privately.

That's when the adventure really begins—and I love a good art-related adventure.

By the time I made the appointment with Levine, who had an office on 7th Avenue, I had secured loans of watercolor pieces from the Metropolitan, Brooklyn, and Whitney museums. It was already shaping up to be a prestigious show.

When I met Levine, the first thing that caught my eye was not the Wyeth watercolors I wanted to see, but the producer's physical appearance. For some reason, I imagined him as a strapping, fit Hollywood type, like a Golden Age movie star or something. You know, Errol Flynn, Clark Gable, a young Marlon Brando—how surprised was I to see before me a short man, overweight and chain-smoking cigars, without extending me the courtesy of asking if I minded cigar smoke. Sure enough, his attitude matched this crass introduction. After I told him about our show, I mentioned how grateful we'd be if he would agree to lend us some watercolors from his collection.

He gave me a hard stare while sizing me up and down like a piece of sliced meat. "Why would I lend my fabulous Wyeth watercolors to a punk kid like you? Who do you think you are?" he asked. I did look like a teenager, and that's what this misogynist saw—a bratty teenager who pretended to know something about art. Not an art history expert with far more experience in her field at 23 than he'd gathered at that early stage of his own life.

Instantly flush with fury at this personal put-down, I stuffed my shock and put on my best museum-curatorial face. "Look, Mr. Levine, I'm older than I look. And this is going to be a highly publicized and prestigious show."

One would think that would assuage his concerns. *No*—he continued to insult me. I realized that within twenty minutes, he would not be furnishing me with the watercolors.

I began to make my way to the door, and then turned around. "Fine, Mr. Levine. Don't lend. I don't need your work. Why Andrew Wyeth is in the show in the first place, I don't know; Andrew Crispo insisted. What I can tell you is that Wyeth is, by far, the weakest artist in the show." He'd roused my fire and anger, and I was going to send some anger and fire back and make him regret it. "What I now plan on doing is borrowing the shittiest watercolors I can find and hang them next to John Singer Sargent's from The Met, glorious Prendergast and Hoppers from the Whitney Museum, and incredible Demuths from the Columbus Museum. The Wyeths will pale in comparison."

I continued staring into his eyes, the way I like communicating with people: face to face, eye to eye. Only my eyes were glowing with a hard-focused anger; he had really pissed me off. I wasn't done. "And what, pray tell, do you think will happen to the value of your Wyeth watercolors when I do that? When I make them afterthoughts in this exhibition? Their value will sink like a stone."

He looked at me incredulously, like the punk kid who trespassed in his office. Finally, I reached the door. "Goodbye, Mr. Levine. It was a pleasure to meet you," I said.

I walked quickly outside and burst into tears, so upset with Levine's barrage of insults and my inability to convince him to lend us the Wyeth watercolors. I quickly jumped into a cab and returned to the Crispo Gallery on 57th Street.

When I got there, Andrew was falling off the couch, laughing. "What's so funny?" I asked, my face probably a mess from wiping off tears. "Did I miss a joke or something?" I was in no mood for this after dealing with Levine.

"Well . . ." Andrew tried hard to contain his laughter long enough to speak. "As soon as you left, Joe Levine called and asked me, 'Andrew, who's the blonde with the balls?"

That brought a smile to my face. So did the next thing Andrew Crispo told me: Levine was suddenly willing to lend us anything we wanted. He knew I was right about the perceived value of his Wyeths if I made them an afterthought, and he also knew I wasn't playing around.

And wouldn't you know? When the exhibit opened, a sterling review came out in the most important of places, the Sunday edition of the *New York Times*. In the lead paragraph, the writer praised the Wyeth watercolors owned by Levine, also stating that it was one of many reasons to see the show. Wyeth might not be the best technically or even conceptually among the ten watercolorists we exhibited, but his name recognition was instant for *Time* readers.

Twenty-five years later, in 1998, I met Andrew Wyeth (who died a decade after that) and purchased some watercolors. We had time to talk, and I couldn't resist telling him the story about my visit to Levine's office.

He burst out laughing. "Patricia, let me get this straight. You were going to ruin my watercolor market with one show on 57th Street?"

A sheepish grin crawled across my face. "Well, I was furious and felt insulted, and said the first thing that came out of my mouth."

Wyeth smiled and then delivered the *coup de grace*. "Well, if it's any consolation, Joe Levine went bankrupt at the end of his life and ended up selling all of those watercolors back to me at far below market value."

It served Levine right. The exhibit served me right, further launching my name and reputation within a hard, male-dominated art world where my toughness, moxie, ability to get things done, and deep love of art and art history mattered every day, where I operated as the blonde with the balls.

How did I get to be this way? Well, like many other stories of how we become the people we are today, it began in my childhood home—and a family that never considered my dreams the least bit valuable. Just as they felt about me.

CHAPTER 2

Where It All Began

A 23-year-old woman, just getting into her career, finds the balls to stand up to a movie mogul. A natural follow-up question might spring from that: where did the toughness, moxie, and directness come from? And the strength to get to where I was trying to go despite the attempts of some to hold me back?

Could it be that Mr. Levine's abusive behavior and attempts to disregard me as an up-and-coming player in the New York art community, or as a serious woman at all, reminded me of home, and the things my father said to me every day he was alive?

Why, yes it did.

I think the first part of my trouble at home came from my position in the pecking order. I was the fifth of six children of William and Lillian Hamilton, who made our family home in Drexel Hill, Pennsylvania, a middle-class suburb of Philadelphia. My father was the youngest of 13 children (eight of whom died in childbirth). By all accounts, he was a bit of a spoiled brat.

My father's father was a doctor and so incredibly young-looking that when he went around to treat people for the Spanish influenza pandemic in 1918, no one believed he was a doctor. He was sober and never took a drink until his wife, my grandmother, died of breast cancer. My father was only 13. The grief and stress of being a widower instantly turned him into an alcoholic, planting the seed of a very big problem in my family. My parents lived with him at the beginning of their marriage, and while my father was in the Navy. My mother was afraid of him in his drunken rages.

My mother, Lillian, was the oldest of two daughters born to William and Helen Smith, also of Philadelphia. Her father was a pharmaceutical clerk who died of the Spanish Flu, the most fatal pandemic in U.S. history until COVID-19 came along. My mother was only three. Her mother, just 19 at the time and caring for two toddlers, soon married Charles Sloan, the first man who proposed. Charles was a parole officer but also a mean, nasty alcoholic.

Thanks to my grandfather's way of dealing with the horrible tragedy of losing his wife, the roots of alcoholism ran deep in my DNA before I was born. It was a most unwelcome part of home life.

My mother's escape from the abuses of her alcoholic stepfather came in the form of meeting my father, a pre-med student at the University of Pennsylvania on his way to becoming a pediatrician. Lillian saw William as her ticket out of her chaotic house and into the charmed upscale life of a doctor's wife. Little did she know that it would become no escape at all, but instead, a place where her own worst behaviors and tendencies would fester, grow, and play out in very cold ways. Especially against me.

When I came along, I was their fifth child in a seven-year span. They were tired of having kids, which did not work out to my advantage. However, that is not what lay behind their hatred of me. In my father's case, I reminded him of his older sister. She was a big, buxom blonde who was interested in art and music and didn't put up with any of his shit. How interesting that I was somewhat of a reflection of her, though I am smaller in stature. In his eyes, she'd returned to life as his daughter to stand up to him all over again.

My mother's resentment stemmed from something that normal, well-adjusted, loving, and caring parents *wish* for their children: I was a happy kid. However, she suffered from depression and did not seek help. While I had my dolls, toy guns, and imagination, surrounded by a bubble of constant happiness, she had her moods, tirades, and periods of sheer darkness. I protected my happiness for all it was worth. I would not allow her to manipulate me.

When it comes right down to it, my father was a raging and embarrassing abusive alcoholic. He told me I was fat, ugly, and stupid nearly every day he was alive. Not to be outdone, my mother was a cold bitch, completely incapable of showing love to most of her children. Most of all, me. Their treatment and constant barrage of negative, demoralizing messages left me with no choice but to batten down my heart and mind, try to survive the household, and forge my own path from my earliest years. My only escape would be to create a truly independent life, get out in the world, and fight like hell to succeed in a job or career that impassioned me. As childhood went on, it built within me a fierce competitiveness and a hunger to always do better than the person next to me. Even as a kid, I knew that my only chance was to work harder than everyone else, too. *If I have to make it on my own, I'm going to have to be the best.*

My first great outlet was swimming. Though my parents belonged to Aronimink Swim Club in Drexel Hill, and took all of us there for hours at a time, they were not the ones who recognized me as a natural in the water. They didn't recognize anything good in me, not then, and not later. When I was six, I was floating in the pool when one of my father's patients, Mr. Hornsmith, noticed me. He suggested I become a competitive swimmer. I took his advice and convinced my parents to let me enter the six-and-under races at the club. When the big day came, I moved from race to race, loving every bit of the thrill of competition and winning everything.

Mr. Hornsmith then suggested that I join the prestigious Vesper Swim Club, a competitive team that swam all winter. The Vesper Swim Club was owned by the famous Kelly family of Philadelphia, among the city's leading construction czars who counted among their illustrious group someone you may have heard about and seen on AMC or, if you're old enough, on the big screen: Grace Kelly, the glamorous young Hollywood actress who later became Princess Grace of Monaco. Grace, a prodigy in her own right, came from some very gifted and hard-working people. Her father, John Kelly Sr., was a four-time Olympic rowing gold medalist, the most decorated rower in U.S. Olympic history. The Vesper Swim Club was run by Mary Kelly, who was married to John's son and Grace's older brother, Jack, himself possessor of a highly impressive Olympic pedigree: four Olympics, a medalist, and later, President of the U.S. Olympic Committee.

Right from the beginning, my lucky stars were connecting me with the best of the best at what they did. It began with sports, and swimming in particular.

Mary was looking for one kind of swimmer above all: the type who wanted to be as good as they could possibly be. She was very serious about extending the family reputation outward and training future Olympic champions. Beginning at age seven, I swam six hours a day. My daily schedule looked more like a college athlete's than a second-grader's: get up in the wee hours for morning practice. Attend school all day. Back to swim practice afterward. Plus, we didn't practice in a community pool or even local high school facilities, but at the *University of Pennsylvania*. That made a big impression on a precocious little girl. It also meant a lot of driving for my parents, who ushered me back and forth the 45 minutes from Drexel Hill to the University of Pennsylvania pool. Soon, they got involved in carpooling, so that the drive was not too much.

My specialty was the breaststroke, one of the most disciplined strokes, and one of the toughest to master because of the precise coordination between two challenging and technical movements—bringing the arms together and out and timing it to the so-called "frog kick," where you pull your legs up, and then shoot them out sideways, like a frog skittering on the surface of a lake. The stroke felt natural to me, so I picked up the technique, learned from my mistakes, and made the adjustments quickly when Mary pointed them out. For example, if your frog kick fluttered above the water, you were disqualified; the breaststroke kick is a pure underwater movement. You would also be disqualified if your head remained completely under the water after popping up from the starting blocks. During turns, if you didn't hit the wall with the hands completely parallel, you were DQ'ed as well.

By the age of 10, I was the fastest age-group breaststroker in the country. I went all the way, winning the Junior Olympics, which made me feel pretty damn confident. Then Mary Kelly introduced me to the whip kick, which I really liked. By whipping my leg out quickly after curling it back to initiate the frog kick, rather than the fluid, measured way I was kicking, I found that I accelerated on every completed stroke. It made me faster. The only problem is that it applied direct torque and pressure to the anterior cruciate ligament in the knee. No one wanted the dreaded ACL tear. Not in those years. An ACL tear could potentially be a long-term crippling injury. To fix it, you needed to undergo a brutal surgery. We were decades away from the advanced sports medicine that sends professional athletes back into competition as soon as nine months after surgery today. Some make it back even faster. Then? It took two years, if you were lucky. Even then, your mobility was not quite the same.

Not surprisingly, because of Mary's influence on the national level, the whip kick caught fire in swimming clubs from coast to coast. Sure enough, reports poured in of numerous swimmers, including some of our own, tearing their ACLs. While I never suffered a full tear, my knees were impacted, too, which I later found out while skiing and playing tennis.

Within a year, the heralded "whip" kick was outlawed for that very reason.

I swam competitively for ten years, logging those six hours a day and building a lot of internal discipline, determination, and desire to succeed even further because of it. I was building the strength, focus, and willingness to do what it took to be the best, the very skills that would enable me to become fully independent from my unloving parents. By the time I was 17, though, I showed up at meets and realized I was looking up at all of my competitors. In competitive swimming, virtually all the women are 5-foot-8 and taller. Height matters in a sport where you can win or lose by your final extended stroke and lunge for the wall. The same was true in the 1960s. Every girl suddenly had six inches or more on me; a 5-foot-4 girl isn't going to beat someone who's 5-foot-10 at that level. When I started losing, I lost interest in the daily workouts.

I also discovered something else: boys and society. Suddenly, I wanted to get out of the swimming bubble and socialize.

I found high school really boring. What do you do if you're a top-level swimmer with interests that have nothing to do with the classes you're taking, as well as a very low impression of yourself outside the pool? The constant put-downs at home were defining my view of myself far more than winning swim meets. I felt totally unchallenged by the classes, and completely bored. Because of that, I did not do particularly well, which limited my college choices.

I thought of my few options. If I could get away to a college that offered classes in something I *was* growing interested in—art—then maybe, just maybe, I would become a better and more engaged student. However, my parents were not interested in seeing me improve my life because they didn't have a future for me. Worse, they didn't care. Even if they had, despite Dad being a pediatrician, they couldn't afford to send me away or pay for tuition. I had to live at home and commute locally to Temple University.

When I arrived at Temple, the swim coach knew of my competitive background and sent me notes, imploring me to join the team. However, I so badly *didn't* want to swim that I took the most final route possible to avoid it, trying out for the women's basketball team. I made the team as a guard, despite being so short. That is when I also learned to play tennis, the sport I would carry through my adult life. I continue playing consistently to this day, at least once per week. Later, I also returned to the pool and resumed swimming four times a week. It's really beneficial for my body and cardio, but I also have to admit, it's pretty boring for me. And I'm a lot slower than I used to be.

While winning races, working with the great Mary Kelly, and finding out about my capabilities and potential to excel in the swimming pool, I learned three things I carried forward into my career: leadership, a sense of competition, and playing by the rules.

My first experience as a swim leader came at age 19, during my first summer break from college. I was hired as a counselor and swim coach at Camp Watitoh, a Jewish camp in the Berkshires of central Massachusetts. I was the token "shiksa," and was also appointed to be the men's swim team coach.

When I met the boys, I took a look at their appearances and expensive swimwear, remembering how threadbare some of my much cheaper suits grew from all the competition. I realized I had never seen such a bunch of spoiled boys in my life. What does a new swim coach do with spoiled boys? I had an idea: I would push them really hard, which is what I did in workouts. My goal was for us to become the summer camp version of Mary Kelly's Vesper Swim Club, the best around.

One weekend, there was a competition among three camps, all boys-only. I arrived with my team in a white swimsuit and coaching gear. Before you knew it, about 1,000 eyes were upon me, because there wasn't another woman around. In a sign of things to come in the art world, it didn't take long for the one woman amongst boys and men to get into a spirited disagreement with a judge over fair play and the rules of competition. Mary Kelly had drilled into us how to win by the rules, it was deeply ingrained in me, and became an essential element of Patricia Hamilton's core belief system.

The dispute happened in a 12-and-under race. Our kid swam a beautiful, winning race, but he finished second. I knew the winner should be disqualified for a number of rules violations he made during the race. To me, the violations seemed clear as day. I would never protest a race result involving kids unless it was that clear. As a counselor, I would never grandstand. So much grandstanding goes on with parents and coaches today. In many ways, I believe it contributes to kids becoming adults without respect, manners, or any particular desire to succeed.

I walked up to the head judge and opened the conversation by getting right to the point. "The kid did nothing right and should be disqualified," I said.

"You're being too harsh," the judge told me. He also told me the boy couldn't wait to write to his parents about winning the race. That stopped me in mid-stride. What could I say to that?

I had a plan. Next up was a 10-and-under competition. I told the slowest of our two entries to abandon the prescribed race stroke, breaststroke, and swim freestyle instead. "When the race is over," I added, "you jump into my arms and say, 'I can't wait to write to my mother.'"

The kid won by swimming freestyle. Afterward, the head judge had the balls to come up to me and say, "Obviously he forgot what stroke to swim, and I will disqualify him."

"No, he didn't," I replied. "I told him to swim freestyle. And if you don't allow this, I will demand again that the 12-and-under winner be disqualified."

He shrugged. "Okay—but Olympic rules from here on out."

. . .

If you are told by your father that you are fat, ugly, and stupid every day, and this continual insult is reinforced by everyone in the family, you start to believe it and grow demoralized and devoid of self-esteem. Also, if your mother makes it clear she doesn't love you, it becomes tough to find love, or to even know what authentic love between two people looks like. My mother reinforced her feelings right to her last days, when she admitted, "We never loved you."

"You made that perfectly obvious," I replied.

Those were the last words she spoke to me.

Of her six children, she only truly loved two: my brother Rick and sister Susan. Rick reminded her of Dad when he was young, before alcohol pickled his brain and made his behavior unmanageable. She loved Susan because, like herself, Susan was smart and manipulative.

I was still under their thumb as my college days began, even though I paid my own tuition that first semester and every semester that followed. The spring before I enrolled, we learned that Temple University would become a state institution. With that new designation, the tuition dropped considerably and was closer to my affordability range. I wanted to get further from them, and into a more prestigious school one day. This was my one option, so I took it to begin the process of moving far away.

After I arrived at Temple, four things happened that completely changed my life and set me on the course to the independent woman I've been since. First, I really immersed myself in the art classes I was taking, and a love of art history formed deep in my mind and soul. Second, I discovered I was not stupid—quite the opposite. I began to re-evaluate and scrutinize my parents' horrid opinion of me. Third, I looked around and jumped right into the fires spreading across campus—the fires of Feminism, the Sixties Revolution, and Vietnam War protests. I became a Feminist and supported Eugene McCarthy, who was chosen as the 1968 Democratic presidential nominee after our world was shattered by the assassination of frontrunner and likely President Robert F. Kennedy (instead, we were saddled with Richard M. Nixon and Baby Boomers and the nation know how that went).

From that experience, I began standing up for myself, realizing that I was a survivor of a constantly abusive, toxic atmosphere at home. As everyone who knows me is well aware, I have never stopped standing up for myself since.

The final thing that happened was that I found a boyfriend. I began dating Terence McInerney, an art history major at Yale. Terry is one of the finest men I have ever known. I pursued a romantic relationship to find whatever that thing called 'love' was and to make up for all those years in the swimming bubble. We did all the things a boyfriend and girlfriend do together, including sex, but I noticed that as time went on, he seemed more and more uncomfortable with a romantic relationship. That's because, years later, Terry realized he felt uncomfortable because he was someone else deep inside. He was secretly gay.

Eventually, we shifted the nature of our relationship and remained the closest of friends and confidants. It hurt me deeply, but it was for the best.

Terry spurred my growing interest in art history, feeding my brain and soul with his treasure trove of knowledge. Because of Terry's obvious passion for art history, which informed and enlivened almost all of our conversations, I took an introductory art history course in my junior year. I loved it so much that I decided to pick it up as my second major. When I made this decision and started getting into the vast history of art and its influences in Europe and America, dating back to the great Renaissance masters, I felt like the prodigal kid who arrived home after a long trip in the desert. The feeling hit me deeply and centrally. I had found something that would define my professional life and, in many ways, me as well.

I came home, excited as could be, and told my family the great news. Well, let's just say their reaction was different than I hoped. It sucked. They didn't like my choice and immediately told me reasons why I wouldn't make it in life. My sister Susan stated, "The smartest people at the University of Pennsylvania major in art history. Who are you, Patricia, to think you can handle art history?" she asked, her voice dripping with hard, thick beads of condescension.

She was talking to the same sister she'd belittled much of her life, but now, she found out she was addressing someone else. I'd learned a few life skills to fend off my family's attacks and condescending comments. These included the first taste of my power and worthiness as a woman and human being, my fellow feminists at Temple, my love of this new major, and Terry's steady confidence in me to exceed anything my family had done. While Susan's comments hurt, they did not deter me.

Quite the opposite. I became further inspired and motivated to master art history. It felt really good to have enough confidence in myself and feel my strength enough to use their harsh attitude towards me as a motivator, and never buy again into their "you'll never amount to anything" mantra.

With each art history course, I loved the subject more. It just kept getting better and better. I knew that I had found my career choice. Realizing that a simple bachelor's degree might not get me into the world, I began to see myself occupying the New York art scene, and I decided to go to graduate school and earn a Master's in art history.

When I made this decision, I learned Rutgers University had just opened an art history graduate program. *Perfect.* Rutgers is in Northern New Jersey, so finally, I was able to leave home for more than just the summer. I lived in student housing and held two summer jobs as a lifeguard and bartender to pay for most of my expenses. My parents were supposed to help with tuition for my second semester, but predictably, they informed me they had no money. The truth was, they had no money *for me.* They thought my graduate studies were unnecessary, a waste of a young woman's time and resources. They decided they would rather help my brothers make it through college.

I was growing into a persistent woman. Persistence is a huge asset when things get particularly tough in life, and it is also necessary to achieve major goals. Their newly persistent daughter broached the subject one more time. I truly hoped my mother's basic sense of humanity would prevail, a bit of heart would rise up, and she would relent.

How wrong I was. "No," she said firmly. "I think you can live at home and take your bachelor's degree and substitute-teach at the local high school!"

That was the sum of my potential, in my parents' eyes. Not only were they miles behind where my head was, but I also realized they didn't even really know me anymore.

· · ·

New graduate programs take years to develop. The process typically involves developing and tinkering with the curriculum to see which courses are most valuable for one's career and the overall program. Of equal or greater importance is finding professors with the right combination of academic and professional or life-experience skills to deliver courses with the insights that send students on their way to successful lives. And make them *want* to succeed. Once the pieces are in place, the chemistry between faculty, institution, students, and the courses themselves needs to develop.

When I arrived at Rutgers, I quickly learned they had not yet ironed out the kinks. I took an early Italian Renaissance class taught by Rutgers University art historian and Giotto expert James Stubblebine, who lived with another art history professor on campus, the flamboyantly gay Martin Eidelberg, a Northern Renaissance scholar who collected ceramics and Tiffany glass. For Stubblebine's class, we wrote our first long essay, and then awaited our grades. I felt I nailed my essay, diving deep into the subject and writing both a strong thesis and conclusion. He generally gave all the students either a "Pass" or a "Fail."

However, he gave me a specific letter grade, a C. In grad school, a C might as well be an F. I promptly went to the head of the graduate department. "If my grade is a C," I asked, "can I please see what an A or a B looks like?"

I didn't get what I wanted. Apparently, Stubblebine had promised to bequeath his prestigious Art Nouveau collection, worth an untold small fortune, to the Rutgers Museum upon his passing. Because of that, the university did not want to rock the boat and cause a stink over his grading rules. Nothing would be done.

Sadly, I realized my days at Rutgers were over. Backbiting academia was not for me. I knew I would never pass my oral exams if Stubblebine or Eidelberg were on the committee. Even though I was offered a scholarship to continue to study for a PhD, I chose to leave. Stubblebine turned out to be quite a turncoat, a lot different than the prestigious professor I deeply hoped to learn from. He never left that Art Nouveau collection at Rutgers.

Despite the fact the graduate program consisted of 90 percent women, which *did not translate* to career opportunities in the art world at the time, Rutgers gave a true misogynist, Stubblebine, such tremendous power over students' lives. He wasn't the only one on the faculty. Gail Levin, who earned her PhD from Rutgers and became a distinguished early Modernist scholar and Edward Hopper expert, was in the middle of applying for the curator position of the Hopper Collection at the Whitney. Highly impressed with her, the Whitney team called her thesis advisor at Rutgers for a recommendation. Rather than recommend her, the advisor put himself forward for the position. Gail got the job, but she never forgot the slight. Rather than encouraging their graduates to pursue their dreams, those early Rutgers graduate program professors were jealous of our abilities and talents and undermined us.

Years later, James Stubblebine visited my gallery on 57th Street, undoubtedly to check out the success of his former student and take some credit for it. Within moments, I threw him out. His rejection of my potential still stung deeply.

. . .

After graduating from Rutgers, it was time to take my big leap into the New York art world. I got a summer internship at the Williams College Museum of Art and met Director George Heard Hamilton. We used to joke that I was his long-lost granddaughter, and I liked that suggestion of having a family member who actually gave a damn about what I did. A highly respected scholar, George wrote the voluminous *Pelican History of 20th Century Art* book. He turned out to be a great and powerful ally.

In the fall of 1971, armed with my master's degree and a brain flush with art history knowledge culled from classes and viewing countless works in museums and galleries, I traveled to New York City and started looking for work. My first stop was the Whitney Museum. I applied for an assistant position to Chief Curator Robert "Mac" Doty, along with at least 40 other women applicants who sat in the waiting room.

During my interview, Robert asked me, "Who recommended the Whitney Museum?"

"George Heard Hamilton," I said.

That was the right answer. Mac Doty had worked for Hamilton at Yale. He quickly called his former boss for a reference. "We'd like to offer you this job, and have you start immediately," Mac told me after the call.

Mac was eccentric and operated with a big heart. He was also willing to teach me the ropes, because he knew I was ambitious. There are few things more valuable to an enthusiastic young person entering their career than an experienced boss, or mentor, who starts teaching you from their direct experience. Besides shortcutting past years of their growing and learning pains (I would still experience plenty of my own, believe me!), he filled me with the foundational knowledge I would use for the next 50 years.

On my first day, renowned sculptor Alexander Calder was in town to celebrate "Calder's Circus," a piece the Whitney Museum owned and was installing. "Calder's Circus" pulled together wire figures of circus stars, clowns, and animals, a wonderful piece and a big attraction for the younger crowd. On a personal note, it was going to be such a thrill for me to meet my very first art star!

At 11 a.m., Calder arrived at the museum, drunk as a skunk, stinking of alcohol, and stumbling all over the place. I was shocked, horrified, and pulled back into the messy scenes I saw every night at home when Dad fired up his drinking. *Is this what renowned artists are like?* I wondered. *Do they get drunk in order to open up to what they are trying to get out of themselves? Or is this how they escape? Or both?*

Looking back on this, I realize I was receiving a very early introduction to the dark side of the lives of many artists. Right off the bat, I was experiencing and witnessing the things that would toughen me up for dealing with the world I loved.

Later that week, William de Kooning called Mac. Besides being a personal hero of mine, de Kooning was one of the greatest Abstract Expressionists of the 20th Century. He redefined abstraction and painted women, who he clearly loved, in an inventive and beautiful form. He was more than a great artist; he was a titan of the art world.

Mac handed me the phone without telling me who was on the other end. "Who is this?" I asked.

"Willem de Kooning."

I nearly fell out of my chair. "Willem de Kooning, *the* Willem de Kooning, one of the greatest painters of the 20th century?"

Willem started laughing. Later, when Willem relayed the story to Mac, he laughed uproariously as well.

I became good at many things, but no one has ever accused me of being a good secretary. From Day One, I was much more interested in chatting up the artists, learning how they regarded and perceived their own paintings, discussing their styles, viewing work, and installing exhibitions. However, my job description was to be Mac's secretary, a true entry-level position.

One day, Mac was looking for correspondence with a certain artist. For the life of him, he couldn't locate where I had filed it. "A for artist," I told him. Since 90 percent of our correspondence was with working 'A for Artists,' he suggested I might consider refining my filing system.

During my time at the Whitney, the most important one-person show Mac organized was the Lucas Samaras retrospective. It opened in November 1972 and ran for a few months. Lucas is a quirky, independent, diverse, and fabulous artist who made paintings, sculptures, boxes, and photographs and later worked with computers. Represented by Arnold Glimcher of The Pace Gallery, Lucas could be very charming, but also very mean. I later found this split personality a fairly common characteristic as I continued to work with artists, but I was baffled at first as to why that was so.

Lucas' show became a major event at the Whitney. It took up the entire third floor, which was given an entirely different look. We borrowed the famous Mirrored Room from the Albright-Knox Art Gallery in Buffalo, which is made entirely out of mirrors and is an artistic piece in itself. The installation included Lucas' plaster figurative work from the 1960s, along with a number of glorious pastels. In the mid-1960s, he started making signature boxes. They included knives, razor blades, and sexual objects. Other than Joseph Cornell, no one was making boxes, but Lucas stuck to it. Glimcher did fabulous installations and knew Lucas' work better than anyone. Glimcher worked with us day and night on the installation, and the show turned out to be one of the better exhibitions of that time period.

The mirrored room needed to be polished after it was put together. I was in the room, polishing away, when I met Robert Wilhite, a California artist who was working at the Pace Gallery. Our paths crossed many times in the future, and we became lifelong friends.

Major art installments and exhibitions receive catalogues that further illustrate and describe the exhibition. When done right, these catalogues are collectors' items and artistic pieces of their own. Late in our Lucas Samaras installation preparation process, while the catalogue was at press, we learned it needed some corrections. I did the best that I could, and then sent the corrections to Lucas.

The next morning, he called me up. "You stupid bitch," he growled. *What did I do?* I immediately hung up on him. He called right back. "We were disconnected," he said in that same angry, accusatory voice.

"No, we weren't," I responded. "Lucas, I hung up on you. Until you apologize, I won't be having a conversation." I hung up on him three more times before he finally apologized.

Standing nearby, Mac heard my entire side of the conversation and asked what happened. When I told him, he said, "Good for you, Patty. No one gets to behave like that."

From then on, Lucas was pretty much a pussycat. It was the first time I learned that fabulous artists could be rude pricks, just like everyone else. In this country, we show a tendency to anoint the best in career or sports fields and place them on pedestals, like Greek gods. It is a cultural matter, part of America's relationship with heroes, or perceived heroes. However, for some of us, we have to deal with the private side of these same people. If we continually hold them up on pedestals, it only reinforces their thinking that they are "above" us. Lucas Samaras reminded me that, yes, he's good, very good, *but so am I at what I do. We've been brought together to do something together.* His manners were abhorrent, but boy oh boy, was he a great artist.

I loved working at the Whitney. Every day, artists would call to talk to Mac and invite him to their studios. While I had them on the phone, usually for an extra minute so I could get some information and learn something, too, they would also tell me where all the hot openings were, as well as the good shows. I followed every lead and took every opportunity afforded me. I wanted to be the best, and being the best means making the most of those opportunities, getting out, networking and being a part of the scene. And working my ass off.

One day, an artist called and told me about an Alfred Leslie show at Allan Frumkin Gallery on 57th Street. It included a painting about the death of Frank O'Hara, a poet and curator at the Museum of Modern Art (MoMA). O'Hara, a darling of the New York art world, was killed in a freak accident, run over by a jeep late at night while sitting on a beach in the Hamptons. Leslie's painting, a close-up of the jeep running over O'Hara, was truly heart-stopping. What stopped my heart was the perspective. This painting came from O'Hara's viewpoint, lying on the beach, looking up at the oncoming jeep. It depicted the last thing O'Hara ever saw. It was shocking, new, and stunning.

I told Mac about the painting. Quickly, the Whitney bought it. That marked the first time they purchased a work off of my recommendation. It reinforced my confidence in my ability to recognize great art and to look for something edgier, with a different perspective than how others might paint the same subject.

We also launched the Whitney Independent Student Program. Fifteen students in art history and fifteen others in the studio were given access to the Whitney for study; the art historians were underwritten by the Helena Rubinstein Foundation. These very bright college students earned school credits, but more importantly, established connections that would last far beyond graduation day if they chose to pursue art as a career. They met with famous artists, critics, and curators. The students were impressive.

During my time at the Whitney, I met Paul Schimmel, Larry Shopmaker, and Jay Gorney in the art history department, and Julian Schnabel in the painting department. Schimmel, an intern in the education department, went on to become a major contemporary curator in Houston and Los Angeles. In my eyes, he is the best curator to come out of California. Larry Shopmaker worked for various dealers and eventually opened his own gallery with Betsy Senior in New York. Gorney later worked with me at the Andrew Crispo Gallery, then much more directly when I opened the Hamilton Gallery. We were all launching careers that would go somewhere.

Another of my tasks was working on the biennial exhibitions of all the *au courant* artists. Even though the exhibition was panned by the oft-fickle media, every artist in America wanted to be in the Whitney Biennial because of its prestigious reputation. To get me started on the project, Mac gave me a list of artists' studios he wanted to visit and a map of SoHo. My job? To set up appointments and make it into a tour of sorts. Good thing he gave me that map, because I have absolutely no sense of direction. He would have been lost in minutes with my "directions."

The installation of Whitney Biennials was quite the raucous scene, with artists vying for key spots. Through the work, I met quite a few of the most important artists, as well as their dealers.

Among them were Chuck Close, Tom Wesselmann, Bruce Nauman, Richard Pousette Dart, and Helen Frankenthaler, to name a few. What could be more exciting?

Well, how about *making more money?* Despite gaining the on-the-job education and experience that launched everything that followed, I was living on $7,000 a year, a pauper's wage almost anywhere. In New York? *Scary.* Further, there was no chance of rapid advancement within the museum. I learned of an unwritten rule: if you wanted a curatorial job, which I did, you had to leave the Whitney—and probably New York as well. In the early 1970s, women were not respected as curators, reps, gallery owners, or even artists. In the art world, their workplace was still considered the secretary's chair.

I had a far different idea of what women should be in the art world, what we could become, and why we belonged on even terms with men. It's time to forge ahead and make it happen.

CHAPTER 3

Art in America— and Bad Boyfriends

My next move in the New York art world wasn't the typical career leap for someone with museum experience and a growing interest in working directly with artists and exhibits and being part of the growing scene. Or maybe it was. Anything is possible, right? Just that it wasn't something I viewed within the realm of possibility while going to college or working at the Whitney.

It happened in the summer of 1972, a wonderful summer in New York when the entire art community blossomed with new momentum after the wild art explosion of the 1960s. Nancy Foote, managing editor of *Art in America*, called and asked if I would be interested in working at the magazine. Nancy was also an editor at the Whitney and, without my knowing it, had taken measure of how hard I worked on all the catalogues to make them perfect. In particular, she noticed my work on the Lucas Samaras catalogue and asked if I would have lunch with her and the Editor-in-Chief, Brian O'Doherty. They were looking for a Senior Editor, a prestigious position on any magazine masthead, especially when covering any specialized subject like art. In the eyes of the readers, Senior Editors are considered *de facto* experts on the subjects they cover. At least they used to be, in a different media era.

As I listened to Nancy, I was stunned, unsure of how to respond. Now you have to understand that I had never edited a thing in my life besides catalogue copy—not term papers, theses, or book reports. Not even school newspaper articles. When I later met with Brian and Nancy, I was very frank. I might as well throw my zero editing experience cards on the table, which in retrospect is an interesting way to lock down a Senior Editor's job.

"Oh," they said, "don't worry. We'll teach you."

They were very convincing, and I was all about learning everything I could about the art world from every credible expert, gallery owner, artist, and museum curator I met. Before me were two esteemed editors. What happens when you learn from great mentors? Usually, great things. It was a prestigious job that paid more than the Whitney. As someone who had received zero votes of professional or personal confidence from home in 24 years, I was deeply flattered and touched by what they saw in me. I took the job.

While basking in the afterglow of my decision, a surprising career leap I was still trying to grasp, I started thinking about the man who preceded me, Dave Hickey. I looked into his background to better understand what he brought to the job so that I could do the same with my quickly gained Whitney experience.

His opening credential was impressive on its own. Dave had been director of the Reese Paley Gallery in SoHo, a New York extension of a short-lived underground gallery housed in the only building Frank Lloyd Wright designed in San Francisco. Their business model spoke to a truly conscientious approach that combined selling fine, radical works of art from the upstairs showroom. Their young San Francisco-based curator, Carol Lindsley, coordinated an entirely new generation of Bay Area artists with classes, exhibitions and space for them to work. She also orchestrated the famous "Plastics West Coast" show at the notable Hansen-Fuller Gallery, promoted as "San Francisco's first total show of the revolutionary space-age media." In it, artists worked with vinyl and resin in complex ways that, true to the word 'revolutionary,' had not been seen before. The reviews for that show were smashing, with *Art in America* among the loudest to applaud. They continued covering activity at Reese Paley until the gallery closed in 1972, just three years after its heralded opening.

Dave had also been the owner and director of another seminal gallery, A Clean Well-Lighted Space in Houston. While gigs at the Reese Paley and A Clean Well Lighted Space verified him as an art expert, his abilities as an editor and writer were just as impressive. In fact, he took them very far after his *Art in America* stint, writing many art criticism books, becoming a seasoned professional in the publishing world, and even earning the nickname: "The Bad Boy of Art Criticism." In 2001, Dave was awarded a MacArthur Genius Grant.

So to replace this rising giant in the art media world, Brian and Nancy decided to hire someone with no experience editing anything but catalogue copy. Me. I shook my head as a whole cavalcade of thoughts and emotions washed over me. I was so excited about this opportunity, yet I wondered more than once, *what are you thinking*?

As soon as I started the job, I realized I was not the only new blood in the *Art in America* offices. Another fresh face occupied the biggest chair of all, the publisher's chair. And wouldn't you know, true to the way things catch my attention, that the newly appointed publisher was a man named Charles R. Lawless? Chuck was 20 years older than me, handsome and dressed beautifully. Think of a good-looking Gerald Ford, the President of the United States for a brief time in the mid-1970s: tall, blond, a Harvard grad, and very bright.

He was also a complete alcoholic. I came from a family of alcoholics. I knew exactly why I shouldn't be around him. *Danger! Keep Away! Danger!*

But that's not how women elsewhere felt about Chuck. He had the looks, the charm and charisma, the swagger, the ability to persuade and seduce, the power, the money—a consummate bad boy. They fell all over him; he was trouble with a capital T. This collided with one aspect of my job: answering the phones. *Great. Lucky me.* I had the privilege, if you can call it that, of being the first voice this endless string of women would hear when they were seeking out Chuck. Some of their voices were sing-song, others deep and sultry, some speaking slowly, others almost breathlessly, but they all wanted one and the same thing—him. The numbers who called became almost amusing.

What wasn't amusing were my secretarial skills. They were just as poor as at the Whitney. One day, Chuck asked me to type a memo to the entire staff with this lengthy, profound message: "Please sign in and sign out." That's it: "Please sign in and sign out." Six single-syllable words we speak and write constantly. Piece of cake, right?

What I typed instead was "Please *sing in and sing out*," as if I were working in the *Music in America* building, not *Art in America*.

Then, a funny thing happened. Funny as hell. Because this official memo came from the Office of the Publisher and not the 24-year-old blonde with paintings in her eyes who typed it, they took it very seriously. Chuck was new; they didn't yet know his managerial style, quirks, or preferences, and they weren't going to test their luck as he was just getting his feet wet. So, for the next week, the entire staff racked their brains to come up with songs. The Animals' massive hit "We Gotta Get Out of this Place" was a popular choice, along with the old favorite, "Good Morning." We learned, among other things, that a couple of people in the office could sing, while most could not. I guess one way to look at this in retrospect is that I was already getting people to think outside the box!

My *faux pas* was not soon forgotten. Years later, when I owned the Hamilton Gallery and the rising blue-chip and other artists in my gallery and exhibitions were covered by *Art in America*, I would see some of my former colleagues on the street or at art openings. On cue, they would break into song.

We had a fun staff at *Art in America*, and if anything, my errant memo drew them closer to me. It didn't take long to feel like a welcomed part of the team. Which of course meant going out for drinks at a local dive every night. Our group included Chuck's charming friend, Dick Brown, whom he hired as a consultant for the magazine. They had both worked at the *International Herald Tribune* (Chuck's background was in journalism, not sales), and regaled me with colorful stories from the old days. Many older journalists reflect upon their beginnings with great nostalgia and sadness, since the ethical, two-sides-to-every-story, old-school journalism that runs through their veins has largely gone the way of the dodo bird.

Not long after I began joining the staff for nightly drinks, I decided it was time to ramp up my social life. Or, to be more specific, my dating life. Out of the men at the bar, who did I end up dating?

Chuck. He of the switchboard filled with wannabe girlfriends. And a gatekeeper was now dating him.

I fell hard for Chuck and swallowed his stories faithfully. As a journalist, he had the storyteller's flair, and with those looks, eyes, and voice? Plus the fact he was my boss? When you're a young woman who never received fatherly affection, or even more than a tacit acknowledgment of existence, attention like this is very hard to resist. Plus, I was charmed and intrigued, and really liked the guy. The age difference didn't bother me at all, and whenever that phone at the office rang with the latest felicitous voice on the other side, I could smile to myself and think, *Taken.*

Only, the joke was on me. He wasn't taken, not in his eyes, and certainly not in theirs.

Soon enough, he started missing dates and making excuses. After one such night, I asked him, "Where were you? We had a date."

"With a sick friend," he'd reply. *Oh, please!*

On New Year's Eve, I learned Chuck had visited another girlfriend in Chicago, which is why he wasn't in New York for us to celebrate together. I cried all night long in the arms of my best friend, Terry McInerney, who I still loved for the compassionate, caring man he was. I was devastated, feeling betrayed and dumped, overlooked for some other woman in another city. I'd made a mistake, and I needed to come to grips with myself. Maybe one day I'd find someone else. Chuck never bothered to call on New Year's Eve. Nor on New Year's Day.

Time to dump him, right? Well, not quite. Yet, I was grateful a few days later when he finally called when returning to New York. Perfectly reasonable logic for a betrayed woman.

Instead of being furious and final and dumping the jerk, I fell for what turned out to be yet another of his lies about his whereabouts. As I began to unravel this, I felt whatever self-esteem and self-confidence I'd developed as a rising young woman in the art world seep away from my heart and spirit. Filling that empty space was a terrible realization that, honestly, I spent much of my adult life dealing with: I had no doubt I was wired and destined to settle for men no better than my father. Men like Chuck. Men are contemptible of women and what we bring into the world—alcoholic men. Sadly, I was walking in the world with my upbringing and troubles, and my father's influence on me was influencing my relationship with Chuck.

As this sinking feeling swirled through me, magnified by the pain of what Chuck was doing, it was clear to me that my days at *Art in America* were numbered. Chuck certainly reinforced that notion. I simply was not an editor, a secretary, a typist, or anyone capable of being chained to a desk all day; I was a people person. *What was I doing in this job?* I had to get out on the streets, meet the artists and gallery owners, see the shows and exhibits, create some noise of my own, and get my finger on the pulse of what was hot. I had no idea what my next step would be, but I had to get out of Chuck's orbit, certainly his work orbit.

For his part, Chuck was not your ideal employee. A grandiose man who routinely saw himself as two or three levels beyond his current station in life (which was pretty damned good already), there were things he would not do. As our publisher, he was expected to bring in advertising revenue. That's what publishers do. They bring it in, or they orchestrate the process. This, however, was beneath him, partially because, as I mentioned, he was a true journalist and not a salesman. So how would he support these opulent, grand ideas he held about the direction of the magazine? Well, he acted as if the magazine had plenty of money, hosting expensive lunches and discussing his visions, sticking *Art in America* with the lofty tab, time and again.

He also insisted on three-martini lunches. "Why three?" I once asked.

"Two," he offered, "are chicken shit."

Chuck was eventually fired after only one year on the job. Rather than give him a standard severance package, the magazine agreed to pay off his American Express company card. I can only imagine how many thousands of dollars that set them back.

Well before Chuck's final drama at the magazine played out, I knew I needed to leave of my own accord before I was fired. Being terminated from a position at *Art in America* would not look good on my resume, nor would it do anything good for the future I was beginning to see for myself in the art community.

Coincidentally, Editor-in-Chief Brian O'Doherty, who originally hired Nancy and me, decided to leave the magazine to pursue a career as an artist under the name Patrick Ireland. Right before he hired me at *Art in America,* Brian, a native-born Irishman, wanted to protest the events of Bloody Sunday, the terrible 1971 uprising in Londonderry, Northern Ireland that ignited decades of sectarian violence. He staged a small performance at the Project Arts Center in New York during the Irish Exhibition of Living Art. As the *New York Times* reported, "he swore to sign all his artworks 'Patrick Ireland' until 'the British military presence is removed and all citizens are granted their civil rights.'"

After leaving *Art in America,* he legally changed his name to Patrick Ireland for the next 36 years, creating mosaics, stone work, and masks. He was supported by his wife and my friend, the noted art historian Barbara Novak. Personally, I wasn't big on his masks. Not at all. Many in New York and elsewhere couldn't figure out what had hit Brian in the head; in 1972, you just didn't switch to your alter ego as a conceptual artist. Conceptual art wasn't understood like it is today. Plus, Brian's work was mediocre, so it wasn't selling on its own strengths or merits anyway.

Finally, in 2008, when he turned 80 and independent Northern Ireland was largely violence-free, Brian decided to say farewell to Patrick Ireland. He did it with pomp and circumstance, a *wake for Patrick,* complete with casket, pallbearers, the works. He held the ceremony at Dublin's Royal Hospital Kilmainham, effectively attending his own wake. The next day, the *New York Times* ran an obituary with the headline: "Patrick Ireland, 36, Dies; Created to Serve Peace." His story, for all its warts (and mediocre works), is truly unique.

But as a human, a man, a leader? Brian was a cad. A big one. It turned really sour between us. As Brian and others were interviewing his replacement, I knew all over again my days were done at the magazine. I think Brian was leaving the option of what to do with me to his successor. That turned out to be Betsy Baker, an experienced editor with *Artnews*.

As they were talking in his office, Brian called me in. Right in front of me, in a cruel moment, he said quite bluntly, "If it were up to me, I would fire her, but it's up to you, Betsy."

Stunned and offended, I decided to speak promptly in my defense. *I needed to leave of my own accord before I was fired.* "Betsy, I was hired with no experience in editing or media and told I would be trained, but it never happened," I said, my eyes trained on hers. "Let me help you out in whatever way I can. I will show your new Senior Editor the ropes, but I have decided I am not going to stay."

With those words, I succeeded in exiting on my own terms and providing some useful assistance to Betsy. The new Senior Editor turned out to be the artist Scott Burden, a well-known sculptor in his own right and a wonderful choice for the magazine. How you leave something is generally more important than how you come into it. After I stayed long enough to help out Betsy and Scott, I moved on. Betsy and I have retained a good relationship in the five decades since.

Still, Brian's insensitive remark to Betsy really angered me, to the point where doing nothing besides standing up for myself in an office was no longer an option. Being a child of an alcoholic, I had mastered the art of holding grudges by the time I was a teenager. Ten years later, I also knew how to act on them. These are unfortunate survival skills in an alcoholic household, a grudge becoming an armor plate you can throw around yourself. I was pretty angry at Brian for humiliating me on a daily basis, lying to me about his promise to train me, and then hanging me out to dry.

I was equally furious at the way he treated his wife, a truly talented art historian. I loved and respected Barbara and fully disapproved of Brian's infidelity. So, being the girl who knew how to act upon a grudge, I struck back. *You messed with the wrong girl, big guy.* After I had made my decision to leave, I started compiling the love letters of one of Brian's girlfriends, a smart, sexy academic who lived in Los Angeles. I sent about a month's worth of these juicy letters to the printer and had them set up in galleys with the headline, "Hot Flashes from the Coast."

The day I left, I rolled four out of five copies of the galleys into Brian's IBM Selectric typewriter in his office. I would have loved to be a fly on the wall when he read them. No one enjoyed this story more than Dave Hickey, my predecessor at *Art in America*, who had the same humiliating and horrible experiences with Brian. It's too bad Dave and I didn't chat before I took the job.

· · ·

Back at home, despite every red flag, warning sign, and *obvious sign* staring me in the face, my Chuck situation was anything but resolved. After he was fired from *Art in America*, he bemoaned his termination in the small studio apartment he shared with another friend, Jack Sebastian. How would he pay the bills? *Well, how about if you don't go out every night drinking, Chuck?* But that apparently made too much sense. On my grand salary of $9,000, he proved a very expensive boyfriend, even to eat at the local burger joint. In trying to accommodate and appease him, I started running up my own credit card bill. We were both in financial peril now. Both of our leases were up, so we did what many couples do when it's time to cut costs—live together. Chuck got a job in advertising, and I'd started something new, so at least we were back to two incomes.

For the Summer of 1974, we rented a school teacher's loft on Prince Street in SoHo, well before loft space became the *de rigeur* lodging of choice for young artists and craftspeople; now they live in nicely appointed loft spaces in all five boroughs. Despite the new living arrangements, Chuck's drinking, lying, and manipulative behavior continued, and I put up with it. That's what also can happen to children of alcoholics. When you think you're in love, your loyalty is strong. Typically healthy, but in this case, misplaced. You do whatever it takes to hang in there, minimize the situation and *just keep the peace.* But not leave. At least, that's what I was thinking.

Ironically, as bad as my choice of men was, I had very good instincts and taste when it came to making friends. More often than not, they would remain friends for years, if not life. A perfect example is BoBo Rockefeller, a glamorous, gorgeous woman with plenty of balls herself, who came to my SoHo loft for dinner. Though she was born in America, she won the Miss Lithuania beauty pageant in 1933, owing to her heritage. We hit it off right away, even though I was far younger. She had quite an artistic, creative mind as well: she was a character actor in old Westerns, including one with the great Walter Huston, along with being a ballet student. She even performed as Pearl in a stage production of *Tobacco Road* in Boston. Twenty years later, in 1960, an aging Salvador Dali painted her portrait.

For my part, I hit it off with BoBo because I was up for anything she could think of, and I cooked for her both at her place and mine. This included the infamous Coquilles St. Jacques story. She called me up and said, "Patty, come over here and make Coquilles St. Jacques." However, I had no fucking idea what it was. I grabbed my *New York Times* cookbook and managed to whip up her requested entrée.

Like me, BoBo was blonde. She loved my art world connections, as she had been friends with Andy Warhol. I was still the Senior Editor of *Art in America* when we met, routinely talking to famous artists on the phone, which impressed and delighted her. One month, Lee Krasner was featured on the cover of AIA. Lee was one of the first artists ever featured with a *Catalogue raisonné,* a very high honor for any artist. Lee had started out associating with Jackson Pollack, then became a fabulous artist in her own right. BoBo regaled in stories about her, both from the magazine article and from me. BoBo was fun and lively. Besides knowing interesting people, I came from nothing and it was fun. She admired all of those things about me.

However, also like me, you could say a number of things about her choice in men. When she died in 2008 at age 91, the *New York Sun* noted she "married well and divorced better." After marrying and divorcing John Sears in a marriage that fell apart during World War II, she married again in 1948. This time, it was Winthrop Rockefeller, grandson of Standard Oil founder and billionaire John D. Rockefeller and later, a two-term governor of Arkansas. That marriage was a train wreck, with all sorts of sordid accusations, and it ended four years before they finally divorced in 1954. Afterwards, Bobo moved back to New York, and was a highly respected socialite and patron of the arts when I came to know her.

When BoBo divorced Winthrop Rockefeller, there was plenty in the press about the scandalous nature of it all. Namely Winthrop's scandalous nature. However, in order to protect the massive $6 million settlement (about $62 million in today's dollars) that she received—the most ever awarded to a divorcee at that time—she never talked about it with me. She had agreed to abide by a gag order, obviously to protect Winthrop's political career and the Rockefeller family, though the Rockefellers and scandals seemed to go hand-in-hand. I later learned she burned through five divorce attorneys before finding the one who secured the massive settlement. During that process, she taught herself divorce law to the point that she became a lay expert at it. She'd caught Winthrop in bed with another man, making her so determined to divorce him that she pawned her diamond engagement ring to get what she wanted.

Unfortunately, and unlike BoBo, I wasn't done with the man behaving badly in my life.

In August, I was walking down 5th Avenue near 11th Street on a typically hot, steamy day when a doorman put out an "apartment available" sign. Finding an apartment in the heart of Greenwich

Village, then *the* center of the underground and young artist community, along with folk music and raconteurs and other people expressing themselves in a variety of ways? *Hell, yes!* I went in, took a look around, and knew it was for us.

When Chuck saw the apartment, which was renting for something like $430 a month, he was equally enthused. It was quite easy for him to sign on the dotted line of the lease, too. He didn't have to! The truth was, he *couldn't sign*. His credit rating was in the toilet. I had to carry it by myself. Somehow, we got through that. I bought the furniture, and a lot of my anxiety melted away as we began to call this place home. Chuck painted our beautiful one-bedroom apartment that also contained a fireplace and a view into a courtyard. By New York standards, it was quite glamorous—and better yet, rent-controlled.

CHAPTER 4

The Crispo Gallery—and My First Shows

While Chuck and I apartment hunted, and I tried my hardest to stabilize and normalize our relationship, I'd already taken my next leap forward in the art world, from *Art in America* to Andrew Crispo. With that, I really began to find my stride.

But not without its colorful moments, of course. They seemed to accompany me wherever I went. I had a knack for drawing in colorful moments and characters like some kind of art magnet. However, I could give as well as I received, as Joseph Levine, Brian O'Doherty, and others had already experienced.

My interaction with Crispo actually began before he brought me on to curate the watercolor exhibit. In the Spring of 1972, while at *Art in America*, I was invited to the glamorous opening of the Andrew Crispo Gallery on 57th Street in the Fuller Building. Andrew opened with an exhibition called "Pioneers of American Abstraction," a curated show of early Modernist artists like Arthur Dove, Marsden Hartley, Alfred Maurer, Georgia O'Keeffe, Charles

Demuth, and Stuart Davis. On any level, this was a prestigious show featuring true titans of American art. Modernist American painting largely preceded the abstract expressionist movement, taking place between 1910–35. Even though all their works are largely categorized as "modernist American art," the styles, inspirations, influences, and motivations of the exhibited artists were wildly varied. Charles Demuth, for example, wanted to represent reality in an industrialized setting. Stuart Davis, who did much of his best work after this time period, created proto-pop art in the 1940s that was influenced by the contemporary jazz of his time. Bebop was emerging from musicians like Charlie Parker, Dizzy Gillespie, and Thelonious Monk, and Davis' works captured the tone and mood, creating abstract still lifes and landscapes in bright primary colors.

But on the whole, these painters thought nothing of challenging social boundaries such as race, class, and sex. They were the predecessors to the literary Beats that emerged in the 1950s, ready to open up to new thinking, new expression, and new possibilities. At the time, not surprisingly, their work was undervalued.

The show was a big success. However, Crispo found it too time-consuming, and knew that while he wanted more of these big-tent shows, he didn't want to be the person curating them, putting them together.

The Crispo Gallery was beautiful. Andrew's lover, the well-known designer Arthur Smith, designed the space, and it seemed every artist wanted to show there. And I loved being there. As often happens in life, my entrée into this position began with a third-party introduction. After telling an acquaintance, Ronnie Caran, that I was unhappy at *Art in America,* he went right to Andrew, whom he was helping with installations. Andrew was a handsome, outrageously gay man, about six feet tall with boyish good looks. He looked like he was in his early 20s, even though he was closer to 30.

He was also an uneducated orphan from Philadelphia on the rise in the art world, which really impressed me.

Andrew's road to the Crispo Gallery featured a lot of twists, along with an inauspicious beginning. After he left the orphanage, in order to survive, he started turning tricks in Rittenhouse Square in Philadelphia. Eventually, he graduated to a richer clientele, including Liberace and Henry McIlhenney, the head of the Board of Trustees at the Philadelphia Museum. That trick proved fortuitous; among other things, Henry introduced Andrew to art. By 1964, at the ripe old age of 19, Andrew felt he had exhausted the resources of Philadelphia, so he moved to New York City.

Andrew's first steps into the New York art scene were, well, modest running steps. While I started out at the Whitney, an entry-level position but still *The Whitney*, Andrew was what we call "a runner" in the art business. He would find paintings from one source, run to a gallery, and sell them there for a profit, putting his resourcefulness from turning tricks to work in a far more positive way. After a few years of running paintings around, Andrew caught his next break, when Sidney Bergen at ACA Gallery gave him a job. ACA Gallery was one of the oldest galleries in New York, dating back to 1932—the height of the American Modernist movement. Not surprisingly, they still specialized in early Modernist pictures. Their newly hired "young blood," Andrew, made a big impression from the start by helping them put on museum-quality exhibitions that brought in plenty of press and clients. With his great street smarts and ability to absorb and utilize information quickly, Andrew picked up everything he could from Sidney Bergen. He worked there for five years.

Then Josephine Zeisler, who owned the Magic Pan restaurants in New York, funded Andrew to open his own gallery. However, this wasn't a multi-layered seed and round funding operation like you hear about today. She gave him enough to open the doors. Andrew had to make it from there on his hustle. He opened with a bang with the "Pioneers" exhibition, his flair for the spotlight apparent, but he needed to concentrate on sales. That meant hiring a curator.

. . .

In the Fall of 1973, Andrew called and asked me to lunch at the Magic Pan. I knew what this could mean, and I was excited. Right on the spot, in the middle of our meal, he offered me a job as curator of exhibitions. I jumped at the opportunity. He hired me on the spot.

Right away, he had a job for me: curate an exhibition of ten of the top watercolorists in America. He thought I could start on January 1 and have the watercolor show open in May. *Not how it works.* Only I didn't really know that, either. Museum shows of this quality take between one and two years to plan, and that is with a dedicated staff. He was looking at me to pull this off by myself, anxious to make a splash.

Andrew wanted me to use all my museum connections to help him put on a quality show. During my two years working at the Whitney and *Art in America,* I had already developed a good network of museum, artist, and gallery connections. The people knew I worked hard, had a good eye, and would not let things slide, right down to the tiniest detail. That's why *Art in America* hired me, because of how meticulous to detail I was, as seen in the catalogs I put together at the Whitney. It always comes down to the details.

However, I knew that no museum would lend us a work unless the show directly benefited a charity. So in March 1974, two months before the show opened, I reached out to Geraldo Rivera's One to One Foundation, and cemented that relationship.

The next relationship to cement turned into a personal highlight. One morning prior to the watercolor show, Andrew came in and told me that Jacqueline Onassis owned a Sargent watercolor. "You should write to her and ask her to lend it to us," he said.

Sure Andrew, no problem. The former First Lady, the living symbol of the Camelot years of the Kennedy presidency that inspired my generation, a highly knowledgeable First Lady with a great eye for art, fabrics, Gucci handbags, and other sublime works—let me just scratch out a letter to her.

Well, I am not afraid of a good challenge, nor do I sit around for days wondering how I'm going to approach the next step, or if I'm qualified enough to take it. Andrew clearly thought I was, so I immediately wrote to her, figuring *what the hell. This is hit or miss.* I didn't hold any expectations of what her response would be, but I certainly was hopeful.

Two days later, on Valentine's Day, the response came. A woman called me with a voice similar to Marilyn Monroe (how's that for ironic?) and said, "I'm Jacqueline Onassis."

I didn't believe her. I thought it was my sister playing a joke on me. I'd told her about Andrew's request. And I responded accordingly. "Susan, cut the shit. I really did write a letter to Mrs. Onassis."

After a sigh at the other end, the Marilyn Monroe voice on the phone convinced me she was Mrs. Onassis. *Oh shit!* I spent the next few moments apologizing profusely.

Then I told her about the show. Suitably impressed, she agreed to lend the painting. Two weeks later, she called again. "Might you consider another Sargent watercolor I own for your exhibition?" she asked.

"I would love to, but I will need to see it," I responded. Two paintings from Jacqueline Onassis? Two Sargents? You bet I was loving my new job already!

"Can you set a date for when you will see it?"

I couldn't resist a moment of levity. I just couldn't resist. "Well, call me crazy, but I bet your schedule is a lot busier than mine, so you tell me when I can come over."

"Please do," she said.

Knowing her impeccable sense of style and fashion, I realized I needed to add something before heading to her 5th Avenue apartment. "We are installing an exhibition right now, and I'm in jeans. I hope you don't mind."

She didn't mind. I took a cab to her apartment on the Upper East Side, which was located right across the street from The Met, around 5th Ave. and 85th St. Upon arrival, the security men frisked me; as the wife of one of the world's foremost shipping tycoons, and the widow of the most charismatic President of the 20th century, she required security.

I proceeded up the back elevator and walked inside to find Mrs. Onassis in the kitchen. Not only was I wearing jeans, but my blonde hair was pulled up into pigtails. "Oh my, you're a lot younger than I imagined," she said; I probably looked like a teenager with those pigtails. Even at that, I was only 25.

Without skipping a beat, I replied, "You, on the other hand, look exactly like I imagined." Which is to say, the striking, incredibly classy woman, now in her mid-40s, who had swept America away with her style and elegance a decade before.

She laughed. It worked.

She then took me to her Sargents and showed them. "Which of these were done earlier?" she asked.

I looked at the labels on the back and the signature on the front. They were both signed and dated. It didn't take much scholarship to tell her which painting Sargent composed first. After the opening, she stopped in to see the exhibition. We walked around the show together; she had already come to value my expertise, which deeply flattered me. We reproduced both the Sargents in our catalogue, in color, one of them a very important work in art history. She was impressed. And she liked me as a person. I introduced her to Andrew, who was unashamedly circling around us like a dog in heat.

Mrs. Onassis made the most of her years in New York, becoming a writer, photographer, influential art collector, and one of the top book editors in the country before her passing in 1994. For years after she provided the Sargent watercolors, I would see her at the movies or in the Fuller Building and she would always say hello. She was an elegant, lovely lady.

The opening was unbelievably dazzling, with plenty of liquor and hors d'oeuvres. Andrew went to great lengths to ensure his opening at his gallery was *noticed*. He rented the Jaguar showroom across the street and brought in a DJ for entertainment. He closed down 57th Street and rolled a red carpet right to the showroom, with strobe lights and all! Three of the greatest stage performers and dancers of the last century were there—Liza Minnelli, Carol Channing, and Joel Gray. They danced the night away. It was spectacular—and cost a fortune.

. . .

It didn't take Andrew long to impose some rules at the gallery and find himself in some trouble. The air conditioner could only be used when a client walked into the gallery. No personal calls were allowed, nor was there any socializing for lunch or coffee. Since my work directly involved socializing and networking, as it does for virtually all curators, gallerists and dealers, his new rules ran directly against the way I do business.

Further, I was in a huge minority—as were all few of us women who were operating in the New York art scene. The gallery staff was all men, and Ronnie Caran quickly became Andrew's "whipping boy." I couldn't understand the connection between the two, nor the amount of responsibility Andrew gave Ronnie, and here's why. Ronnie was a serious drinker who never had a dime to his name. When I met him, he was homeless and routinely crashed on friends' couches. He told colorful stories about his rich Long Island family, all of which proved to be lies. Furthermore, he was uneducated and could barely read or write—and had none of the street smarts or motivation to excel that Andrew possessed. I found that Andrew would trust this man to talk to clients about art unfathomable.

I also shook my head at some of his other hires. Operating the front desk was the handsome and well-mannered Caleb McKenzie, but looks and manners don't translate to the knowledge of art one needs (in my opinion) to work and help sell paintings at a hot new gallery. Frankly, Caleb didn't know a thing about art. Our press release writer, George Perret, was an elderly gentleman Andrew brought with him from ACA. Last but not least was Jay Gorney, who I'd met at the Whitney, now our registrar. Jay *did* know about art. He matriculated at Oberlin College and studied with Ellen Johnson, a renowned art historian and respected scholar. He was her pet, and they went on to become lifelong friends. But he looked downright disheveled, and a bit geeky, weighing maybe 135 pounds and wearing large boys'-sized clothes. He was also notably gay. Outside of Crispo and myself, he was the only one at the gallery who knew about art.

Unfortunately, Andrew was pretty mean and brutal to him. He turned out to be that way with a lot of people—and those weren't his worst transgressions. More on that later. One day, Jay arrived at the gallery wearing fresh contact lenses, and Andrew screamed, "Oh Miss Thing, you are so beautiful, isn't she?"

Andrew had a strong sexual appetite and loved to banter with the boys. On many occasions, I had to scream to make them stop talking about their exploits at the S&M bars in Greenwich Village. There were some things I just did not need to know. They literally discussed how many guys they slept with at the baths, their venereal diseases, and literally who gave the best blowjob. They were, by all means, part of the gay sex explosion in the decade prior to the outbreak of HIV and AIDs. Like I said, this young curator needed none of that.

· · ·

Two of Andrew's prominent early clients led to my next great experience: Dr. Victor and Marylea Johnson D'Arc. Victor was a psychiatrist and Marylea was one of the Johnson & Johnson heirs. They wanted to host an outdoor sculpture exhibition on their Merriewold West estate in Far Hills, New Jersey. "Can you recommend a curator?" Andrew asked.

I suggested Jim Monte from the Whitney. However, the D'Arcs were unimpressed with Monte. At that point, I was offered the job, which I accepted, and then I was asked to put together the show in six months. As mentioned earlier, major shows generally take at least one and up to two years to put together for a variety of reasons—contacting, contracting, and dealing with the artists (or people holding the sought-after works), acquiring the works, arranging shipping, building concrete or wood bases, setting the space, producing the catalogue, writing the all-important lead essay, and engaging in the well-orchestrated publicity campaign that brings everyone through the doors.

To compound this rather compressed timeline, Hugh Davies was doing a monumental sculpture show in Newport, Rhode Island, just up I-95, at the same time with many of the same artists. He was the director of a museum at the University of Massachusetts at Amherst. With Davies running the show, I knew there would be a lavish catalogue. The sculptures in Davies' show would be placed all over Newport, a hot spot as it was for the elite yachting set. We were competing for the same pieces—and some of the same audience.

While I had always been interested in sculpture, my curation of the exhibition for the D'Arcs cemented my passion. Plus, I was able to overcome the very large shadow of Davies and pull it off. The show was a fiesta of noteworthy sculptors circa 1974—Ronald Bladen, Alexander Calder, Jose de Rivera, Mark di Suvero, Raoul Hague, Alexander Lieberman, Clement Meadmore, Louise Nevelson, Isamu Noguchi, David Smith, and William Zorach. I wasn't merely trying to rock the D'Arc estate with a great sculpture exhibition. I was attempting to put together a mini-history of Modern Sculpture. For me, it was all about shooting for the stars and landing as close to them as I could, all on behalf of my new clients.

And historically rich it was. William Zorach was an early 20th-century pioneer in Modern American Sculpture who worked figuratively, carving only with stone. His pupil, Raoul Hague, an Armenian born in Turkey, came to the United States in the 1920s. He worked in all sorts of wood, like butternut, locust, and elm, but later in life, he sculpted almost exclusively in walnut. He made only abstract work. Alexander Calder, who I'd met in a drunken state on my first day at the Whitney, was perhaps the biggest household name among sculptors, a titan who made sculpture move in such a beautiful way. He studied engineering, which probably helped with his feats of magical balance. I couldn't help but be reminded of that great story about Michelangelo, then the papal sculptor, who'd been conceptualizing *the perfect sculpture* for years while searching far and wide for the right piece of marble. Finally he found it in the Tuscan mountains. While sculpting out the shape he envisioned into human form, he became distracted for just a moment, perhaps because of his exuberance over the masterwork he was creating. He then nearly cut the stone in half. He spent the next two weeks in bed, suicidal, depressed beyond measure over ruining his perfect piece of marble. During his moment of darkness, he received inspiration. He worked around the nearly amputated lower half of the marble, created torsion and movement, and *voila!* The David. A masterpiece of magical balance. Calder had that same quality.

For his part, Noguchi, a Japanese-American artist, was the only pupil of Constantine Brancusi, the masterful Romanian who worked in the first half of the 20th century and was considered by many the patriarch of modern sculpture. Noguchi carved in granite and marble, and his work was elegant and sophisticated. He was one of the smartest businessmen I ever encountered. He not only made abstract sculptures but also worked in theater, architecture, dance, lighting, furniture, and gardens. A true creative genius with a very practical, business-oriented side as well. That's a rare combination.

While pulling the exhibition together, I realized no contemporary sculpture show could be complete without the work of David Smith, the father of American Abstract Expressionist Sculpture. He was the first American to work in welded metals, sculpting directly with iron and steel. A master of structure, rhythmic movement, and dramatic content, he constantly experimented with new techniques. The one woman in our show, Louise Nevelson, made metal collages. First known for her boxes, she later started to put metal together at the Lippincott Foundry, in North Haven, CT. She took ordinary objects, stripped them of their identity by painting them black or white, placed them in a box, and began to build a wall.

While Nevelson looked to ordinary objects for inspiration, Alexander Lieberman looked at gas tanks. He thought of constructions and made preliminary drawings. He then would cut away areas of the tanks and weld them together. There could be up to six or seven pieces in each work, and some as long as 40 feet. He had a striking perspective and vision.

Yet, the hottest sculptor in 1974 was not any of these great artists. It was Mark di Suvero. The crane served as his paintbrush, and he got off to an inauspicious start with the machine, nearly killing himself installing his first sculpture show. A hero to the avant-garde, he constructed junk sculptures using rough planks, beams, and steel rods. Another sculptor originally trained as an engineer, the Canadian-born Ronald Bladen, made massive abstract sculptures in simple colors and shapes. They had a real architectural feel.

It just seemed to get better and better. Australian-born Clement Meadmore did steelworks that twisted and turned. The basic design is that of a square and a circle. The works have a linear emphasis and an energy of their own. Like Meadmore, Jose de Rivera's sculpture looked at first glance like a simple twist of stainless steel; however, he varied the width of each twist and turn. The piece seemed to move in space.

Installing a sculpture show is an art unto itself. Not only do you have to make sure everything fits within the space given, but the pieces need to be located so they flow and move in a complementary way to each other. It's a very precise operation. For the D'Arc exhibition, it began with Lieberman's gas tank piece, which was enormous: 40 x 60 x 40 feet. I knew that everything else had to be placed around it. But it almost never happened.

On our way to New Jersey, the truck carrying the Lieberman sculpture was stopped by the cops. They took one look at the monstrous sculpture inside and were sure this was something illegal. I had to convince them it was, rather, a work of art for an exhibition. "Gas tanks, Lady?" the cop asked. "Are you kidding me?"

"No," I said, "but let me ask you guys—do you think Andy Warhol's Coca-Cola Bottles were works of art?"

They admitted I had a point and let us proceed.

That was just one challenge. When setting exhibits, artists often have plenty of say in their preferences for the presentation. Noguchi wanted his pieces on marble bases, rather than the concrete sleeves with wooden bases I was building. I priced them; they were not merely expensive, but exorbitant. Victor D'Arc came up with the idea of marble sleeves on concrete bases, but we had to give him the bases after the exhibition closed. Raoul Hague lent us a large walnut piece that he swore could go outside for the duration of the show. His dealer, Jill Weinberg from Lennon Weinberg, later told me the weather permanently damaged the piece. Good thing Raoul wasn't a meteorologist!

For his part, Bladen hadn't fabricated his work and was showing a wood piece. It came apart in sections in boxes, and he reconstructed it onsite. He lived in one of the guest cottages in Merriewold West for two weeks while installing the piece, which turned out to produce a hidden benefit. Like me, Bladen was an avid tennis fan, and the US Open was taking place at Forest Hills in Queens. The two of us were glued to the TV, watching Rocket Rod Laver play in the US Open for the final time in his illustrious career. One of the classiest men to hold a tennis racket, he remains the last man to win all four Grand Slam tournaments in the same year. However, his 1969 mark was thoroughly tested in 2021 by Novak Djokovic (who five months later made an arrogant ass of himself while trying to get into Australia unvaccinated to seek his 10th win in the Australian Open. He was deported back to his native Serbia). Rod, now in his 80s, and possessing none of Djokovic's arrogance, watched from Arthur Ashe Stadium as Daniil Medvedev finally stopped Djokovic in the finals.

One of our featured sculptors also happened to be the editorial director of *Vogue* magazine, and you wouldn't believe who it was. Lieberman, he of the gas tank sculpture for which we were stopped by the cops. Lieberman was also one of the most charming men on the planet, and he took me under his wing. To promote the show, he wanted me to organize a symposium at Merriewold West that also included art writers Barbara Rose, Dick Bellamy, and Clem Meadmore. I rented buses at the Plaza Hotel that would pick up anyone who wanted to go. It was a beautiful early fall day, and there was plenty of food and wine to go around. The symposium went off so well. Lieberman also persuaded me to go to *Arts Magazine* and promote the show—Lieberman's sculpture ended up on the cover. Alex was as charming as he was ambitious. He knew I would push to get him on the cover.

As it turned out, the sculpture exhibition looked beautiful, but Victor d'Arc was no art dealer, and nothing was sold. Despite the elite cast of featured sculptors, people weren't going to travel to Far

Hills to buy sculptures. Years later, even the great sculpture dealer Andre Emmerich was unable to sell sculptures from his farm in Upstate New York. Still, I had my first sculpture exhibition under my belt, and my reputation was truly on the rise. A great position to be in for a 25-year-old woman just getting her career going.

· · ·

After I installed the sculpture show, Andrew came right back to me with another idea for a glamorous exhibition. He wanted me to curate a show about the work of Edward Hicks, America's most beloved folk artist, who lived in a very folksy time in our country's nascent history, from 1780 to 1849. A Quaker, he painted the famous *Peaceable Kingdom,* depicting life as he felt it should be, which was an idealized version of the much rougher early life he endured. Born in Bucks County, PA, his mother died when he was 18 months old. His father could not afford to keep Edward, so he sent his son to live with David and Elizabeth Twining, a very loving Quaker couple. His inclination to create first appeared a decade later when, at 13, he apprenticed for a coach maker (think horse and buggy) and began painting signs. He hung out with the other apprentices and enjoyed something a little less Quaker in nature, drinking and frolicking. After a brief time of that, he returned to his spiritual roots and became a Quaker minister, always deeply involved with the church.

For me, Hicks' paintings took on a religious feeling with varied phases as he evolved as both a person and an artist. All of the *Peaceable Kingdoms* I gathered for the show were hung together so you could see the progress he was making as a painter. At first, in the 1820s, the paintings had a wood frame with quotes from the Bible around it. Later, in the 1830s, he dispensed with the frames and included the father of the Quaker movement and religion, William Penn, as well as Native Americans in the pictures. These late paintings were my personal favorite. They were beautifully and elegantly painted.

When Andrew tasked me with the show, no one had yet written a book on Hicks. That in itself astonished me, but in any case, we didn't know how many *Peaceable Kingdoms* actually existed. I had a detective's job to do, which involved a lot of time and expense. Still, the art historian in me was ready to go. There was only one problem with this idea: Andrew was flat broke. This was going to be one of the most expensive shows anyone had ever put together, a great show, and Andrew knew it. He began scrambling around New York looking for loans.

Besides not knowing how many *Peaceable Kingdoms* we were looking for, we had a very big inventory problem: Andrew did not own a single Edward Hicks painting. And we were doing a Hicks show. *Okay*—Andrew got us started by contacting Hirschl & Adler Gallery; he knew a Hicks painting was hanging there. However, Stuart Feld, the longtime owner of H&A, was shrewd and would not consign the painting to Andrew. "If he wants to borrow the painting," Feld told me, "he will have to buy it."

In his own mad way, Andrew was piecing that money together. He finally found Martin Ackerman, a patron, who gave him a loan at very high interest rates. Ackerman was a New York lawyer famous for buying companies cheaply, reaping the profits, then closing the companies. In a way, you could consider him a shrewd, ruthless early-era merger and acquisition guy. When I came home and told Chuck about it, he sensed Andrew was in trouble. "If he's doing business with Ackerman, you need to keep your eyes open," he said. It proved very sage advice.

I started to work on the show. Most people who have taken an art appreciation class or thumbed through basic art history books know of one or two *Peaceable Kingdoms*. Well, from my research and calls, I learned there were actually *62 Peaceable Kingdoms*, every scenario a painting with children and animals living peacefully, subsequently placed in every significant art museum in America. I managed to pull together twenty of them—more than Edward Hicks had seen together in his lifetime. My treasure trove turned out to be the Quakers in Philadelphia, who held many of the works. During this search, I was told about a strange man who owned some of Hicks' *Peaceable Kingdoms*. I had to convince the Quaker I would never reveal his name to Andrew, I wouldn't borrow them for the show, and my purpose in seeing them was purely as a scholar.

I took the train to Philadelphia to meet the man. He was very old, wore tattered clothing, and looked like a homeless person. About five minutes after we began our drive from the train station to his place, I was blindfolded, truly a surreal moment—I didn't realize I'd plopped myself into the middle of some dark mystery or caper. We drove to a farm, where he showed me two previously unknown *Peaceable Kingdoms*.

"Look," I emphasized during the drive, "I do not drive, I have no sense of direction, and I could not find your place again if my life depended on it."

After spending the day together and giving him my word that the works would be carefully handled, the strange man lent the paintings to the show. As you might expect, art history aficionados attending the show were properly blown away.

After returning to New York, I also met the distinguished former curator at the Museum of Modern Art, Dorothy Miller. Dorothy and her husband, Holger Cahill, were noted contemporary art and folk art collectors. She owned two more important *Peaceable Kingdoms* and was a legend in the art world. Her best friend was Louise Nevelson, who she discovered and showed in her famous 1956 "Twelve Americans" show at the MoMA.

Dorothy knew every famous artist, curated fantastic shows, and was as classy a lady as I had ever met, right up there with Jackie Onassis. Her stories were fantastic.

Dorothy and Holger lived in a rent-controlled apartment in Greenwich Village on 8th Street, right around the corner from the Cedar Tavern, a popular gathering spot for *avant-garde* artists for 140 years until it closed in 2006. It was the New York art scene equivalent of Pete's Tavern, which also opened in the 1860s a mile up the road in Irving Plaza (named for early American novelist Washington Irving), and became an illustrious literary hangout when O. Henry and later Dylan Thomas, among others, frequented it. On many nights, Dorothy and Holger would get calls from Jackson Pollock, Willem de Kooning or Philip Guston, who were drinking at the tavern and wanted to come over. On occasion, they let them inside.

During our work together, I introduced Dorothy to the woman who wrote the catalogue essay for the Hicks exhibition, Eleanore Price Mather. That began a collaboration that filled a major hole in art literature: the two women went on to write the definitive Hicks book for Harry Abrams.

My job continued. In the process of curating the show, I kept writing to Richard Stuart Teitz, the director of the Worcester Art Museum, asking him to loan us a Hicks painting. Strangely, despite the fact we'd worked together before, he refused. I couldn't figure out why; it didn't make sense to me. I decided to travel to Worcester to see him. When I got there, I asked point-blank, "Why won't you loan us the painting?"

"Well, very simple," Richard replied. "When I lent Andrew that Edward Hopper painting for the watercolor show you organized last year, Andrew never paid for the crating and shipping of the piece. We ended up having to pay the bill."

Fuck. What was with Andrew and these financial problems?

Highly embarrassed, not to mention *pissed,* I pulled out my checkbook. "How much does he owe you?" I wrote a check for more than $350 from my personal account, leaving me with $5 in my account to get home.

When I returned to New York, I screamed holy hell at Andrew. Instead of apologizing for putting me on the spot with Richard, or showing any contrition, he laughed it off and reimbursed me. His next question: "Did you get the loan from Hicks?"

That's why you have me doing this, Andrew. I got the painting.

But sadly, this wicked dance with Andrew and his wicked nature only intensified. When the Hicks catalogue for the exhibition went to press, I spent a lot of time talking with the printer and became friendly with him. One Saturday afternoon, he called me at home. "I just want you to know Andrew has removed your name from the catalogue as curator and substituted his own name."

I was flabbergasted, hurt, and pissed all at once. The catalogue is the most important published piece connected with a major exhibition. It's the guide to the exhibition, a historical document in its own right. The best ones, as I mentioned earlier, are art pieces in and of themselves. I'd overseen a similarly beautiful catalogue for the show, with my passion not only for Hicks and the beauty and significance of his works coming out, but also the search far and wide I'd undertaken for *Peaceable Kingdoms*. Plus, Eleanore had written a magnificent essay. While my primary concern was always to honor and promote the work, promote the gallery, and inform the public of the work, I also appreciated receiving credit in the catalogue as the curator who put everything together.

I didn't know what to do. Crispo was blatantly stealing the credit for all of my hard work, which was a very low move. I was so furious that I couldn't think straight. Thankfully, after spilling my very wounded guts to Chuck, he put his vast experience in the art world to work and helped me manipulate the situation.

The following Monday, I walked into the gallery and told Andrew the printer had called me at home. "There was a terrible mistake," I began, keeping my cool. "Your name somehow appeared as the curator of the exhibit. Naturally, I changed it back to my name because you know how I struggled to put this show together."

Andrew was caught red-handed and knew it. Plus, I'd made sure my comments had an impact: I spoke to him in front of the entire staff. Andrew didn't dare try to remove my name again.

However, true to the financial chicanery he was already engaging in, he never paid the printer for the catalogue.

. . .

Great openings can make bad feelings and ridiculous behind-the-scenes moments like this vanish. At least temporarily. And our opening was very elegant. It would have made Edward Hicks so proud to see such a large set of *Peaceable Kingdom* prints, put together like this, with the audience response we received. We staged the opening as a benefit for the Jr. Diabetes Foundation, which would have appealed to Hicks' Quaker sensibilities, and Dina Merrill and Cliff Robertson were our honorary chairs. They came to the opening, as did a number of collectors to whom I introduced Dorothy Miller. The affair was black tie, completely packed, as crowded as a museum. Andrew was in heaven.

The world found out about our show very quickly. We received great press, highlighted by rave reviews in the *New York Times*. We also landed a full-page color spread in *Time* magazine.

During what should have been a warm, celebratory afterglow period, where I could smile widely and reflect on everything that came together to create this smashing success of a show—and the challenges and obstacles I overcame—I knew my days were numbered at the gallery. Not a typical afterglow feeling. For one thing, the ever-sensitive and insecure Crispo felt I was getting too much personal press. Somehow, he felt threatened. Of course, the press mentioned me; I put the show together! But Andrew was simply incapable of seeing that my motivation for curating the show, and the press it generated, was for the work, the show, the gallery, and to honor Edward Hicks. I never made it about me. Sadly, narcissists cannot recognize that.

Moreover, I was convinced the gallery was going to close. I had no idea what was really going on, other than the continuing challenges of trying to get things done, owing to his financial irresponsibility. He grew increasingly secretive and never let anyone know about his business, what sold, or what didn't. We fought daily about his unethical business practices. No one was getting paid, and people were calling the face of the gallery with whom they were used to dealing—me. Also, Andrew instructed the staff to "clean up" the provenance on paintings, removing labels of other galleries and making false provenances. Truly fraudulent behavior. He left me continually embarrassed and afraid that his sleazy behavior would affect my reputation.

That summer, when the heat and humidity ramped up in midtown Manhattan, Andrew again informed us that no air conditioning was to be turned on unless a client was in the gallery. Well, clients visit galleries only for part of the day. His staff had to work in that sweatbox *all day, every day.* I promptly threatened to call the New York State Bureau of Employment. Not surprisingly, that did not go over well.

Because they needed places to show their work, and keep their reputations clear of any notoriety as difficult to work with, contemporary artists were not about to make demands on Andrew. He put one or two of us in charge of working with a contemporary artist. I chose Fred Eversley, a Black bi-coastal sculptor who made works in cast resin that allowed them to appear either opaque or transparent. He was part of California Light and Space, a Southern Californian movement in the 1960s, which John McLaughlin influenced. Basically, it melded together elements of op art, minimalism and geometric abstraction. Fred was trained as an engineer, creating very well-made works, and I knew the show would cost a fortune. Unfortunately, Andrew didn't want to make sculpture bases or pay for shipping, insurance, or photography—the most basic ingredients of a good show, besides the works themselves. We fought every day.

The final straw, however, was when Andrew decided on his own to extend the Hicks show not once, but twice—each time for a month. He did it on a whim both times. Upon the second extension, I looked at him incredulously and said, "No, the lenders will never agree." That led to yet another screaming match—and I walked out.

I left with a new idea for a business lined up, my own this time, but Andrew wasn't done with me yet. True to his insecure, paranoid self, as I was walking out the door, Andrew grabbed the manila envelope I had filled with my personal bank statements and a few other things. You know, my *personal* effects. He was afraid I would steal his clients. *What clients?* I thought to myself.

Rather than closing that summer, though, Andrew just went bigger, expanding his gallery to the next floor. He did this despite not having money or paying his bills. From where he got the money, I will never know. Andrew's only significant client was Baron Thyssen Bornemisza, from Lugano, Switzerland. How could Andrew possibly afford this glamorous gallery in the Fuller Building on 57th Street, not to mention keeping up with his expensive lifestyle? Simple, in his mind, he wrote daily letters to Thyssen offering him works.

Thyssen Bornemisza, known as Heine to the gallery staff, first visited us during Andrew's first museum-quality exhibition, "Pioneers of American Abstraction." Andrew convinced him that the Modernists were undervalued, and Thyssen began to collect them in depth. The Baron had plenty of money to spend; his great-grandfather was the Andrew Carnegie of Europe. He had the biggest steel and iron fortune in Europe, not to mention a huge collection of Old

Master paintings. He was charmed by Andrew and very interested in collecting American art. He put himself in Crispo's hands.

Thyssen worked with another dealer in Europe, Franco Rappeti. Evidently, Rapetti was having an affair with Thyssen's fourth wife, Denise, and he tolerated it. One day in 1975, Rappeti walked into the gallery and tried to shake down Crispo for a commission on everything the Baron was buying. "No," Andrew said bluntly.

Three years later, in quite a real-life mystery, Rapetti was sent flying out a window in a Midtown apartment building, dying instantly. Andrew arranged for the body to be flown back to Europe. Thyssen was so happy to have the help that Crispo became his exclusive dealer. During the course of their working relationship, Thyssen bought over 400 American paintings from Andrew Crispo to the tune of $90 million.

• • •

Sadly, Crispo did not improve himself with age. His peccadilloes and outrageous behavior swung well into criminal activity. When the 1980s rolled around, long after I had left the gallery, he started using cocaine and indulged in a very risky S&M sex life. He would call phone booths in the Village and invite young men upstairs for a cocaine party, where they would be routinely drugged and tortured. One night in 1985, he and his "henchman," Bernard LeGaros, went to the Limelight Disco and picked up a Norwegian model named Eigel Vesti. They brought him back to his house, then later suggested they go to LeGaros' parents' home in Rockland County. Andrew and LeGaros also brought along a rifle, intending to kill Vesti. While evidently high as a kite, Crispo ordered Vesti on his knees, put a Nancy Grossman sculptural leather mask on his face and ordered LeGaros to shoot him, which he did.

Hikers found the charred and mutilated body. The murder weapon was found in the air conditioning vent of the Crispo Gallery.

Later, LeGaros confessed to the shooting. Amazingly, Crispo was never charged with either murder or conspiracy to commit murder. LeGaros, on the other hand, got the sentence that truly should've gone to Crispo: 25 years in Attica, not the place you wanted to spend 25 seconds, let alone 25 years. Then or now.

A few years later, Crispo eventually went to prison for tax evasion. The original sentence was reduced to five years, and he served three. In 1989, he was released. Shortly thereafter, a massive explosion ripped apart Crispo's house in Southampton, a house filled with art. In 1992, a jury awarded him $8.6 million from Long Island Lighting Company, because they admitted at the civil trial that there was a gas leak under his house. When I heard the news, I shook my head. How many more chances was the world willing to give this guy?

Andrew paid off his debts, but by the end of the 1990s, he was out of money again and declared bankruptcy. When Arthur, Andrew's lover of many years, passed away, Arthur's family, suitably fed up with Andrew, refused to let him stay in the apartments the men had shared for 30 years. That's not all. Andrew felt his attorney was not getting the money from Long Island Lighting to him fast enough and blamed the judge in his case. So, in a twist of thinking only a brain like Andrew Crispo could conceive, he tried to kidnap the judge's four-year-old daughter and hold her for ransom.

It didn't work. He was convicted and sent to prison for 11 years. Currently, he lives in Brooklyn, but his once formidable art world presence is no longer a presence at all. No one I know will do business with him.

But for me, the end of my days with Andrew Crispo meant the beginning of a new chapter, bolstered by my very solid reputation and my own growing dreams.

CHAPTER 5

A Travelling Exhibition Service

In the Summer of 1975, I left Crispo Gallery with three notable assets: my brains, my reputation as a young woman who curated great shows, brought in the best artists, and stopped at nothing to get the job done right, and my ideas. You might notice that none of those assets included anything of a financial nature. I had no money. I'd walked from Crispo and his increasingly amoral operation with little more than a box of catalogues and some personal mail. And I was about to start my own business.

My idea? To start a traveling exhibition service. I would curate shows and send them to museums all over the nation, acting as both curator and registrar.

Traveling exhibitions had been around for quite some time, in a formerly very basic form. Centuries, in fact. They first sprung up during the Renaissance, when works of one or more artists would be exhibited in different village centers, palazzos, or other locales in Italy. Traveling exhibits helped spread the spirit, energy, and sense of freedom that accompanied that remarkable period of creativity, much of it originating among the artist guilds, artists, and apprentices of Florence, funded primarily by the ruling de Medici family, the patriarchs of art patronage. They again became a main source of spreading a movement in the late 19th and early 20th centuries, when salons, museums, and other locales served as hosts for various Impressionist works.

In the United States, the traveling exhibition took flight in a more organized way. On May 11, 1909, the National Academy of Arts' Board of Regents convened a meeting; among the attendees were President William Howard Taft, former president Theodore Roosevelt, industrialists Andrew Mellon and J.P. Morgan, patrons of the arts, and other esteemed government officials. They called for the formation of an agency that would send "exhibitions of original works of art on tour to the hinterlands of the United States."

Believe it or not, a century ago, the highest-level government officials and the biggest private money in the country believed that seeing and learning about art was essential to the intellectual growth and education of the citizens. They viewed it as stoking one's vision, sense of possibility, and wonder, looking at the world in a deeper way and seeing the beauty in it. It makes you wonder whether we've evolved or devolved in our current world of reality shows, video games, and the near-extinction of art classes in high school when you look at the way it was 113 years ago, doesn't it?

Out of that came the Academy of Fine Arts, the AFA, which devoted itself to promoting the visual arts as a vital component of the nation's cultural life. The AFA's first president was Charles L. Hutchinson, the President of the Art Institute of Chicago. Hutchinson envisioned the AFA's mission as "bringing the museum to the people" since nearly all US-based art at the time was concentrated in the northeast, primarily New York, Boston, and Philadelphia. So, they did, offering original paintings at small rental fees to small art and educational organizations, producing nationally broadcast radio programs about art during the Depression, distributing allowances to museums to purchase original art, and a select number of exhibits that went from location to location.

It was out of that service of the AFA's legacy, the traveling exhibit, that I was preparing to fly—solo. I wanted to try it, and I sure tried hard, but it turned out to be short-lived.

. . .

Never, to my knowledge, had anyone taken it upon themselves to operate such a service as a one-person band. And certainly not in the mid-1970s in the United States. I felt like a pioneer in many ways, breaking a new trail from the AFA's foundational efforts, which others would follow when they saw the success and reception of my exhibits. Sure enough, a decade later, Independent Curators International (ICI) formed to bring together curators of all stripes to support not only their creation of exhibitions but also arts community leaders and organizers who generate public interest in the arts.

I had been thinking of traveling exhibitions for some time. When I curated the shows for Crispo and the Merriewold West sculpture show, I brought together the works of the nation's most esteemed artists and sculptors of the last fifty years, sometimes the last one hundred years. Or more, in the case of Edward Hicks. As I curated the shows, put together beautiful catalogues and watched the satisfaction, approval and, at times amazement on the faces of patrons in Crispo Gallery—not to mention the delight people like Jacqueline Kennedy Onassis took when viewing my shows—I thought, *why does this have to be confined to New York? Why can't people all over the country see this where they live?*

Now, to be real, I knew I couldn't personally take one of these supershows around, like the works of ten of America's greatest watercolor artists, or ten sculptors with many different forms and materials and pieces as long as sixty feet. But I *could* take around the artists with whom I'd already formed relationships, including some of the very best in their genres—and soon-to-be blue-chip artists. I could use my now substantial network of contacts among gallerists, museums, and art institutes, trade on my reputation, and put together themed exhibits that would travel well and draw plenty of attention wherever they landed. I knew the artists would be interested; their livelihoods depended on as many would-be buyers and admirers seeing their work as possible.

Since I thrived on the energy, intellectual, and inner resources needed to take on a mighty challenge, no matter how impossible someone else might think it was, this was right up my alley. It reminds me of something filmmaker George Lucas once said while irritated at a LucasFilm employee: "I built this place on people telling me what was impossible." Translation: It *motivated him to prove them wrong.* I'm not positive anyone was personally doubting my chances of succeeding in this new endeavor, but I'm sure a few were out there thinking, "She'll never pull it off." And, possibly a few also musing, *"If anyone has the balls to pull this off . . ."* Like maybe Joseph Levine, who got an early taste of my determination to succeed and gave me the nickname that stuck!

I knew what to do, how to do it well, how to envision and execute shows, and how to button down all the details. I had the tireless energy of the 25-year-old that I was, the drive borne of both my ambition to spend my life in the art world, and also the survival instinct of knowing I had to make money, no matter what, since my alcoholic live-in boyfriend was very hit-and-miss on that subject, totally unreliable and irresponsible.

I got right to work. I organized a show with an artist I knew, Chet Boterf, called "Drawing Today in New York." We arranged for it to open at the University of Texas in Austin, where he was a professor. Jumping on my network of artists, I assembled quite a cast for my debut exhibit with the service that included Nancy

Grossman, Nancy Graves, Alex Katz, Joan Snyder, Deborah Remington, and Neil Welliver. This was quite an impressive group. Grossman became well-known for her work with wood and leather sculpture of heads, and in later life, received the Women's Caucus for Art Lifetime Achievement Award. Graves was a prolific cross-disciplinary artist in her short life (she died in 1995 at age 56), focusing primarily on natural phenomena as a sculptor, painter, printmaker, and filmmaker. Katz's landscapes and portraits used flat planes of rich color; he became famous for the portraits he made of his beloved wife, Ada. Welliver made his biggest mark with his large, vivid paintings and woodcuts of the Maine wilderness he cherished.

Then there were Joan Snyder and Deborah Remington, who stayed with me for years and were blue-chip artists, two of the six blue-chippers whose careers I helped along or downright shepherded. Joan, who is still painting into her 80s, made her breakthrough in 1969 and the early 1970s with two very famous stroke works, "Lines and Strokes" and "Dark Strokes Hope." She was already established when she participated in my exhibit, which led to my carrying her in the Hamilton Gallery and promoting her career. In a nutshell, "stroke painting" isn't as general as the term implies. Her website describes it as "using the grid to deconstruct and retell the story of abstract art." By the late '70s, when she was showing in the Hamilton Gallery, she'd moved on from strictly stroke painting, but she left an indelible impression in the history of modern art—and was just revving up into the heart of a now highly decorated career.

Deborah Remington, who passed away in 2010, had even earlier beginnings, as part of the West Coast Beat movement in San Francisco in the 1950s. While best known as a poetry and literature nirvana involving visiting New Yorkers Allen Ginsberg, Gregory Corso and Diane diPrima, poet and City Lights Bookstore owner Lawrence Ferlinghetti (the man behind the 1961 Supreme Court ruling to lift censorship laws on art and literature in the United States) and West Coasters Gary Snyder (a future Pulitzer Prize winner), Kenneth Rexroth, Joanne Kyger and Michael McClure, among others, it also had a vibrant art component. Deborah was right in the middle of it. She started as an abstract expressionist, learned calligraphy in Japan, moved to New York in the late '60s, and shifted to, as her website puts it, "illusionistic with hints of figuration . . . the compositions are structured, centered, and tightly controlled." More on Deborah and Joan later.

After a successful opening at the University of Texas, I traveled "Drawing Today in New York" to a number of universities and smaller museums, including the Dayton Art Institute. Each event was well-received, and the artists received plenty of new exposure "in the nation's hinterlands" to coin the AFA's 1909 phrase. People and the press were taking notice of me as the traveling curator, but something else was happening as well: the more I worked on the shows, the more I met artists who were unhappy with their current gallery affiliations. As I continued talking with them, hearing their frustrations, and identifying what was specifically frustrating them, I made sure to stay in touch with them. I would later focus on picking up the best of them to open the gallery.

I also worked with my old boss, Robert Doty, now director of the Akron Art Institute, to organize a sculpture show. The premise of the show was about sculptors who made monuments that became symbols for cities. I asked each artist to make a maquette for a monument, like the Saaranin (Gateway) Arch in St. Louis, Missouri. We received a National Endowment Grant for the show, and it traveled to a number of museums opening in Akron. Some of the artists we selected for the show were Mark di Suvero (who had also exhibited in my sculpture show at Merriewold West in 1974), Clement Meadmore, Robert Murray, and Lyman Kipp.

Another person to whom I offered my traveling exhibition services was Larry Fleischman from Kennedy Galleries. He agreed to let me work for him as a consultant for the first year, curating shows and aiding my service. I organized exhibitions of inventory from the gallery and traveled them to museums.

There was a catch: after one year, I would agree to come on board as a full-time employee. Like so many in the art world, Fleischman was looking for the right angle to get him over the top. He was very curious about Andrew Crispo and all of his clients—fair enough—but he was also very controlling. If there was one thing I completely understood about myself when I came out of my childhood home and dysfunctional family dynamic, it was this: I did not handle controlling people well at all. Nor did I want to be around them except when utterly necessary, which is ironic, because the art world is full of controlling people. Being the full-time employee of a controlling person was not going to cut it. I knew I would never be able to work for him full-time.

However, Kennedy Galleries represented the estate of one of my favorite artists, Charles Burchfield. I knew Burchfield well from the watercolor show. Burchfield painted from 1910 into the 1950s. I was very familiar with his oversized watercolors and crazy about them. One afternoon, I walked into the packing and shipping area in the back of the Kennedy Gallery and found two employees cutting down the large Burchfields to a more saleable 18 x 24-inch size. *What the fuck!?* I gasped audibly, shocked by this sacrilegious carnage happening before my eyes.

The employees turned around and freaked out. "We forgot to lock the door," one of them said.

"Great," I said, "but what are you doing?"

Their biggest fear wasn't that I'd seen them cutting down the Burchfields, or what I thought about their awful act. It was that I would reveal to Larry what I had seen. *Why are they worried about that?* I thought. Clearly, they had been told to do this by Larry. He was trying to sell more Burchfields.

It was a scene I never forgot.

While trying to keep my traveling exhibition service going on a shoestring budget, and developing and building shows to make it work, I was dealing with my personal life. And it was grinding me down to the bone, at exactly the time I needed my boyfriend to be a bedrock of support both emotionally and with my new endeavor. Nope—not happening. I received little or no support. I was living with an alcoholic who was completely and totally irresponsible about the bills. He would cash his paycheck and go to the 21 Club—only the best for Chuck, right?—and buy everyone drinks. Of course, among other bills that never saw their way back to the sender with checks in the envelope, there went the rent money. You know, the roof I counted on for what little sleep and rest I was getting in the midst of making my service work.

But when I'd get on him about his non-support and financial irresponsibility, Chuck would turn on the charm, and it still had its effect, as well as his way of making me seem clueless and powerless, elevating himself to the high priest's seat in the process. Typical manipulative male behavior, but I didn't see it so obviously from the outside as I do now. Specifically, he told me I'd be nothing without his sage wisdom. Frankly, I believed him. He also knew that my family was toxic and unloving. With the exception of my brother Rick, I received no support at all from the family.

Chuck knew I depended on him emotionally and, to an extent, financially, as I had nothing and nowhere else to turn. So he kept pulling the puppet strings, and without any other options in my mind, I carried on.

CHAPTER 6

The Hamilton Gallery

Wouldn't it be nice to open an art gallery? In midtown Manhattan, right in the middle of another red-hot New York cultural, artistic, and musical era as the Baby Boomers were moving through their own version of the Roaring Twenties, no less? Any number of people entertained this dream, me certainly included. However, it takes a specific set of skills, moxie, ambition, relationships with artists, agents, and the press, and the ability to envision how a piece of art would look on a buyer's wall, for an art gallery to prosper. Plus the financial wherewithal. Especially in New York.

I knew I wanted to open a gallery. I also knew I had all of the necessary skills and ambition. All but one: the financial wherewithal.

After working my tail off for not much money in the traveling exhibition service, and realizing it was a very difficult way to make any money at all, I decided it was time to open a gallery. Even though I was only 25, with no background as an entrepreneur (or any business background at all, really), I knew what I wanted. And I was ambitious. Further, through my quickly growing number of different jobs in the art world, from the Whitney to *Art in America* to curating for Andrew Crispo Gallery and the side curation for Merriewold West,

I'd spent a great deal of time in galleries and had an idea of how to operate a successful one. Further, while doing the traveling exhibition service, I'd heard from many of our exhibiting artists about what was wrong with the galleries with whom they'd had relationships.

In business, as in life, you often learn far more about how to do something correctly, and well, when you hear about the *wrong* way to do things, or the many things that can go wrong. I spent many hours listening to and digesting those experiences from a wide variety of exhibiting artists, including Deborah Remington, and then figured out how to make sure their bad experiences would not be repeated in my gallery. For one thing, she told me I would *not* have to give stipends to artists that I sought out. She was very helpful. More than any other, she told me what not to do.

I brought all of that very recent input into my preparatory work.

In the Summer of 1976, some friends were in town, and we decided to go to the hot new restaurant Windows on the World at the World Trade Center. At this rooftop dinner, I met Dennis Miller, who I eventually hired to be the architect of the gallery. The evening was a disaster—from the service overall, to bringing main courses before appetizers, not to mention the lousy, cold food. How hot could a restaurant like this really be? I was infuriated and wrote a scathing letter, which I threatened to copy to the *New York Times*. Windows of the World management offered me a free meal sometime in the future with a few friends. *I sure as hell hope it's a lot better than this,* I thought to myself. However, I also thought something else: this complimentary dinner for four could be useful while trying to raise money for the gallery.

. . .

I began to set my idea into motion. I started figuring out how to get from idea to grand opening. The first thing I needed to do was to put together a stable of vibrant artists whose work would draw visitors, the press, and, most importantly, sales to keep the doors open. I already had strong rapports and relationships with quite a few artists who ticked off all of those boxes, so that looked good. Many of them, in fact, were already friends and openly encouraged me.

Since I had no money of my own to throw into the 5,000 square feet of fledgling gallery space I sought, I needed to rely on my relationships, persuasiveness, and sales ability, which gave me some confidence. It had worked well with putting together the shows I'd curated, that's for sure. And everyone knew that I would definitely put on great shows at my own gallery.

But money is a funny thing: you just don't know what it can do to any relationship, business or personal, when it enters into the equation. No matter how well-received all the other things I planned to do.

My effort swung into full motion with the first vital piece of the puzzle—my business prospectus. I developed and wrote it in May and June of 1976 with the stakeholder breakdown of a Broadway show; in other words, those who participated financially would receive shares in a Limited Partnership. Here's how I set it up: I would solicit a number of investors who would own a small piece of the gallery (3 percent apiece, a maximum of 16 participants), and I would retain a 51 percent controlling interest. For their contribution, they would receive art discounts, and I would negotiate discounts on all work they wished to purchase from other dealers. They would also get tax deductions as long as I showed a loss. However, an art gallery is *not* where you want all these proverbial sous chefs dipping their hands into and ruining the main course, so I stipulated that they were not to interfere with running the business. Nor were they to bring in their favorite artists—or any artists. Hence the designation of "limited partners." I would be the general partner, assuming all operational and other responsibilities. If the gallery closed, it was my responsibility and mine alone to pay off the debts.

My prospectus was complete with a list of the artists, the location of the space, the costs of running a gallery, cash flow charts, and a resume for me. I decided to hire Jay Gorney, my friend from Crispo Gallery. After he was fired from Crispo, I felt unfairly, he worked for ACA gallery—and was fired again. However, I was convinced he was a smart, capable employee. I also knew I needed some business advice from a trusted hand, and I turned to my family, particularly my older brother Bill, an investment banker. Rather than give me business advice, though, he wanted a 3% interest in the gallery and to become the business advisor. He knew nothing about art or running a gallery, and he redefined the word "cheap." Quickly, I knew that this was a bad idea. So much for leaning on family. Frustrated, I did turn to the one family member I knew I could trust, my brother Rick, who suggested I ask his friend J.B. Doherty to read the prospectus before I submitted it to backers. He was very helpful.

By August, I was ready to present the prospectus to investors. Deborah Remington introduced me to Paula Hughes, the first vice president and director of Thomson McKinnon Securities Inc. and the first full-time woman member of the New York Stock Exchange. Paula was a powerhouse indeed. She became my first investor, and asked me if I would be putting the check in an escrow account. "Of course," I said—then ran to a phone booth in her building and called my brother Rick. "What is an escrow account?" I asked.

We got through it—and I promptly deposited her check in my newly opened escrow account. Paula was enamored with my prospectus and my vision for the gallery, and promptly turned me onto her attorney, George Cattallo. He, in turn, sent me to his friend and client, Ann Nappa. They all became investors. So far, so very good.

Deborah also introduced me to one of her collectors, Frank Mandlebaum. I was never sure of what business Frank was in, but it always seemed to involve a lot of cash. Not only did Frank invest, but he added a $10,000 cash investment for his Aunt Bernice.

Then Frank introduced me to his friends, Alan and Carol Baer. They owned the Art Registry Service, a business in which works of art were registered in case of theft. Unfortunately, it never got off the ground. Both Huntington Block, my insurance agent, and Ed Schiff, my attorney, warned me against taking any of this money. I was so focused on collecting the needed investment funds and backers that I didn't listen. Not surprisingly, it cost me later.

I'd already played my Chuck Lawliss and Verna Mott cards to rousing successes in my endeavor, so it was time to throw down the third ace in my deck—the Windows on the World Dinner card. I invited Paula Hughes, Frank Mandlebaum, Deborah Remington, Chuck, and Jay for a lavish dinner. In the middle of the dinner, Frank asked me, "Will you be putting this on the gallery tab?"

"No, I will pay for it personally," I said, gulping. Sometimes, you just had to reach into your own pocket to thank the people who were helping you. Not that Jay or I had deep pockets. Jay sat there with holes in his socks, and after I paid, I barely had enough cab fare to get home.

As my effort continued, I asked seemingly everyone I had ever met to help me raise the money. Mac Doty, my old boss from the Whitney Museum, introduced George Green to me, and he in turn introduced me to Doris Weintraub and June Kraft. Doris was married to Jack, and June was a widow; the two women emotionally adopted me as the daughter neither ever had. They were sweet, nice, and supportive in that special, doting Jewish mother way, which I had never experienced before in my life.

Even though I lived with my current boyfriend, my old boyfriends were fair game as well. I called upon them to help me raise the money. Years earlier, in a bar on the Upper East Side, I met Nicholas Rassias, who claimed to be a rich Greek businessman. He was extraordinarily handsome, and I went home with him. Later that night, he had some sort of attack. Whether it was anxiety or a heart attack, I don't know, but I called 911 and went to the hospital with him. I saved his life; I figured he owed me. When I contacted him, he introduced me to a very classy lady from Washington, D.C., the sculptor Hilde van Roijen. Despite possessing a very nice collection of her work, she never once pushed her art on me for an exhibition, as a condition of investment. Or at all. That's class. She also owned and kept a wonderful home, sat on the boards of a few museums, and was very well-connected. Through her, I secured the investment of her relative, Albert Gordon, a partner at Kidder-Peabody. He bought two shares.

The last original Hamilton Gallery investors I sought were the Jacksons. Ann Jackson was an old girlfriend of my brother Rick's. When Ann's parents met me, they said, "If you ever open a gallery, we want to invest." Needless to say, I followed through. Virginia, Ann's mother, put in $7,000 and Ann added another $3,000. But amidst this apparent success, another red flag popped up: my attorney warned me I would end up having trouble with Ira, Ann's father and Virginia's husband, who was not even an investor.

Once again, I didn't listen. Ira, a doctor, felt he was a businessman and began demanding a lot for his wife's investment. Further, Rick was furious that I had taken money from his old girlfriend and her mother and made no bones about telling me. Quite frankly, in hindsight, I don't blame my brother for feeling that way.

After escaping the Jackson home with the $10,000, and the ire of Rick and Ira billowing at my back, I had what I needed to open the gallery. So, armed with $110,000 in an escrow account, I found my architect, Dennis Miller. Then I found my contractor, Ron Lusker, through Denise Hare. As they got to work, planned for the inauguration in February, 1977, at 20 West 57th Street. We started construction in October.

. . .

As I moved forward, I took a look at the art gallery landscape in New York. There were about 150 galleries in New York City, and not that many were in SoHo, as became the case later. The three most powerful galleries were Pace Gallery, Emmerich, and Leo Castelli Gallery. I wanted to be on 57th Street, right in the heart of Midtown Manhattan, because I was convinced that clients from the Upper East Side and Midtown would not go to SoHo. Nor would out-of-town clients who stayed in the Midtown hotels, from the Waldorf-Astoria to the Plaza and everything in between.

Also, 57th Street has quite a history. Once known as the Rue de la Paix and the home of Theodore Roosevelt, 57th Street had been synonymous with art in one form or another since The Art Students League established in 1892 and built its headquarters in what became known as the American Fine Arts Building, under the vision and direction of Rosina Florio.

Around 1970, after a number of ups and downs, the art scene again took form, built on the foundation of the ubiquitous Fuller Building that housed Andre Emmerich, David McKee, Zabriskie, Andrew Crispo, Marisa del Re, Jill Kornblee, Brooke Alexander and Pierre Matisse, among others. Also on the street were the Stable Gallery led by Eleanore Ward, the Greene Gallery headed by Dick Bellamy, dubbed "the eye of the Sixties," the Janis Gallery, and all the great galleries in the Fuller Building. As I was getting ready to hang my shingle on that iconic street, it was definitely feeling new energy.

"Fifty-seventh street, which over the years has had its ups and downs as a contemporary art scene, is making a thunderous comeback . . ." proclaimed Grace Glueck in her Art People column in the December 10, 1976 *New York Times*. ". . . within the last two years, enough new starts have been made on 57th Street by galleries debuting or moving from other locations to assume the proportion of a trend."

I'm proud to say Hamilton Gallery was going to be one of them—as was duly noted in Grace's article. She went on to add, "Attracted by the street's re-emerging elegance, its offer of more space for less money, and—yes, its spillover clientele from the fashionable stores, no less than nine new galleries have opened or are opening there this season, and almost as many are moving there from more expensive sites in the reaches of upper Madison Avenue."

Then I looked at another demographic: the representation of women. In particular, how many women-owned art galleries in 1977 New York? The answer was disappointing: less than 10 percent. Most of those were owned by wealthy women who "played" at being art dealers. It was not exactly the way I would be doing things, starting with the fact I was running on knowledge, connections and moxie, certainly not my money. One of the only women who did not come from a wealthy family and successfully sold work was Paula Cooper, whom I greatly admired. She had a great stable of artists and was very loyal; further, she never stole artists from other galleries. All these years later, she is still in business.

During her 50th anniversary as a gallery owner in 2021, Paula told a story of how Dick Bellamy would pat her on the head as an art dealer. Talk about condescending! He reflected the attitude of the times; they didn't take her seriously, yet she was incredibly serious. And look who got to 50 years as a successful gallery owner? That's right. She had great taste and built careers from the start. Out of all the dealers, she is the one I most admire, and I know every woman wanted to be like her. Proudly, I was one of them.

Was it an advantage to be a 25-year-old single woman opening a gallery with fresh ideas, perspectives, and an already established name among artists and representatives? You'd think that would be a no-brainer, an absolute "yes"—but I think not. Clients felt they could beat me down and get the best price. Artists, especially men, felt they could manipulate me. They saw the picture: young, blonde, small in stature—and a woman. But in a way, I have to thank them for their boorish behavior and attempts to manipulate me, because I became one of the toughest dealers in New York. I gave no discounts to people when they bought for the first time, and after that, only 10%. I was aggressive but honest.

Apparently, none of them had talked to Joseph Levine before dealing with me.

. . .

No matter how successful my fundraising or how forward-thinking my prospectus and vision for the gallery were, its success hinged on who I worked with and the works I showed. I got the right to work on the artists. One of the great galleries in the early '70s was Bykert Gallery, led by Klaus Kertess. He showed Brice Marden, Chuck Close, Deborah Remington, and Dorothea Rockburne, with Marden and Remington being his biggest sellers.

I already knew Deborah from my days of curating at the Crispo Gallery. She was friends with one of the Crispo artists, Lowell Nesbitt, and she courted my friendship. Deborah was a direct descendant of the iconic Western cowboy artist, Frederic Remington. As mentioned earlier, she was also part of the AbEx movement out of San Francisco and was quite well-respected. I already knew her work quite well. Her paintings were intensely colored machine-like shapes emanating from a central form that radiated light. They were theatrical and extremely complex.

The creator behind these works was as overwhelming as her paintings; Deborah had a strong, demanding personality. She was in her mid-40s and in need of a new gallery to show her work. A representative from Pace Gallery on West 25th was interested, but he could never get Pace founder and owner Arne Glimcher to visit her studio, and she was ready for a show. She wanted my gallery to open and to install her exhibition. Motivated by my enthusiasm and her own ambitions, she then introduced me to a number of other good artists.

One was the well-known Kenneth Snelson, who made tubular abstract sculpture out of rigid pipes and flexible cable. He studied with the visionary architect Buckminster Fuller (creator of the geodesic dome, a staple of late-1960s "back to the land" living, among many other innovative designs). He invented a concept called "tensegrity." The beauty of his elegant work lay in the tension between the pipes and cables. Everyone loved Snelson's work, and it sold well. He was also very nice. While I preferred something more wholehearted, he half-committed to work with my gallery and agreed to be in the opening show. He even said he might do a one-person show. Working with him would be a coup, and I knew it.

I also sought out the sculptor Clem Meadmore, who I knew from showing him in my 1974 sculpture show at Merriewold West. An Australian, he was instrumental in Max Hutchinson's Sculpture Now gallery opening in 1974 on Greene Street in New York. They also had another important link; Hutchinson founded Gallery A, one of Australia's most iconic galleries, and Clem later became a director of it. At Sculpture Now, Clem picked all the artists, designed the logo, and was, in essence, a business partner. Max must have gotten sick of it because Meadmore was looking for a new gallery to serve in this way. Since I was only 25, he likely thought he could do the same work for me. Unfortunately for Clem, every artist he recommended, except for one, was uninteresting. However, he made beautiful sculptures, and I planned on giving him the first one-person show.

Clem introduced me to another sculptor I liked, Robert Murray, a Canadian who fabricated large painted abstract aluminum pieces with Donald Lippincott's foundry in New Haven, Conn. Unlike the artist John Chamberlain, who worked with car parts, they did not look like crushed objects. His work was boldly painted and elegant.

He built the models and enlarged them at Lippincott. Murray was a wonderful artist who spent most of his time either with his lovely family in Pennsylvania or on a Canadian island.

The Merriewold West show not only introduced me to Clem Meadmore, but also to Isamu Noguchi, who has become renowned historically for his art and landscape architecture since his passing in 1988. I think Noguchi liked me, but wasn't about to join a gallery in the conceptual phase or run by a young kid (he was 70 when we met). He did recommend I visit his friend David Hare, a well-known Surrealist sculptor from the 1950s. He was a member of one of the wealthier New York families, the Goodwins, who were among the founders of the Museum of Modern Art. As a young man, David was strikingly handsome and the subject of a very famous photo taken by Arnold Newman, the renowned photographer. In 1942, David co-founded the short-lived but influential *VVV* magazine with Surrealists Marcel Duchamp, Max Ernst, and Andre Breton. They only published four issues before the magazine folded in 1944, but their coverage of the New York surrealism movement was very important.

After *VVV*, David started painting *The Cronus Series*, a project that lasted ten years. Cronus was the Greek mythological figure who ended up eating his children. Hare illustrated most of the myth. The paintings were uneven but interesting, surreal and frightening—and very unique. Before the gallery opened, I introduced him to Tony Alessandra of the short-lived Alessandra Gallery in SoHo. He had a one-person show there with a catalogue, and Tom Messer, director of the Guggenheim Museum, saw the work. He immediately planned a one-person show of *The Cronus Series*.

David was an absolute character but also into drugs and a known womanizer. He was married to Denise Brown, known as Dencie, an extraordinary French woman in her own right who traveled the world as a professional chef, writer, and photographer. They had a son, Morgan, and lived on LeRoy Street in the Village with a vacation home near Jackson, Wyoming. She knew what a bad boy David was, but loved him. She also lived for the peace and quiet they shared together when they spent summers out West. I learned an incredible amount from her about not only cooking—always a favorite pastime of mine—but also about life.

Denise had been married before and had two children. Sadly, she sacrificed her relationship with her eldest daughter over her love for David. Tofer, the daughter, did not get along with David and, as a teenager, went to live with her older brother in San Francisco. She never forgave her mother for choosing David over her. Well, in a sense, Dencie's loss of Tofer was my gain, although no one can truly replace a lost daughter. Dencie became a more nurturing mother figure to me than my own mother. It always struck me as a sad, tragic irony that her own daughter hated her, because my experience with her was one of love.

. . .

The last two artists I felt I needed for the initial artist roster were Walter Dusenbery and Janet Stayton, who were married. Little did I know that you should never represent a married couple, but I was certainly about to find out. It's like the old barroom adage: a married couple (or siblings) can fight like cats and dogs, but if a third party's relationship sours with one, it sours with both. They will go back-to-back against you—or, in this case, me.

I met Walter through Isamu Noguchi as well. He was a talented young sculptor with great potential who worked in marble and bronze. His biggest skill, however, lay in schmoozing with rich people and executing real estate deals. Walter and Janet owned a place in Pietrasanta, Italy, on the northern Tuscan coast where Michelangelo had worked; he even made his marble sculptures in the same foundry as Michelangelo. I can't think of too many more impactful historical connections than that! He also had a large loft on Broadway and Houston that he later traded up to a building on Lafayette Street. As I said, he was very clever with real estate.

For her part, Janet Stayton made abstract paintings that didn't really appeal to my tastes. However, her works on paper, called "worksheets," were marvelous. She was originally from Lake Charles, Louisiana, and carried a great deal of Southern charm wherever she went. But boy, oh boy, was she high-strung. I gave her a one-woman show, but after dealing with her through the course of that, I couldn't bear to give her a second. I tried to do what Leo Castelli suggested, which was ignore her, but you did not just ignore Janet Stayton. Not a chance. Leo was one of the most important dealers in the 1960s through the 1980s, a friendly acquaintance, and a man I could always call when I had a problem involving an artist or an industry-related question.

So, I called. He advised me not to return her calls, not to plan visits to her studio, or to send a photographer anymore. The artist's ego, he surmised, would be large enough that she would get frustrated and leave for greener pastures rather than feel any sense of shame or neglect. Not Janet Stayton. She appeared in my office and promptly confronted me. When I told her that I was not behind her work anymore, she left. Unfortunately, that soured my relationship with Walter permanently.

In the end, I found my artists. I gave them and they signed a letter of intent stating that if I opened a gallery on 57th Street, they would join the gallery and be represented.

* * *

Now that I knew who would show in my nascent gallery, I needed to work on finding a space for the gallery, writing a business prospectus, and raising money. The first thing I found was the space, some 5,000 square feet on the sixth floor at 20 West 57th Street, just across Madison Avenue from the Fuller Building and next to Grace

Glueck of the *New York Times* called "another hive of galleries." It was renting for $6 per square foot (imagine that!). I figured I would be walking into an ideal situation, as this area of West 57th was transitioning from tailor and garment firms into gallery spaces. "On Madison, you get half the amount of space for twice the money," 57th Street pioneer Rosa Esman told the *Times*.

I had some nice forward momentum going, and a location for my gallery, but there was just one problem. I hadn't raised a dime yet. I decided to talk with my banker, Verna Mott, at Marine Midland Bank. "What would happen if someone called to ask about my credit and history with the bank?" I asked.

"Well," she said, "we could tell them that you have been with the bank for three years and keep a balance in the high three figures." She further explained they would never be specific.

That, I realized, would do me much good, no matter how flexible the landlord was or how willing he was to work with a new tenant.

I didn't catch either of those two breaks. The owner of the building was an older gentleman named Harrington, who was well into his 90s. The first thing that struck me was his very distinctive voice. His face drew into a deep concern when he met me, for the same reason so many others seemed to be concerned—I was only 25. What was it about age? Didn't anyone believe that young people could have the brains, balls, ingenuity, ambition, and wherewithal to succeed? The other problem lay in my request for a 10-year lease, to establish some stability with my gallery, and let it be known that *this* 25-year-old planned to be a fixture for years to come. Harrington was afraid I was a bad credit risk.

So I pulled one of the cards available to me. I brought Chuck, who dressed for the occasion in his snappy Paul Stuart suit, looking every bit the suave, debonaire middle-aged gentleman versed in business. "We are engaged," I told Harrington. That appeased him.

Later in the month, Harrington called my home phone, thinking he was reaching Verna Mott at Marine Midland Bank to check on my financial status. I recognized his voice, and quickly snapped into character, pretending I was Verna Mott. I told him, "Patricia Hamilton is from the wealthy Hamilton Family from Philadelphia, a direct descendent of Alexander Hamilton and she has plenty of family money." (You can catch a glimpse of Alexander Hamilton, our nation's first Secretary of the Treasury, every time you pull a $10 bill out of your pocket). I went on to add, "She keeps a steady five-figure balance in her account and is a good credit risk. Furthermore, she is engaged to the distinguished Chuck Lawliss, who has kept her on the straight and narrow."

My historical representation of Hamilton as the builder of a wealthy estate was a bit off. Alexander Hamilton died broke, as the multitudes of us who saw Lin-Manuel Miranda's fabulous *Hamilton* show on Broadway were reminded.

Talk about tall tales—I got the lease.

• • •

Four months later, on February 3, we opened the Hamilton Gallery. The space was huge and gorgeous.

Chuck, being Chuck, suggested we have two openings: one for the general public and one black-tie event for investors and collectors. The first opening was packed with 700 people. Absolutely every artist in New York was there, as well as a few celebrities, the great Russian ballet dancer Rudolph Nureyev to name one. Each one of the gallery artists had their own guest list to add to my already prodigious and power-packed mailing list. During the night, one woman put her mink coat over the Robert Murray sculpture, which I quickly scooped up and hung in my office closet. In our 5,000 square-foot space filled wall-to-wall with people, there was a lot of excitement. Everyone was buzzing about the hot new gallery on West 57th.

Well, almost everyone. My Aunt Ruth and Uncle Frank, my father's brother, gave my parents a very hard time for not coming to the first opening. My parents' excuse? "It was snowing." Now that's supporting your daughter. My mother, chastened by her sister-in-law, who hated the way my parents treated me, did show up for the black-tie opening. Rick accompanied my mother, and of course he was supportive.

Before dinner, Mom came to my apartment to help me get dressed. "If I hadn't had six kids, I would have opened a gallery on 57th Street," she said, already trying to knock me down a peg.

"But Mom," I countered, "you don't even like art."

Two nights later, we hosted the black-tie opening with a preliminary dinner at the 21 Club. Dorothy Miller and Tom Messer attended, which was a real coup. I learned a lot more about the artists I represented from how they behaved that night. Clem Meadmore brought a date with enormous breasts and a plunging neckline, a destination into which he seemed to be plunging all evening long. I sat Walter Dusenbery next to Doris Weintraub, which took another direction, developing into a lasting relationship as a patronage for years.

After dinner, we all went to the gallery to find sales moving briskly. We landed a great review in *The New York Times,* but the backers were unimpressed; they didn't realize how hard it was to get reviewed in the *Times* at all, let alone the golden lights and shining stars their words seemed to me. In *Artnews,* feature writer Phyllis Tuchman (and still feature writer 45 years later) wrote about how the money I raised for the gallery was similar to the way angel investors were secured for Broadway theater, an analogy I have used since to describe my strategy. She also noted how young I was for being this far along in the business. When Phyllis interviewed me, I told her that when any potential investor asked me my age, I said, "I was '30- ish.'"

"They in turn asked, 'What kind of an answer is that?' And I replied, 'What kind of a question is that to ask a lady?'

Phyllis and *Artnews* loved that.

I opened Hamilton Gallery with a group show of gallery artists, but followed with one-person shows. The first two artists to feature their own shows were Clem Meadmore and Deborah Remington, the two most difficult-to-deal-with artists in my group. In fact, Clem was very negative. During the show, he told me he wanted to leave the gallery. Let me tell you that does not inspire a dealer to knock themselves out to sell out a show. Though I enjoyed reasonably good success with him, it made no difference. He wanted to leave. *Just go,* I thought. Clem thought that, with a young female dealer, he could pick the artists and logo for the gallery, and run the place. He was sadly mistaken.

Deborah's show was next. Despite her instrumental involvement in connecting me with Paula Hughes, my first investor and the one who got the investor snowball rolling down the hill, Deborah was a real pain in the ass. For this, she wanted a contract that gave her veto power over who could buy her work. She invited Paul Cummings, the curator of drawings at the Whitney, to install the show without asking me first. No one I could sell a painting to was good enough for Deborah, and she rejected one client after another.

Among them was Hilde van Roijen, one of my backers and a very classy lady, as I noted earlier. Why? Because, evidently, Deborah had once been Hilde's houseguest and, in her opinion, Hilde had a "poopy collection." That's a nice thing to say about your classy, elegant hostess, isn't it? By the way, Hilde also happened to be on the Board of Trustees of the Corcoran; among the paintings in her "poopy collection" was a Brueghel.

I got through that ridiculousness and got Deborah's show up—and she landed on the cover of *Arts Magazine* with a long article by

Corrine Robbins. The feature story amounted to more press from a single source than Deborah had ever received, but unfortunately, Deborah thought *Arts* was as important as *Time*. She was absolutely impossible.

As if that was not enough, Deborah started to cause trouble with my backers. Suddenly, Alan Baer wanted approval power over every check I wrote. Not legal, since he was only a limited partner. They threatened legal action, but it never amounted to a thing because they were just being bullies and trying to take over the gallery. Carole Baer, his wife, was bone thin and about five-foot-six. She was so heavily made up that Jay and I nicknamed her "Vampira." She wore expensive designer clothes but had horrible taste. While they were threatening me, she actually said, "Pat, you won't look good in stripes." (as if I would go to jail for not going along with two of the limited partners' ideas of how to run a gallery.)

In the end, they filed a nuisance suit and sued both the gallery and me personally. I had to hire an attorney and found the lawyer, Jack Scherer. He got the case dismissed rather quickly and was a real mensch. You can imagine how I felt about Deborah after all of this trouble. While none of them had a legal leg to stand on, it really fucked with my stress level.

Not to mention my self-esteem and body image. One was too low and the other too fat, in my eyes, despite all the acclaim and attention my new gallery was receiving. Janet Stayton, with whom I was then still on good terms, told me about a bizarre treatment from a diet doctor that would inject you with urine from pregnant women, and it would kill your appetite. This doctor apparently guaranteed you would lose ten percent of your body weight in the first month. Also, my primary source of food needed to switch to shrimp. Let's see—shrimp and the urine of pregnant women. That's a pretty novel dietary program!

Yet, the weight poured off, and I dropped 30 pounds, getting to a point where I was downright thin. I never ate another shrimp for many years, though, and don't even ask about urine from pregnant women.

. . .

That of course led to trouble on the homefront. Not one to ever take kindly to being upstaged by a woman, let alone the one he was living with, Chuck was pretty threatened by all of my success. When I became thin, I also grew more desirable to other men. Not exactly what he wanted to see. In the Summer of 1978, a little over a year after I opened the Hamilton Gallery, he was trying to raise money to start a theater magazine—another of his grand ideas. I was sick of his get-rich-quick schemes, and the 20-year age difference was starting to feel huge. To clear my head and gain some perspective on my rising profile in the art world, and my relationship, I traveled to Europe for about six weeks while he stayed in New York, fundraising for the magazine.

I returned just in time for my brother Rick's wedding to Dola Davis of Wilmington, Delaware. The entire family was there, including all of my aunts and uncles, with plenty of drunk anecdotes flying around the place. Before, during and after my brother's big day, Chuck and I were fighting like cats and dogs. When I would complain he had no rent money, he would threaten to kill himself. The icing on the cake—and the closing chapter on our tumultuous relationship—came on my birthday, when friends wanted to celebrate with me.

"I have no money," Chuck announced.

"For something new and different . . ." I snapped.

Well, allow me to unpack this exchange. I had helped him raise $10,000 in August for his magazine, and he had managed to spend all of it. Not only did he not have money to help me celebrate my birthday, but he didn't have money for September rent, either. In reality, the relationship had been emotionally over for a year, but I was too afraid to throw him out in the middle of the frivolous lawsuit the Baers filed against me. I wasn't the least bit attracted to him anymore, physically or as a person.

So I threw him out.

On his way out the door, he fired off one final salvo: "If I had known you were going to throw me out, I never would have gone to that stupid wedding." He always had to have the last word.

When he moved out, he also left me a really nasty three-page letter outlining my defects of character. He added that I should be more like my mother, and more tolerant of his behavior. (Yes, that's exactly what I "wanted" to be. Miserable and unhappy, supporting a drunk for the rest of my life, just like my mother.)

. . .

After Chuck left, I threw myself into work, which wasn't so hard to do. There were always studios to visit, openings and events to attend. My gallery also started to take on more artists. Just before opening the gallery, I had lunch with Dorothy Miller, who recommended I represent John Willenbecher, who made gorgeous black constructions and objects. I was very excited about the work, and it helped that John was an extraordinarily nice person. Jay and I explained that we planned on selling the work, but then John insisted that his work did not sell.

Well, it didn't take us long to prove John wrong. On opening night, we sold a piece to the Hirshhorn Museum—every dealer's dream. Andre Emmerich always said that if you sell one piece to a museum, you sell four others to people who see it on view there. John's sales prospects took a decided turn upward.

John had a wonderful loft downtown, the site of many dinners and parties throughout the Hamilton Gallery's existence. He was in a long-term relationship with J. Patrice Marandel, a European art curator at the Chicago Art Institute, who he eventually married. Patrice was one of the smartest and funniest men I ever met. Recently, he retired as the curator at the Los Angeles County Museum of Art, where he accomplished a great deal for the museum's collection. His exhibitions were beautifully curated, tasteful, and well-received.

The next artist the gallery represented was Joan Snyder, with whom I'd originally worked while running the traveling exhibition service. Joan was a feminist who made really tough, important abstract paintings. She became prominent in the early 1970s with a series of works called "the stroke paintings," long, separate strokes in bold colors on white ground, as I further described earlier. The work is intensely emotional and hard to categorize. She was written up in magazines and newspapers as the next big thing. The minute she got bored with the strokes, she stopped making them and turned to other imagery.

When I met Joan, the work was deeply personal, intensely emotional, and feminist. When we spoke about showing in my gallery, she had finished a 40-foot painting about rape and wanted to show it. I, too, was a feminist, and personally thought it important to show, but the businesswoman and gallery owner in me did not think it would be easy to sell. Joan was very demanding and persistent, though; in this case, it was worth it. I thought she was a genius.

Joan also had a big heart. As tough as she was when it came to business, she was sympathetic and warm on a personal level. While I was representing her, she gave birth to her only child, Molly Fink with her then-husband, the photographer Larry Fink. One night while she was pregnant, I got a call from her. She was living in a loft in Chinatown and had no bathtub. She was dying for a bath, so she came to my 5th Avenue apartment to take what felt like a luxurious bath to her in my tub. Later, I loved spending time with Joan and her daughter Molly, and on several occasions, I even babysat Molly. She was a wonderful, loving mother with a smart, well-adjusted, and balanced daughter.

So, we were off and running on the adventure of a decade—I hoped.

CHAPTER 7

A Star is Born: Louise Bourgeois

Blue-chip artists are the *crème de la crème* of the art world. They're the artists whose works draw attention far and wide, who dealers and gallery owners fawn and sometimes fight over in their respective (and sometimes joined) quests to represent or show their work. Their reputations and fame grow as they get older, or die, their works taking on huge and sometimes oversized stature in the grand scheme of things. When it comes to buying their works, these artists can sell paintings, sculptures and other expressions for exorbitant prices to private collectors and at auction. To use an analogy from my favorite sport, tennis, they represent the Hall of Fame of modern artists.

I've had the distinct pleasure of helping launch six blue-chip artists in my career, substantially advancing their statures and legacies. All of them created work that stands the test of time. And all of them were characters that alternately thrilled me, made me laugh—and had me tearing my blonde hair out, more than once.

When I opened Hamilton Gallery, I'd already worked with

three blue-chip artists—Ron Gorchov, and the two I described earlier, Joan Snyder and Deborah Remington. They were all well-established, Deborah and Joan for decades, and my representation of them, showings of their work and support in getting them great press helped take them over the top into true blue-chip status. But there was a woman older than all of them, born in Paris before World War I, who had yet to gain much notoriety at all. She became perhaps the most enigmatic and interesting—and often difficult—blue-chip artist with whom I worked. To give you an idea, take her answer to first question about her in the beautiful art book: *"Let us get something clear before we begin. In general I don't need an interview to clarify my thoughts. It is absurd, a pain in the neck! Interviews are a process of clarification of other people's thoughts, not mine. In fact, I always have to know more about you than you know about me. All the same I like to be crystal clear when we speak. I like to be in a glass house. There is no mask in my work. Therefore, as an artist, all I can share with other people is this transparency."*

Now that's the way to get the press and collectors interested—but maybe it is. It's the art world, after all.

Then 68-year-old Louise Bourgeois wasn't even *at* the blue-chip level when we met. In the spring of 1978, I was at Max Hutchinson's Gallery opening in SoHo and spotted Louise, whose work I admired. Knowing a good addition to my gallery when I saw one, I suggested a studio visit in the future. She was a pioneering feminist artist, her work as emotionally disturbing, perverted and witty as any I had ever seen. Plus, she was versatile, working with many materials such as marble, bronze, wood, and paper. And the titles she chose for her pieces? Naming a piece *Cunt I* didn't faze her at all. Penises also showed up in many of her pieces; she was an equal opportunity shocker. There is a famous Mapplethorpe photo of Louise holding an enormous bronze phallus that she made—typical.

I knew Louise was an important artist, but her reputation was still pretty underground at the time. Certainly nowhere near the highly visible levels of Joan Synder and Deborah Remington. I had seen her pieces in group shows at the Modern Museum and the Whitney, but she was truly off-grid, relatively speaking: she had not featured in a one-person commercial gallery show in nearly 15 years.

Because of this, when I arrived at her studio in Chelsea on 20th Street, I had no idea what my latest adventure into the life and work of an iconoclastic artist would bring. After meeting and seeing some of her works, both complete and in progress, I knew what my eyes and instincts told me. I immediately offered her a show, but she wanted to come up first with an idea and present it to me. I definitely appreciated that.

About a week later, Louise made an appointment to visit Hamilton Gallery to talk about a possible show. True to form, she walked into my gallery and out of the gate with a somewhat off-the-wall idea: she wanted to do one large piece in the main space and show smaller pieces in the back gallery. I thought about it for, oh, a few seconds. "You can have the opening show of the season in September," I said, referring to the time of the year when New York's art scene relaunched in full after summers spent in Woodstock, the Catskills or the Hamptons. The best time of the year. Louise was in.

While many artists and others in the industry migrated out of busy Manhattan and into the bucolic countryside or sweeping beaches of the Hamptons, Louise spent the summer in town. Throughout the summer, she kept asking me if she could come to the gallery to sit and contemplate the space. What was she going to do? Meditate? Draw pictures in her head? Size up a remodel and then pitch it to me? I had no idea.

Well, what she had in mind was to install her work early—as in a week before the scheduled opening. She also called me at 8 a.m. every morning with updates on how her main piece was coming, what she needed to complete the work, and so forth. It got to the point that when the phone would ring at 8, I would answer, "Good morning, Louise." She'd giggle and say, "How did you know it was me?"

"Lucky guess."

My other concern, and upcoming issue, was pricing her works in the back of the gallery. She employed only student assistants, who had no idea how to set prices. Nor did she. Consequently, she was self-managing, or shall we say, *mismanaging* her own career. When I'd ask her for a price, she'd suggest $50,000, like it was a standard price for the work of a then-underground artist out of any gallery in two decades.

"Louise," I'd say, "that's ridiculous." We settled on $10,000.

Fortunately, her work didn't need her faulty intercession. It spoke for itself. She was developing quite an exhibit. The one large piece for the main space was titled *The Confrontation*. The installation comprised a large banquet table adorned with latex body parts—you know, parts such as breasts, phalluses, testicles and arms. She was not shy about cutting to the chase! Surrounding this anatomical feast and its table were 66 empty coffin-like structures. As for Louise's vision for such a strange but amazing work, that now rests in the collection of the Guggenheim? Well, besides knocking people in 1978 New York sideways, this work is sometimes compared to Brueghel's 1567 masterpiece panel *The Peasant Wedding*. That's vision. To put an even more bizarre spin on it, she also envisioned the family *eating the body parts*, thus addressing some deep-seated emotional issues within the family. As well as herself. Her father, who owned a tapestry foundry in France, was a notorious womanizer. She hated him, and it came out in her work all the time.

I could relate to her.

The morning of the opening arrived on a bright September morning, with New York alive and kicking, the art community back from a summer of partying and cavorting. My phone rang for my now-daily 8 a.m. coffee call with Louise.

This time, though, Louise was in tears. "I cannot finish the piece," she cried, "and so there will be no opening that night."

Clearly, she didn't fully appreciate that *opening* didn't merely mean *opening when she and her work were good and ready according to her timeline*. It also meant the promotion and marketing I'd done for her, the build-up I'd given her show, a noteworthy event because of her unique art and because it was her first commercial appearance in 15 years. I wasn't going to let her or any artist fuck with the hard, supporting work I'd done on the back end because of incomplete work or stage fright.

It was time to get tough with Louise. She'd had all summer to come up with a show and work on the piece, and she was not going to cancel out on me at the last minute. "Okay, Louise, don't finish," I said, my voice particularly firm. "It's your name on the wall. Everyone told me I was nuts to agree to show your work, so no one will be surprised to come to an opening seeing unfinished work—this one's on you." Then I cranked it up a notch, my irritation approaching red-line status, not caring at all that I was talking to a 68-year-old woman. I only saw an artist trying to bail out. "I don't care who you have to call, and what help you have to hire, but get your ass to the gallery and finish the damn piece."

When I arrived at the gallery at 10 a.m., eight hours before showtime, Louise was indeed there and crying her eyes out—had she stopped in the past two hours, I wondered? But she'd listened to me and brought along plenty of help. Nancy Graves painted boxes. Her son, Alain, a judge, pitched in, along with some students. I was impressed. Come hell or high water, *The Confrontation* would be ready to take center stage, and all the other works with it.

I left the gallery at 4 p.m. to go home and change for the 6 p.m. opening that was at 6 p.m. When I returned, not quite knowing what stage I would find her big piece, Louise and her crew were in the process of leaving. She'd pulled it off. The piece was done.

Sadly, we didn't receive the one piece of publicity every artist and gallery owner covets on opening night, but it was through no fault of our own or Louise's. The *New York Times* happened to be on strike during her show, but the city's other newspapers showed up and covered it. In fact, Louise's work and the opening appeared in every other newspaper in town—blanket coverage. It doesn't mean I was able to sell a thing, but the gallery was certainly crowded. Among the crowd was Deborah Wye from MoMA, who found much to like about Louise's exhibit, so much so that, four years later, she gave Louise a one-woman show at the Modern in 1982—making her one of the first women ever to have a show there. (Georgia O'Keeffe had a show there in 1946.) It was a watershed moment. *The Confrontation* was included in the show.

. . .

Despite our somewhat bumpy run-up to her opening, I found Louise such a fabulous character that she became part of my inner circle. I threw dinner parties at my 5th Avenue apartment, which always featured the regulars. Paul Gardner—who lived around the corner—was an art writer I met through John Willenbecher. So it was usually Paul, John, and my associate at the gallery, Jay Gorney, along with whoever he was dating, plus one or two others. Louise soon ingratiated herself to the group, became a regular, and even threw dinners at her own place. She was a lot of fun.

Louise's townhouse in Chelsea was three floors, plus a sub basement; you entered on the first floor. All the ceilings were low. I mean Venice in the 15th century low. Louise was only five feet tall. She told me she had the ceilings dropped before she moved into the place. I could never truly understand why. Even I, at five-foot-four, had to bend down to get through some of the doorways. What her doors lacked in height, her kitchen more than made up for in size. It was quite large, both the cooking and eating areas. I soon realized that, like the doorways, the kitchen perfectly matched and reflected Louise's stature in that particular room; she was an excellent cook who loved champagne.

One afternoon, she turned to me and said, "Pat, would you like to see a new sculpture?" We went downstairs. I beheld another banquet table, much, much smaller than *The Confrontation*, but covered with all-male body parts. And an ax with lots of blood. She dedicated the piece to her father. I gasped in shock.

"Ah, but Pat," she said, "I hated my father."

She definitely knew how to express her deepest feelings through art.

One Sunday, during our exhibition at the gallery, Louise called. "Can you, Jay, and I have brunch together?" she asked. "I have a fantastic idea."

We went for brunch at the Empire Diner in Chelsea. After ordering coffee, she said, "I want to do a performance piece in the gallery."

"A performance piece?" I asked. "What's on your mind?" I knew that with Louise, literally anything could come out of her mouth next, and likely, it would be strange. Or certainly different.

"I want to hire 66 Black angry dwarfs willing to perform in the nude. I want them to stand in empty wooden boxes, and then end up fighting over the latex pieces." Well, my reaction was a step away from the height of embarrassment: I almost shit myself. Jay as well. No way 66 Black angry dwarfs were walking into my gallery to perform in the nude in some macabre performance.

Still, I played along. If you can call operating in a mild state of shock playing. "Louise, where the fuck am I going to find 66 Black angry dwarfs willing to perform in the nude?" I asked.

"Small People, Inc.," Louise replied, apparently referring to Little People of America, which prominent actor and activist Billy Barty, a 3-foot-9 dwarf, founded in 1957. I say "apparently" because Louise didn't have a clue. But certainly, she was clued in as to who she expected to pay for these people. Me.

"Well, I don't think that's going to happen," I said when I finally gathered control over my bodily functions.

I could just picture my backers' faces if we allowed 66 Black angry dwarfs to take out their aggressions, mock or otherwise, to satisfy Louise's vision. I could also imagine a few things they would say to me, none of which would enhance my business or reputation.

We did, however, settle on putting human beings in the boxes. We agreed they would not be dwarfs, but art-world personalities. We even tried to present it as a real honor to be asked to be in the box. When we reached that agreement, Louise said, "Patterson Sims must be in a box, but he must be tied up."

Nice try. There was no way I was going to tie up the curator at the Whitney. Louise and I got to work on the tamped-down version of her bizarre concept. We designed the invitation like a ransom note, with cut-up letters inviting people to the performance. She wanted the best-looking bartender that I could find and also marijuana joints on the table at the opening. That's pretty heady thinking for a nearly 70-year-old woman (no pun intended), but I could not go along with the joints on the table. It was 1978, after all, and today's legal recreational status was yesterday's felony. We did, however, have an open bar. Now I needed to find the right person to tend the bar. On the subway to work one day, I saw a gorgeous man. I walked up to him and told him about the show. "You *must* be our bartender," I stated in closing. Not "Will you be our bartender?" or "Do you know how to tend bar?" but simply and affirmatively, "You *must* be our bartender."

He was working in advertising at the time and loved the idea; Louise approved. On the invitation, we added another wrinkle to the evening: "Wear your uniform," it read. Louise wanted everyone to wear their fantasy outfit. So, they did. Some people arrived in black tie; Jay was in leather. I wore satin pants with a white silk vintage blouse and 5-inch gold heels; it felt good to be 5-foot-9 for a night. Grace Glueck of the *New York Times* (and later *ArtNews*), came in a tennis outfit. Bill Lieberman and Lowery Sims were there from the Metropolitan Museum; John Elderfield, Deborah Wye and Cee Brown from MoMA; Patterson Sims from the Whitney; and collectors Herb and Dorothy Vogel, Elaine Dannheiser and Gilbert Kinney showed up. There to dress some of the performers in her piece was art collector and philanthropist Vera List.

All of a sudden, before we knew it, people were fighting to get into the 66 boxes! Louise added to the spectacle by dressing those who didn't have a fantasy costume, or those she self-appointed, in costumes of her own making, with loosely fitted body parts. Gert Schiff, a well-known art historian, was one of the models. She called it a fashion show. Suzan Cooper, one of her young friends at the time , sang a song called, "She Abandoned Me." Louise had a filmmaker from Harvard University shoot the event for posterity. I had no idea how famous the movie would be; it was a film of the performance itself, including every person involved. There was no script, no set-up or developing shots. Just the performance. The photographs of the performance are in every book on Louise, including the definitive *Louise Bourgeois*, by Robert Storr, Paulo Herkenhoff, and Allan Schwartzman. In the photo of *The Banquet/A Fashion Show of Body Parts*, the foreground is occupied by *The Confrontation* table and body parts, while guests are on both sides of the work, most in fantasywear, others not.

Now more than forty years later, people still want to hear about it.

. . .

In 1981, she turned 70. I decided to throw her a birthday party on New Year's Eve in my apartment. Unlike what my ex, Chuck, did to me a few years before, I was actually going to celebrate her birthday *and* pay for the party. When she gave me the guest list, I nearly died when I saw the names. It included performance artist John Cage, iconic Neo-Dada painter, legendary American dancer Merce Cunningham, Pop art forerunner and art legend Robert Rauschenberg, *New York Times* art critic Roberta Smith, feminist writer Kate Millett, and more.

After a second, I gathered myself. "Great, Louise, but where the hell will I get the phone numbers for these people?"

She looked at me shyly. "Well, you could ask me."

Well, okay then . . .

The party took place, and her list of esteemed guests showed. I served homemade desserts and champagne. Everyone hung their coats on the coat rack in my hallway. Not surprisingly, the party was a sensation and the talk of New York. I think at one point, there were over 70 people crammed into my one-bedroom apartment. Still, people actually found room to dance! And some people loosened up their otherwise tight inhibitions a bit. Richard Martin, a very buttoned-down, proper New Yorker and editor at *Arts Magazine*, got rip roaring drunk and started kissing everyone.

As the last of the guests left, some seven hours after the ball dropped in Times Square, Ron Gorchov invited us all to breakfast at his loft on Broome Street.

Soon after, in February , Louise was awarded theAward for Distinction by the College Art Association. The annual conference was held in New Orleans and she wanted to go, but didn't feel she could travel alone. I understood, so I volunteered to accompany her. Well, not that it was any surprise, but my simple trip to New Orleans to support Louise as she accepted her award was an adventure from beginning to end. It began when we boarded the flight. She was desperate for a Perrier. When the Delta Airlines flight attendant tried to give her a club soda, Louise would have no part of that.

Later, we checked into the hotel. When the registration desk host politely asked her for a credit card, Louise said equally politely, and elegantly, "Ah, but for me, this is free." I explained that the College Art Association would later reimburse her, but she had to pay for the room herself. However, Louise literally had no credit card. I put her charges on my card.

As part of the event, Louise was asked to give a lecture on her work. The night before, while sitting in our hotel room, she handed me a garbage bag filled with unlabeled slides. I saw pictures of her work, her life, and various animals and landscapes. What works were they? Who were these people? What about these animals and landscapes? Well, your guess is as good as mine; no identifying or caption information was available on any of the photos.

Then, Louise made a simple request: she asked me to put them in order. Seriously? I did the best I could, but where does a photo of a rabbit go?

This very *unique* slide show accompaniment to Louise's lecture only got better. When Louise gave the lecture, she was constantly saying to the side, "Oh, Pat, how could you put this slide here?" It was pretty funny. But her lecture was great and everyone loved her.

The next morning, Louise wanted to attend a lecture on 17th-century painting being held at the conference. I sat through it but couldn't find her. Later, I bumped into her. "Louise, where the hell were you?" I asked.

"It was so boring I left and went to the most fantastic movie, *Six Unnatural Acts*, a film about the Lesbian movement." Not what you'd normally hear from a nearly 70-year-old woman in the early 80s in America.

I folded my arms and grinned. "What was one of the unnatural acts, sex with a man?"

That cracked her up.

A month after we returned to New York, Judy Chicago was exhibiting the "Dinner Party" at the Brooklyn Museum. Along with that installment came a number of dinners all over Manhattan for famous feminists. Louise jumped into the excitement and was the guest of honor at one dinner, held in the SoHo loft. All the photographs were taken by the conceptual feminist artist and photographer Mary Beth Edelson. We were all told to dress like a famous feminist. I had a friend who asked Calvin Klein to make a black and silver sequined dress, which his wife wore. I borrowed the dress, wore a black floppy hat with a feather and a cigarette holder, and went as the ever-so-sultry and headstrong Mae West.

During the night, Mary Beth took pictures of all the attendees. When I saw my picture, I thought, *this is too great not to share*. I made a Christmas card around the photo and added the caption, "Come up and see me sometime." Mae West . . . the New York gallery owner.

. . .

As my personal friendship with Louise deepened, along with my staunch support of her work, her status in the art community continued to skyrocket. She was now, in artists' eyes, a blue-chip artist, though I could never sell a thing of hers. I wanted only one thing more: to be her exclusive representative. I'd largely gotten her this far, and I wanted to make sure she received the full acclaim—and sales—for her amazing work. Whenever I'd ask, though, she would say, "I do not understand this word exclusive."

She was crazy like a fox. Her show had gotten an enormous amount of long overdue attention that she craved. The next show I planned was for the following February 1980. She developed a friendship with Paul Gardner and told him that she was planning shows in three different galleries in New York—and of course, not telling one dealer about the other. There was a little complication:

Louise told Paul in confidence she was in love with him, but since Paul and I were loyal friends, he informed me.

For starters, Louise wanted to do another performance piece at my gallery. On top of that, she planned to show drawings at the Max Hutchinson Gallery, and some older sculpture with Xavier Fourcade, a well-known Uptown dealer who, like Louise, was French. Supposedly he had represented her for years, but I'm dubious as to what level and form that representation took. I do know he was never willing to give her a one-woman show until I did.

I thought I should call Fourcade to discuss the situation. Perhaps if we coordinated the shows at the same time, and shared advertising and clients, then maybe someone could sell one of her pieces.

So in August, I made the appointment to see Xavier and brought with me a copy of the legal contract that Louise had signed, promising to do a show with me the following February. Xavier kept me waiting for 30 minutes because he was out to lunch. It turns out, he was dining with Louise—which I learned when the two of them walked into his office.

Xavier decided to approach the matter like most insecure, egotistical men who feel their property is being threatened: he was unbelievably insulting right off the bat. He told me flat-out that "your little piece of shit gallery doesn't represent Louise—but I do." Clearly, he had no intention of cooperating with me and sharing clients. Then I told him about the contract she had signed and showed it to him. He promptly grabbed it from my hands and ripped it up in a brazen move.

I shook my head. "Xavier," I said, "Do you honestly think I brought the original?" Not to be outdone, Xavier quickly forbade her from having the show with me. Louise sat silent, apparently deciding the best approach was to not speak. I knew she was desperate to have a show with a gallery that represented Willem de Kooning, Joan Mitchell, and others. Meanwhile, I was completely dumbfounded by Xavier's move, one that ended up in a screaming match. It got to the point where I thought I might slap him across the face, so I knew I should leave. I was not yet a member of the Art Dealers Association, and that would never be tolerated by the ADAA.

As I was leaving, Xavier turned to me and said, "This was the most unpleasant meeting I have had in 30 years as a dealer."

I was not going to be upstaged. "I seriously doubt that," I said. That marked the unfortunate end of my working relationship with Louise.

· · ·

Louise's career and reputation kept its upward trajectory right through the 1980s, particularly the latter part of it, when she was well into her 80s and 90s. Xavier Fourcade continued to show Louise's work until 1980. He later died of Aids. Later, she went with the Robert Miller Gallery, then with Cheim & Read Gallery. It was really when she switched to Cheim & Read that her work started to sell. It was always critically acclaimed, and artists loved it, but sales only began in the 1990s, when she was in her 80s. Some thirty years have passed since then, but Hauser & Wirth Gallery continues to represent her world-renowned work. It sells for a fortune. The confrontation with Xavier Fourcade, and my loss of my friend and wonderfully eccentric artist as her representative and host gallery, left me feeling . . . well, I can't tell you. Not only had I shown Louise for the first time in 15 years, but I also stirred up interest in her work and got her a show at the MoMA in 1982—as mentioned, one of the first women's shows MoMA had ever held. The press coverage was enormous. For all of that hard work and exposure—and believe me, it is *hard work* to break down the wall that separates artists from their future exhibiting successes, not to mention women artists—I was being dumped for two men who had never been willing to commit to a show with her prior to her big shows at the Hamilton Gallery.

Later, Xavier Fourcade admitted to Patrice Marandel that he didn't even like the work. Neither Fourcade nor Hutchinson ever made it into seeing my show. I was, in a word, devastated and felt completely betrayed by Louise.

CHAPTER 8

The New Wave at the Gallery

As the 1970s neared their close, New York was again the center of the cultural world. We younger people drove the fashion, lifestyle, music, experimental art and cinema, and everything else that made New York one of the hottest places to play and to create. Imagine taking in a day of diverse, edgy, and truly amazing art at the galleries on 57th or the Whitney, dinner at the trendiest restaurants, then maybe a campy off-Broadway play or crazy punk or New Wave show—and then letting it fly at Studio 54 or CBGB's until the rising sun burned your glassy eyes.

We worked hard, we partied hard, and we created and did business at full tilt. We operated with complete conviction, as though tomorrow was a day too late and an hour of sleep was a wasted hour. Talk about living in the present—*What a time!*

Within this bustling scene, the art world came out to play again in full force. I witnessed the resurgence from front-row seats, if you will—a very busy 57th Street on both sides of Madison Ave. The street was absolutely rocking, ending the 1970s with twice as many galleries as it had begun, hitting a peak it had not seen since. SoHo and its dirt-cheap lofts were becoming hot places to live, paint, and show your work. Then came the East Village. Since then, like other trends and scenes in New York, the galleries have hopscotched around various neighborhood districts and even to another borough; today, you'll find the catchiest work in Chelsea, Tribeca, the Upper East Side, and Brooklyn.

But I was on West 57th in boom times. Amidst all this action, the Hamilton Gallery of Contemporary Art enjoyed full stature as a major scene-setter and exhibitor of important, smart, and creative works you will never forget. We were one of the city's hottest and most sought-after galleries, parked right in the middle of all the fun.

Thanks to Louise Bourgeois helping me set the table with future blue-chip artists, I became known as a gallery owner and curator who knew how to take someone's career to the next level, as good as it might already be. A few times, I even took artists into the industry stratosphere—blue-chip status. Even though I was hurt and stunned by the treatment Xavier Fourcale gave me, I was determined to move forward with this kind of work. I wasn't about to let a narcissistic asshole like him stop me from showcasing the artists I believed in. Nor was I going to be stopped from showing works I knew would give their new collectors and/or owners great pride and pleasure for years to come—and put valuable dollars into my business bank account.

My next major artist to represent was not a painter or multimedia artist like Louise, but a sculptor. When I pursued him, Isaac Witkin was represented by the Marlborough Gallery. From his very first solo exhibition at the Rowan Gallery in London in 1963, his brightly colored fiberglass works and what the *New York Times* called "their witty, Pop Art-like look" made him a darling of the critics. And a scene-setter. Two years later, right before moving to New York, he was part of one of Great Britain's most important shows of the '60s, "The New Generation: 1965." One year later, he appeared in one of minimalism's defining exhibitions, "Primary Structures" at the Jewish Museum in New York.

That's two defining shows, in one year, on both sides of the Atlantic. He was off and flying.

Thirteen years later, I learned Isaac was looking for a gallery to sell the work. While Marlborough Gallery provided him a sufficient stipend to make the art, they were not able to convert the more lucrative end of the deal—selling it. My timing was fortuitous; by this point, my instincts were finely honed, though some would say they were pretty good throughout my career. Thanks to my previous successes, everyone who mattered knew I could sell sculpture. In some circles, I was already being called "The Sculpture Lady."

The stars aligned for me. It was a big coup to steal Isaac away from Marlborough, and I was very excited to be representing him.

The press was fascinated with Isaac's background, his previous shows, and the large organic sculptures he created. His story intrigued me very much as well. What goes for art goes for writing, music, movies, and many other life pursuits: no story, no success. Originally from South Africa, he studied in London under a pair of famous sculptors, Anthony Caro and Henry Moore. So he knew his stuff. He assisted Moore until 1965 when Caro brought him from London to America to teach sculpture at Bennington College in New Jersey. He later found a great place to make his art—a 22 acre blueberry farm in New Jersey, where he lived out his years. "He was proud to be part of a group of new artists from London who were breaking away from formal traditions," his daughter, Nadine, told the *Burlington County (NJ) Times* after he passed in 2006.

Isaac also had the type of personality and intellect I really enjoyed, which was not always the case with the artists I represented. He was a South African Jew from a wealthy family. Most of his siblings were involved with the arts. One brother was an opera singer and the other an actor; later, one of his two daughters, Tamar, would become a professional composer. The Witkin men were charming with a great dry English sense of humor, and I found Isaac one of the most endearing, humorous, and thoughtful men I have ever met. He even looked like a sculptor: tall, burly, bearded, and well over 250 pounds.

When I sought out Isaac, I was well familiar with his sculptures. All were large-form, topping out with the 55-ton granite piece, "Garden State;" he also worked in bronze, steel, and other forms of stone, along with the aforementioned fiberglass. He made large-scale constructivist abstract sculpture and made it well.

But something else captured my attention—and it is in those glimpses that I sought to make my mark, whenever I had the opportunity. It began with my eye for spotting greatness, whether obvious or not yet realized. There is a difference between having a "good eye" and a "trained eye." Someone with a good eye can talk to you about the work, pointing out the features, how the artist manipulated color to create a painting or form, and the material to compose a sculpture. Someone with a *trained* eye, however, can put the work in a historical art context and see its greater potential.

Both my associate at the gallery, Jay Gorney, and I were schooled in art history—and that made a difference to clients.

Grace Glueck, the great *New York Times* art critic, wrote something quite poignant in the mid-1980s about Isaac's work with the smaller pieces that I loved—the pieces I spotted with my eye—and brought into my gallery:

"There are a number of extraordinarily smaller pieces that demonstrate Witkin's cleverness and scale," she wrote. "Though they are similar in form to the bigger works, he hasn't simply effected simple transitions from large to small. It's the delicate adjustments he makes, in the thinness of forms and their close massing, that gives these smaller pieces the weight and authority of the large works."

Which speaks to the difference between having a good eye and a great eye. We made this connection where others might not have—

and that's why we were the first to show Isaac's smaller bronzes.

Here is how it happened: about two months after we started working together, Isaac called and asked me to visit his West Side studio, where he had started to make new bronzes. I was expecting a fall show of large-scale sculpture, so I went to his studio with a little fear in my heart. *What massive piece would I have to try to install in my main room now? What would it take?*

When I walked through the door, though, I spied the most glorious small bronzes I had ever seen. Instead of traditionally casting bronze, Isaac was pouring the bronze directly into the sand. After it set, he would paint on a patina. Each bronze was unique.

I agreed to do a show of the small bronzes and knew it was a tremendous risk, but that's where his heart was. What other gallery owners would have opted to exhibit Isaac with small bronzes at the time? None. But I had the balls to give it a shot—and, as we got closer to opening, my heart followed suit.

The show was the first to open the 1979 season. We exhibited about 15 small bronzes and again earned the cover of *Arts Magazine*, with an article by Gene Baro. Hilton Kramer from the *New York Times* also came in and raved about it. The show sold out. A major factor? We sold 14 of the 15 pieces, leaving one remaining—the largest piece, which I thought was the best bronze in the show.

Remember my comment about the necessity of a story? Here we go . . .

One Saturday, Isaac came into the gallery with a white-haired woman who looked just like him. His mother had flown in from South Africa, and what a powerful force she was. In no time, she took over my office, aglow over her son's rave review in the *New York Times*.

Later in the day, while Mrs. Witkin was hanging out in my office, who walks in but renowned Hollywood film and TV producer-director Bud Yorkin? Bud made lots of movies in Hollywood, most famously *An Evening with Fred Astaire* in 1958 and *Blade Runner* a quarter-century later. However, my generation knew him far better for his message-driven, hilarious, and irreverent TV comedy with Norman Lear in shows like *All in the Family*, *The Jeffersons* and *Maude*. He had major chops.

It seems Bud was also an art collector. Andre Emmerich, a rising industry legend, told Bud to see the exhibition; Andre had been parked on 57th Street in the renowned Emmerich Gallery for 25 years. He personally thought Isaac's exhibition a landmark show.

When Bud walked in, his first reaction was disbelief: he couldn't believe all but one sculpture had been sold, a large window I had featured in the installation. I showed him the *New York Times* review. "I like the one that hasn't sold yet the best," I said.

"Why?" he asked.

"Because most collectors are too stupid to realize it's the best piece." It took 15 minutes to sell the piece to Bud.

Afterward, I walked back into my office, where Isaac sat with his mother and girlfriend. I threw out my arms in my best imitation of a showgirl. "Ta-da!! Sold it!"

Later, after Bud was divorced, I asked his ex-wife, Peg, if she wanted to sell the piece back to me. "Do you have a Witkin of your own?" she asked.

I nodded. "Yes."

"Is it for sale?"

"No."

She rested her case.

During the opening night selling frenzy, one of the clients wanted to pay us in cash for the piece he bought. Since I was reporting all my income, I didn't think the cash would help me, but I thought it could really help Isaac. I called him at the studio. "I need you in the gallery—now!" I demanded, acting like I was pissed off.

He walked into my office sheepishly and sat down. I reached

into my desk drawer and threw $12,000 in cash in his face. He roared with laughter. Then he and his girlfriend left the gallery, went straight to a Cadillac dealership on 57th Street and bought a big, bronze gas guzzler that he nicknamed "The Bronzemobile." He owned the car until the day he died.

. . .

The Bourgeois and Witkin show and all the press really put the gallery on the map. Many artists began approaching us about representation, while other artists received suggestions to do so. One stood out for me: Ron Gorchov, a mid-career artist whose seminal work influenced an entire generation of painters. He was one of the first artists to take a painting off the traditional stretcher and put it on a curved-shaped stretcher, which is often compared to a shield or a saddle. He made gorgeous emblematic abstract paintings with two marks in the center and beautiful stretches of paint. One of his many admirers was Julian Schnabel.

Ron's show at the gallery opened in October 1980, the month he was also getting married for the fourth time. Sidney and Frances Lewis bought the largest painting in the exhibition, and the money created a very nice wedding present for Gorchov and his bride. However, I found his work very difficult to sell.

Ron was charismatic and extraordinarily smart about art. We spent hours talking about painting, during which he shared an idea for another show he called "Color & Structure." It would include many artists who had broken the boundaries of traditional stretchers, including Sam Gilliam (who we already represented), Elizabeth Murray, Ralph Humphrey, Richard Smith, Joan Snyder, and Lynda Benglis. The show addressed two questions: What is painting? Does a canvas need to be on a stretcher? I thought his idea was fantastic.

While I began my gallery by working with artists with "safe markets," as I termed it a few years later to authors Laura de Coppet and

Alan Jones in the contemporary book *The Art Dealers*, I started feeling the need to go out on a limb once I got established. My first venture onto the proverbial gangplank (actually, a thrilling leap, since I'm always up for a great new challenge) was "Color & Structure," which had evolved from Ron's idea to combine two-dimensional paintings with sculptural elements that came off the wall. "I began to understand the phenomenon of the hot artist, the hot show," I said in *The Art Dealers*. "A new breed of collectors started coming in, and that's when I knew it was going to happen."

. . .

Isaac Witkin offers a perfect example of how I blended my more conservative side as a gallery owner with a fair to large degree of risk, in his case showing small bronzes. Without strong press and some market appeal, you can have the greatest gallery and art show in the world, but it's going to land few or no sales—and in the end, sales keep the doors open. In *The Art Dealers*, I described my approach, as well as my thought process in bringing in an artist—a process that begins long before we open the show, typically six months or more.

"I don't show many artists who haven't shown before, so there is a history already. Still, I talk to critics before an exhibition, write a good press release, call the *New York Times*, and ask them to see the show. I talk up the artist to my best collectors six months ahead of time. If I'm trying to sell you a picture, I better know that it's more than merely beautiful, and they are often not pretty. In those cases, I provide the collector with the reasons why that painting will compel him to look at it for twenty years; a merely pretty picture loses its interest within a year."

Within this one paragraph, you can see my formula for success with the Hamilton Gallery: A past history and existing market, with some (or a lot of) name recognition. Prime the pump with critics from the key media, especially the *New York Times*, to ensure favorable press. Tip-off the art collectors so they will know what to expect and be more inclined to buy. Create an element of surprise or even shock value: Louise's phallic body parts in *The Confrontation,* and boxes into which she originally wanted to stick 66 black angry dwarves (before we settled on 66 art world personalities wearing their uniforms) and Isaac Witkin's sterling collection of small sculptures. Both exhibitions hit home on that front. As did the works of most of my other featured artists.

We sailed at full force into the 1980s with interactions with Ron Gorchov and Sam Gilliam, as well as fellow illustrious artists John Torreano, Rafael Ferrer, Richard Hennessey, and Grace Hartigan, whose drunken bender at my apartment one night was legendary—I'll get to that.

That summer, I went to Washington and visited Sam Gilliam's studio. Sam was a well-known colorfield Black painter whose drape paintings from the late '60s redefined abstract painting. However, he hadn't been featured in a show in New York since 1968; like Louise, we needed to find a dynamic way to capture the attention of the press and collectors and bridge his dozen years out of contemporary gallery view with the present moment. He was a lovely man and married to a fantastic *Washington Post* reporter; they had three of the brightest daughters I have ever met.

Sam's beautiful character really captured me, just as Isaac's had. I wanted to be the one to bring him back into a gallery exhibit, to offer that second chance I spoke about earlier, so I decided to give him a show. He made a series of metallic, iridescent black paintings. I gave Sam two one-person shows and several group shows, and even sold some of his work to the Met and the Museum of Modern Art. He was also featured in an important Barbara Rose exhibition. Much as I loved Sam and his paintings, though, I faced some stiff headwinds on the homefront; both my associates, Jay Gorney and Rafael Ferrer hated the work. They pressured me to drop him.

What a mistake. Rafi was jealous of the rapport between Sam and me—seriously—and Jay just didn't understand the point of the work.

I used my pull as the owner and ultimate decision-maker on all artists and shows to press forward, finding Rafi's reasoning ridiculous and childish, and Jay's a matter of his own personal taste. In Rafi's case, he was an enigma to begin with; he believed that you had to read Gabriel Garcia Marquez's literary work to understand his art. *Okaaaay.* As for Jay, I didn't like several of his preferred artists, either. Besides, when the chips were down, I was the one on the hook for the financial success or failure of my gallery—and I was going with Sam Gilliam. We received fantastic press. Furthermore, Tom Messer, director of the Guggenheim and a real scholar, had called our "Color & Structure" show a "museum quality" exhibition. These were heady times.

Buoyed by that wonderful success, the gallery now surging with momentum and my own star twinkling pretty high above the Manhattan skyline, I turned to Joan Snyder and brought her in for another exhibition. The great artist had just given birth to her daughter and was ecstatic at receiving the invitation. So ecstatic, in fact, that she threw her soul into it. She created a show of very beautiful paintings; the cover of the announcement was titled, "Welcome to this World, Molly Fink." We proceeded to sell everything, and her work was wait-listed. I felt so fortunate because she was riding high as well and was included in shows at virtually all of the museums. However, she was a meticulous painter, now with a child, who only made nine paintings a year. When I sent her a particularly big check, I included a note that said, "Paint, Joan, Paint." She loved it and put it up on her bulletin board in her studio.

In November, an article by Carter Ratcliff came out in *New York Magazine* titled "The Art Establishment: Rising Stars vs. the Machine." In the piece, he grouped the galleries into three distinct categories: Blue-Chip galleries, Mostly for New Artists, and The Armory Show to the Present. The Hamilton Gallery was rated #1 among "Mostly for New Artists." He'd dialed not only into the work and exhibits he saw in our space, but also the core of my process and style as a person and a gallery owner. He wrote, "Patricia Hamilton has an eye for tomorrow's heavyweights today."

I gushed. Who wouldn't? Any contemporary gallery owner, then and now, would feel like they'd gone to heaven when attached to those nine words. To the collector or well-informed buyer of art, they translate roughly as, "She knows what's hot, what's going to stay hot, what's going to rise in value, and what we will keep enjoying for many years to come."

The day the article came out, I walked into the gallery to find the phone ringing off the hook. *What the fuck?* I was completely baffled, since I didn't know about the article yet. Then my new friend, Mary Boone, called and informed me. Laura Bloom, my secretary, quickly ran to a newsstand and bought the magazine.

"How did you get a Number One rating?" Mary asked me, her voice just as green with envy as I imagined the rest of her.

"I don't know," I said, shrugging my shoulders.

This inspired her to hire a publicist.

. . .

Since there was no way I was going to show Louise Bourgeois again after the Fourcade incident, I had to think of an interesting show for February 1981, when I had originally scheduled her return appearance. Enter Isaac Witkin again. While fabricating his work at the Johnson Atelier in Hamilton, New Jersey, he came into contact with a multitude of new and interesting artists making bronze sculptures. "I recommend you have a show that re-examines the use of bronze," he said.

"That's interesting . . ."

I liked his thinking, but at the time, bronze was considered such an old-school, traditionalist form that few gallerists would carry much of it, let alone invest in an entire show involving quite a few heavyweights in the work. Still, I knew Isaac wouldn't recommend anything to me unless he saw something new and captivating that would draw the press and buyers.

I decided to run with it. I would make damn sure there was nothing traditional about *my* show. If it went well, I thought, then they'd be talking about bronze as the hot new form of sculpture when we were finished.

I got to work. I brought in 15 heavyweight sculptors, including Isaac, Robert Murray, and Ron Gorchov, all three of whom I represented. The contemporary sculptors had diverse styles and tastes, some old-timers and others new converts, but all shared one thing in common: they worked in bronze. And they were all great.

What a response! It was a big hit.

As the *New York Times* reported in Hilton Kramer's long review in "Art View," my three-week exhibition stood out for its stylistic diversity. For starters, I had quite the lineup: Isaac with his "The Looking Glass," figurative works by Martin Silverman, Nancy Grossman and Marisol, abstractions by William Tucker and Gorchov, and "in-between" sculptures by Nancy Graves, Bryan Hunt and Lynda Benglis that fell somewhere between representational and abstract. We even had the great Roy Lichtenstein in the show. Silverman's "Run Around Sue" caught plenty of attention with its dancing figures, turquoise patina, and catchy title inspired by Dion's early 1960s hit song.

What I probably loved most about the review of the show was that Hilton Kramer couldn't quite *define* it. He couldn't pin it down. "If there is a trend to be discerned in this exhibition," he said, "it is definitely not a matter of style. Nor do notions of 'tradition' and 'innovation' quite apply, either."

In other words, I curated a presentation no one had quite seen before—just how I like it.

After Kramer's review came out, my neighbor Caroline Alexander said, "Oh good God, you got a Sunday review, and a 'think piece' at that. You will be impossible!"

People came into the gallery in droves. The bronzes looked great on the slick white floors, and it was installed beautifully. The show had a powerful impact, solidifying my reputation as a "sculpture dealer."

. . .

Hilton Kramer's review in the *New York Times* also made quite the national impact. How big? How about the *White House big*?

One morning, a few months after the bronze show, I got a call from the White House. Ronald Reagan had recently been inaugurated as president, and his staff was preparing to throw an official State Dinner for the Egyptian President, Anwar Sadat. In October 1978, Sadat and Israeli Prime Minister Menachem Begin had agreed to peace between their nations through the famous Camp David Accords, brokered by then-President Jimmy Carter. This would be President Sadat's third official State Dinner at the White House; he'd also been the celebrated guest in 1980. Now, the White House wanted me to put together a bronze show for this illustrious fete, setting small contemporary bronze sculptures on each banquet table. You can imagine how thrilled I was. I started planning the show, and I was also invited to the dinner with a guest, who I decided would be Jay.

However, my preparations, the show, and the dinner halted abruptly in October 1981, two weeks before the event. Like so many others who aspire to lasting world peace, I was crushed by the news on October 6: Sadat was assassinated. What a disappointment. What a great loss to the world.

From that would-be show, though, I took on the young sculptor Martin Silverman. Despite my own relative youth, I had never represented a young artist, and this guy brought along plenty of young-person bravado, attitude, and ego. He made charming figurative work in the realm of the folk artist, Elie Nadelman; I found it highly appealing. Martin, however, was having another child and wanted money, money, money. To help him spend less money, I agreed to pay the fabricating costs of his bronzes, along with his Washington dealer, Diane Brown. I got him into a show at the Milwaukee Art Center with a piece lent by the gallery.

During the show, the curator called me. "Martin just sold the piece to a private collector and wants the credit line changed," she said.

When I found this out, I was done. I took the proceeds from the piece I sold, deducted all the expenses Martin owed, secured my commission on the sale out of the studio, sent him a check for $10—and threw him out. My ears rang with one of his famously arrogant lines: "I am the best sculptor of my generation; I should not have to teach." He had been offered a teaching job at Princeton, for God's sake—and only for one day a week.

Many young artists don't realize that good shows are no guarantee. Nor are you guaranteed that an early success leads to another good show—ever. Truly, you can have one or two good shows, and that is the most success you will enjoy in a lifetime.

I truly believed in his work. Before I was done with him, I arranged for him to show in Toronto with Jared Sable from Sable/Castelli Gallery. Jared was a sweetheart, which only made me feel worse when I heard that he, too, had a horrible experience with Martin. Jared let him stay in the guest room in his house. Jared's maid later told him she had never seen a room so messy. Of course, Martin never said thank you for the hospitality.

He carried his reputation as being arrogant, rude, and impossible wherever he went. Years later, the famed gallerist Miani Johnson gave him a one-person show with the Willard Gallery in New York. One show was enough for her as well; she would not tolerate his behavior. How sad, because he truly was a talented sculptor.

No one understood the "15 Minutes of Fame" concept more than Robert Colescott. I saw Colescott's painting *The Potato Eaters* in the dining room of art historian and curator Robert Rosenblum after he bought the piece. It was a spoof of the famous Van Gogh painting of the same name, and Colescott put a truly timely touch on it by adding black characters. He made colorful paintings addressing social and racial inequality, which looked great in the gallery. I even sold a painting to United States Senator Bill Bradley, the former New York Knicks basketball star who later enjoyed an illustrious political career. I introduced Lowery Sims from the Met to the work, and she later organized a retrospective and wrote a book on him. Oh, if Colescott, who died in 2009, could see what his market is now!

. . .

Martin Silverman and Robert Colescott marked a big sea change for me. As my stature grew as a gallery owner who represented well, showcased striking new work and sold it, we started taking on new artists. It was clear that some of the original artists were not working out anymore. As noted earlier, one of my initial champions in opening the gallery, Deborah Remington, started trouble with a few of my backers, telling them I was incompetent. This did not endear her to me. The minute I could, I threw her out of the gallery. Later, she had a show with the Jack Schainman Gallery, and finally with the Mitchell Algus Gallery. She was an impossible bitch, and no one would put up with her. Ironically, before she died, she left her estate in the hands of Margaret Matthews Berenson, who is as nice as Deborah was bitchy. She gets along with everyone. Now Deborah's work is highly sought after; most recently, a showing of her work at the Bortolami Gallery in New York sold out. A major book is being planned as well. If she were alive, none of this would be happening.

There's a lesson in this: some artists should not manage their careers.

In the meantime, Jay was constantly asking me to become a limited partner in the gallery. I would still own 51%, while he wanted 3%, like the financial backers. I had 3% held in reserve, felt he deserved it, and agreed. I presented him with partnership papers, but he was too nervous to ever sign or even see a lawyer about signing. Unfortunately, Jay's idea of a partnership was to reap the benefits when times were going well. He was not interested in being responsible for any of the problems or debts if and when things headed in the other direction. He would only open checks if I was away, and never open any bills. Even though he never signed the partnership papers, he was only too happy to tell people he was a partner in the gallery.

We marched forward with my plan, taking on four new artists: Grace Hartigan, Rafael Ferrer, Richard Hennessey, and Austé Peciura, known simply as Austé. Grace was the only woman who was well-known in the '50s as an Abstract Expressionist. (Though she'd been painting since the Great Depression, Lee Krasner's long-due fame and notoriety did not take hold until the mid-1960s, after her husband, Jackson Pollock, had died.) Owing to the misogynistic art culture in New York, especially in the '50s, Grace originally started painting as "George" Hartigan so that she could get shown. However, everyone knew the paintings were Grace's. She also married a brilliant immunologist named Wynn Price, who discovered the cure for the common cold and had moved to Baltimore so that he could practice at Johns Hopkins.

When I met Grace, she hadn't shown in quite a while. She became yet another artist to whom I was giving a second chance in a new, contemporary art scene. She made a series of really beautiful figurative-washed paintings. I knew it was going to take some time to rebuild a market for her, but she was a good painter, and I liked her enormously. Grace had the best stories, which she told in a hilarious, animated way whenever she got tipsy. One night, she told me the story of going to bed with Franz Kline. While they were about to make love, Franz yanked out her diaphragm and said, "Grace, you know I hate sculpture."

Sadly, her husband, Wynn, died right before her opening in New York. Perhaps understandably, Grace went on a drunken bender, the likes of which I hadn't seen in some time. The only problem is that she got very drunk while staying in my apartment, in my bed. She drank everything in the apartment, including the cooking sherry. I was pretty appalled by her behavior, but felt compassion for her and reserved judgment, believing she was doing so out of a new widow's profound grief and sense of loss.

Well, six months later, Grace's bender showed no signs of slowing down. She made a series of watercolors that were awful. Since I felt too emotionally involved to trust my judgment, I called John Elderfield from MoMA and asked him to stop by and see the watercolors. He confirmed them to be as bad as I thought.

Finally, I confronted Grace. "I really can't show these," I said.

"You're not allowed to edit my work," she snapped back.

"Grace, if I don't believe in the work, I can't sell it. Since I'm the one paying the gallery expenses, I won't be able to show them."

She left the gallery and remained angry with me for the rest of her life.

In hindsight, I could have been more sensitive about telling her I couldn't show them, but I honestly don't think it would have made a difference.

Later, when David Hare had a show at the Guggenheim, I was invited to a dinner at a private home after the opening. Seated at the table were Harold Rosenberg, the foremost art critic of Abstract Expressionism, Saul Steinberg, the great American artist who made the famous cartoon of the United States that represented an over-sized New York as 90 percent of the country, and the enormously talented painter Philip Guston. He was more than talented; he was a legend. I was shaking in my boots just to be seated next to him.

Philip came to New York in the 1930s to do WPA murals with his childhood friend, Jackson Pollock. He hung out in the Village with all of the Abstract Expressionist painters and eventually became one of the most important painters of all time. His paintings are in every major museum collection. By the end of the '60s, he returned to his figurative roots and made political drawings and paintings about the war, Nixon, and even himself. The critics turned on him, failing to understand what he was doing. But all of the artists knew how important Guston was. He influenced generations of artists. And there I was, sitting next to him. What a thrill!

Philip was with Marlborough Gallery, and his handler was David McKee. When McKee left Marlborough to open his own gallery, Guston went with him. He had several shows at McKee, but he hated the space. McKee's gallery was on the Upper East Side in the Barbizon Hotel building. Philip was looking for a chance and liked my space, parked in the center of the action on West 57th.

One Sunday, Jay and I took a bus upstate to Woodstock, a bustling artists enclave (and namesake of a pretty good open-air music festival in 1969), which turned into quite a day. Philip took us into his massive studio and showed us enough work to make my head spin. He had numerous figurative paintings and drawings, along with many of the Ku Klux Klan works. When his show opened at Marlborough Gallery, he knew it would be controversial. He immediately got on a plane and left for Europe, but even in Rome he heard about the scathing *New York Times* review. Thus chastened, he stuck with the figurative paintings, and now they were finally being sold and accepted.

When Philip spoke with me about showing at the Hamilton Gallery, he wanted to do an overview of drawings with a catalogue by the poet Bill Berkson. Quite frankly, he could have asked me for my first-born child, and I would have agreed. We agreed to a five-week show in October and November, with a catalogue by Berkson.

Then one day, Philip called me. "I dreamed I had a heart attack," he said. This notion was not completely unfounded; he previously had suffered a heart attack. He became paranoid and felt he couldn't leave his estate with someone he didn't know, no matter how much he liked me. He also did not believe I was 30 years old. It is hard to argue with someone after such a horrifying dream. So he switched gears and did the show of drawings we'd planned—but at McKee Gallery, not mine. Nonetheless, I went to the opening.

Afterward, he came up to me and threw his arms around me. "Patricia, I was hoping you would come. This shows real class."

Three months later, Philip Guston dropped dead of a heart attack. I spent the day weeping.

Around this time, Ron Gorchov recommended I consider the work of his friend, John Torreano, who had been showing in New York for years. He made large abstract paintings embedded with jewels, as well as columns of paint covered in jewels and cruciform. I first saw his work in a Pattern and Decoration show at the Alessandra Gallery, then more recently at the Frank Kolbert Gallery. A lot of galleries were after him. John was a nice guy who performed standup comedy when he wasn't painting. Quite a diverse man, he also held a teaching job in Las Cruces, New Mexico, for part of the year. It made sense: the cruciform carried a very Southwest feel.

John did a wonderful first show with my gallery, and it sold well. His second show was even more experimental, featuring paintings of jewels made in a Pop Art fashion. They were not good, but I showed them anyway. Predictably, nothing sold. Later, John destroyed the series. Nonetheless, he became a good friend, and I thought of him as a real brother.

Rafael Ferrer was of Puerto Rican descent and came from a very wealthy family. His brother was the actor Jose Ferrer, from whom he was estranged. He made installation art, eclectic sculptures, drawings, and paintings. I first knew the work from the early '70s when he showed a sculpture made of ice. Well, the fates stepped in: we experienced an unusually warm winter and the ice melted. I teased him about the weather, which brought us onto friendly terms. I followed his work from then on.

Rafael made paper bag drawings of portraits, kayaks, and maps, brightly colored and lively, thus bringing in his Latin heritage. He had been with Nancy Hoffman Gallery for years when he approached me. His reason was clear: he didn't like the other artists in her gallery but admired the artists that I showed. I gave him a one-person show. When it took place, Carter Ratcliff had written a large cover article on him in *Art in America,* a heady press placement. The cover image was a marvelous tent painted on the inside and the outside with figures and myths.

There was trouble in gallerist-artist paradise, though. While I loved the work, the chemistry between us never turned out to be good. He was macho, a perfectionist and hard to please. And he really spun my head by claiming no one could understand his work unless they read Marquez's literature. I still supported his work and wished him well after we had a very mutual parting of the ways. He returned to Nancy Hoffman, only to leave her again. Maybe he would've done best as his own dealer.

Then there was Richard Hennessy, who had been included in Barbara Rose's "Painting of the Eighties" show at The Grey Art Gallery. Barbara Rose was a very well-known art critic, professor and author who had written for all the prestigious art and culture publications. She was an expert on minimalism and championed the work of Donald Judd and Dan Flavin. J. Patrick Lannon, the well-known collector and former head of ITT, approached her about doing an exhibition of paintings in the '80s. She included a number of artists from my gallery and some unrepresented artists. Because of who she was, the press was everywhere. Not all of the press was good, but they wrote.

I put Hennessy in the show, as I admired his work at Kolbert Gallery for a year or two before the Barbara Rose show. His abstract paintings were beautiful and always had an unexpected element and a twist. He was a character, intelligent and well-read. He lived on 96th Street and East End Avenue, keeping one apartment for his studio and another for his home. He painted the walls of his home, as well as murals for Charles Ludlum's Theater of the Ridiculous in Greenwich Village. Of some concern, Hennessy was not plugged into the current art scene at all, referring to himself as Rip Van Winkle. Well, 20 years of continuous sleep in the Catskill Mountains does not give your gallery owner much to go on.

Also, Richard and Jay did not get along. At all. Mostly, I think it was because Richard didn't treat Jay like an equal partner. Well, he wasn't. Richard was correct, and he made that clear. Eventually, the two began to hate each other, which became obvious when we made a studio visit to pick out paintings for his final show. Jay didn't like some of the paintings and was quite vocal about it. Richard promptly went nuts, and he and Jay started screaming at each other like a pair of kids fighting for the ball at recess. The shouting match was so loud and nasty that I fled the studio. They rarely spoke after that, so I became solely responsible for dealing with Richard.

I showed Richard's work twice, and it moved. It's always a good thing in the gallery business. Later, he published an article in *Art in America* about painting, taking care to name the three most important painters of the century: Jackson Pollock, Willem de Kooning—and Richard Hennessy. Not many people agreed with the final third of that assessment.

My other new artist in the early 1980s was Austé Peciura, known as Austé, a student of John Willenbecher in Chicago. She was a punk artist and made very strange but interesting drawings in charcoal. They had to be framed in a dramatic way. She and her boyfriend, Aigueres, were from another generation, and Jay glommed onto them. He claimed Austé as his own personal artist, and he was her champion. She gave him one of her most important drawings. After the gallery closed, she and Jay had a falling out, during which he was extraordinarily mean to her. She always regretted giving Jay such a generous gift.

. . .

During this bustling time with my gallery and career, my personal life began looking up again. Until it didn't. Long past Chuck, I was now dating Tom Bergen, who I met originally through the Crispo Gallery as a money lender to Andrew. He called me, and I invited him to the Provincetown Art Association Annual Benefit.

Tom was a tall, beefy guy. Originally from Minneapolis, he held an undergraduate and graduate degree from Harvard and was very proud of it. Right before I met him, his family planned an intervention to try to get him to stop drinking. His wife said if he didn't get help, the marriage was over. He chose not to get help. What a 'perfect' guy for me to get involved with, right? Ironically, he was one year behind Chuck at Harvard.

The good news was that it didn't take me five years to get out of this relationship; I realized how sick he was pretty quickly. He wasn't just an alcoholic, but he had mental problems, too.

Things between us first came to a head one night at dinner. I was trying to fix up my friend, the psychologist Margarita Bailey, with another friend, Dick Sage. Margarita was one of the most balanced and put-together women I'd ever met. She started out as a friend of my sister Susan, but quickly realized Susan had a drinking problem and dropped her. Susan brought her to an opening at my gallery, where she bought a work on paper. I knew Dick well since he was not only an art collector, but an old boyfriend of mine. We had remained friends.

Susan and her current boyfriend, Ron Paige, were at the dinner as well. Tom wanted to talk about something absurd, like, why didn't I try and join the Daughters of the American Revolution and do volunteer work? As if I had extra time to do volunteer work. I finally turned to him and said, "Tom, no one is interested in this shit. Just shut up."

Typical of Tom, he never said another word and proceeded to pay for the entire meal.

In the cab to my apartment, we got into a shouting match. The cab driver told us to shut up—or get out. When we reached my apartment, Tom started storming around, packing his bag. He yanked the shower curtain rod out of the wall, slamming so many doors that the paint started to crack. I finally called 911 and asked for assistance.

That threw more fuel on the fire. He promptly grabbed my Louise Bourgeois pink Alabaster sculpture and threw it. Luckily, I caught it. He then threw my keys about 20 feet into the apartment. It was then and there I got the distinct impression he might have hit women in the past. By this point, between my family, Chuck, and others, I'd seen enough bad behavior to read more deeply into how it might progress from here.

I was through.

Generally, after these big fights, he would check into the Harvard Club, take a sleeping pill, then call in the morning and apologize. This time, it didn't matter. I was done. I don't think he believed me. It took another year and a half before he actually accepted that I was finished with him.

There was an undercurrent to our relationship—a very distasteful one. While Tom and I were together, he became quite friendly with his new drinking buddy—my sister Susan. After we were finished, Susan and my mother occasionally had dinner with him. My mother was convinced he was rich and could help Susan get a job. It didn't matter how many times I explained to her that Tom was not rich, but he *was* a hard-core drinker. "Tom's ex-wife is rich, not Tom," I added.

No matter. My mother and sister continued to cultivate a platonic relationship with him. My mother sucked up to him so badly, it was ridiculous.

Years later, while in California doing an exhibition, a highly flattering article came out in the *New York Times* about agents for artists, which I initiated. There was a large picture of me, Michael Klein, and Karen Amiel. On my way back to New York, I called Susan's apartment.

My mother answered. "Have you seen the *Times* article?" I asked excitedly.

"Tom called earlier and told me about it," she replied.

When I got back to New York, I called my mother. "If you want to continue to have a relationship with Tom, then you can," I said. Silence on the other end. "However," I added, "there will be a price if you do this. You will forfeit your relationship with me."

I paused for a second, then admitted to her what freaked me out even more than the obvious perception of *my mother* taking up with my ex-boyfriend: "I am in fear for my life with him. He threatened me physically."

"I didn't know that," she said. What a complete and utter lie.

I was so sick of being betrayed by my own mother. I stopped speaking to her.

CHAPTER 9

ArtTable

Despite my career and reputation flying high, it was not an easy time for women in the art world. Even during the best times on West 57th and the New York gallery scene in general, less than 10 percent of galleries in New York were women-owned; the rest were owned by men. Furthermore, you had to be a strong, tough woman, willing to put up with any and all amounts of shit, to get your work shown or represented as an artist. Besides their obvious talent as artists, it is no secret why Deborah Remington and Joan Snyder carved out such prestigious careers—they put up with no shit, and were tough enough to fight through the rampant chauvinism and misogyny. Likewise, gallery owners like Miani Johnson, Paula Cooper, Mary Boone, and myself fought many battles to get to our positions of respect in the industry. It should never have come to that, but we simply were dealing with the hand we were dealt—and damned determined to win that hand.

The reputation of the male dealers and their attitudes towards women were appalling. No matter how good you were, whether an artist, curator, or gallery owner, being a pretty receptionist was considered your primary function. I guess I blew my "primary function" early on at *Art in America*, where they learned I couldn't even type correctly! Going back to my epic early battle with Joseph Levine, my skirmishes with Crispo over receiving proper credit for shows I curated and catalogues I produced, and numerous smaller confrontations with men in the industry, I knew I would have to scratch and claw for everything I received. What these men continuously failed to release when they dealt with me was that I had already been toughened up by my childhood successes in swimming, dealing with my alcoholic father and uncaring mother, and the indignity of dealing with misogynistic professors at Rutgers. Their put-downs, demeaning comments, and attempts to subjugate me only made me tougher, more resilient—and more committed to helping other women move past this behavior so their own careers could advance. I had amply demonstrated I was tough enough to fend off these pricks.

A perfect example of what we faced—what I faced—came during my first year at Hamilton Gallery. We were exhibiting a rather scholarly show called "Sculpture in the Constructivist Tradition." We brought in a large piece by Robert Murray that was so big it had to be hoisted up the front of the building and through my office window. The artist sent his studio assistant, who he was paying for a lengthy amount of time while we awaited the delivery. Only one trucker in New York, Ernie Auer, could hoist sculptures up the face of the building.

That's when the antics began. First, the truckers were several hours late. When they strolled in—without apology for being late, I might add—they took one look at me in jeans and a casual shirt. One of them, Eddie, said, "Hey, big tits, where do you want the sculpture?" Like I was some road warrior woman, they'd met at a truck stop or popping into a honky-tonk bar.

I was shocked. "What did you say to me?"

The man looked at me and said, "Where do you want the sculpture, *big tits*?" He actually had the balls to repeat this disgusting slur, with zero self-consciousness about it, like he wanted me to be sure exactly how he saw me!

I asked for his name. Then I told Eddie which window would have to be removed and started the procedure.

As he got to work, I called Eddie's boss. You know what amazed me the most? The boss was barely upset. I then asked the boss, "Do you call Andre Emmerich 'Little Dick' or Leo Castelli 'Mr. Impotent'?" When I got nowhere, I asked him for the name of this man's union, the phone number and address. I wanted the man to receive a reprimand from the union, and I wanted a damn apology.

Needless to say, the Ernie Auer crew did a horrible job. They took a big chunk out of my wall in the office and were grumpy and irritable throughout. I demanded a reduction in the fee, and that they pay Bob Murray's assistant for all the hours he waited for them to arrive. I prevailed on the fee reduction, and the artist's assistant was paid.

I never received an apology. The trucker, however, did get a reprimand from his union.

Interestingly, about eight years after the incident, Eddie went to Peter Reginato's studio, and asked who his dealer was.

"Patricia Hamilton," Peter said.

"Bitch," Eddie said.

As I moved up in stature, dealing with incidents like this seemingly on my own, I began feeling a little lonely. Was I really one of the only women working as a gallery owner and dealer in this unapologetic good-old-boy world? How could I get in touch with women artists, gallery owners, representatives, or others in the art world to share stories, give strength to each other, and *empower* ourselves and the artists we dealers represented to build their careers on their own merits—without having to put up with this shit any more?

Things were about to take a turn.

In the winter of 1978, I received a call from Joyce Pomeroy Schwartz, who was in charge of public art at Pace Gallery. Some women were talking about putting together a women's networking organization. The idea resonated with me. After all, men had clubs they could go to, like the Harvard Club and Yale Club, but there was no place for women in the art world to network. We needed some strength in numbers, badly, and I liked what I heard from Joyce.

In February 1979, she invited me to a dinner at Peng's Restaurant, which I attended. I met nearly a dozen interesting women, all with impressive credentials, including veteran journalist Lila Hartnett of *Cue* Magazine; Liz Robbins, a PR person who worked for the ad agency that represented the Parke-Bernet Auction House until it closed in 1964; Caroline Goldsmith from Ruder and Finn PR agency; Carol Morgan from the Museum of Design; Mimi Poser from the Guggenheim; Manuela Haelterhoff from the *Wall Street Journal*; Liz Shaw, involved with publicity and other vital efforts for a number of key museums since the 1950s; art critic and historian Alexandra Anderson-Spivy; and of course Joyce. The room featured a cross-section of long-time members of the art media or business, young women already in prominent places as gallery owners or curators, and a collective burning desire to create something that fused our work and expanded opportunities for women in the art business—and of course, the artists themselves. Holly Solomon, owner of the Holly Solomon Gallery that opened two years before mine, did not attend the dinner but was also an original member.

In the book *ArtTable*, Judith Brodsky, founder of the Center for Innovative Print and Paper at my graduate school alma mater, Rutgers University, summed up what we were looking to do in a succinct way: "We had a vision: to use the power of ArtTable as a positive force in the art world, to leverage ArtTable's prestige, to help advise on government policy, be in touch with Congress . . . not to remain a resource just for our members . . . (we) put on advocacy programs to educate the public."

When the evening was over, we had become the founding members of an organization whose name we also settled on—ArtTable.

The first thing I did at the dinner was point out that, while we had women in the room from all parts of the country, we had *no* women of color. I recommended Lowery Sims, the Associate Curator at the Metropolitan Museum. Everyone agreed, and Lowery became our 12th founding member. We'd go on to have monthly meetings, usually focused on a topic or an opening of a museum show, with the respective curator leading us around.

We formed ArtTable at the end of a decade in which women made incremental headway in the New York and overall art scene—and by incremental, I mean mostly baby steps. The women who preceded me, including several of the other ArtTable founding members, intended them to be much bigger steps—and certainly put in that degree of energy and effort. However, when you're trying to knock down a previously impenetrable brick wall (or glass ceiling), a few swings of the sledgehammer alone won't work. There need to be many swings on different parts of the wall. And the male-centric art world's wall was particularly thick.

The road to ArtTable began in 1969, when one of the earliest women's art organizations, Women Artists in Revolution, began to form out of the Art Workers Coalition. That was a perfect name for the times! It lasted less than a year. Why? The Whitney Museum's 1969 Annual included only five women out of 143 artists shown. Coupled with that, 75% of undergraduate art students and 50% of MA students were women, but only 5% of faculty were women. That's how bad it was, and I was one of those MA students at the time being taught by a decidedly male, chauvinistic faculty.

Things got moving in 1972. Judy Chicago and Miriam Schapiro joined forces to create the Feminist Arts Program at the California Institute of the Arts. Artists Schapiro, Ellen Lanyon, and art critics Grace Glueck and Lucy Lippard were instrumental in forming the East-West Bag, a cross-country network of women artists. What followed were many non-profit arts organizations and alternative spaces, including A.I.R. and SoHo 20 in New York, Artemisia and ARC in Chicago, and HERA in Rhode Island, all of which showcased women artists. Art centers and artists series followed, leading to The Women's Caucus for Art (WCA), the first national organization for women in the visual arts, now celebrating its 50th anniversary. Indeed, 1972 was a breakthrough year for women artists—to a degree.

Still, it was tough sledding. In the early 1970s, women earned 50% of the PhDs in Art History, but virtually none of the faculty jobs. (By 1996, more than half of faculty jobs were occupied by women.) And, a 1976 panel sponsored by the Women's Caucus for Art reported on a study of women involved with 1,800 U.S. museums: of 30,000 total employees, 11,000 were professionals. Only one-third of those were women.

There was enough of an opening, though, for assertive businesswomen to begin making a hard push, and we did—into galleries. Women dealers moved into the art scene in bigger and bigger numbers. Betty Parsons and Virginia Zabriskie had been around for years, along with Marcia Tucker in the museum world, but now, they were joined by Paula Cooper, Nancy Hoffman, Holly Solomon, Mary Boone, and myself in New York, along with art dealers in Washington, Chicago, L.A. and San Francisco. By 1977, all of us were in place, bringing women artists to go with the men. As the 25th anniversary commemorative book, *ArtTable: Changing the Equation* points out, we also brought in a fresh new perspective to art, incorporating photography, installation, performance art, and representation. I think my decision to exhibit Louise Bourgeois right off the bat, with a most demonstrative installation with performance art elements, speaks quite clearly to that.

Our gathering to create ArtTable drew in all of this rising momentum. We were still in the huge minority in the overall picture, but now we had a framework for how to advocate, educate, and influence the art business, as women actively in the business and as advocates for women artists—and we were all driven and toughened up by our respective battles and swings of that sledgehammer to break down the brick wall. Now, we were swinging it together.

. . .

Seven months after our formation dinner, I went to Holly Solomon's house—and was overwhelmed by how many people were there. There were well over 30. I realized we were no longer just 12 Type-A personality women trying to forge a broader path we might have to walk all by ourselves; we were becoming part of something new, important and increasingly widespread; as Lila Hartnett later wrote, "We didn't convene at hotel bars; we sat at lunch, at dinner, tables, or homes . . . we became a mutually helpful society."

This was an idea whose time had come.

All credit for the concept of ArtTable and its initial movement as an important networking organization goes to Lila Harnett. She got the ball rolling. Lila had her own tell-tale story of life in the business before women could develop a reasonable presence and strength in numbers; she began her journalism career in the 1950s, signing her byline as L.M. Hartnett, obscuring the fact she was a woman. (The painter Grace Hartigan, who I represented, did the same thing to sell art early in her career, signing her works as George Hartigan). After our meeting, Lila became our Founding President and made it her job to fly to other cities and open chapters there; she began with Los Angeles, Washington, Chicago, and Boston, all with significant art presences and—of equal importance to any nascent undertaking—significant and understanding press contingents.

As we moved forward, we arrived at an early decision that surprised a lot of people: we did not welcome women artists into our networking organization. Why not? Weren't the artists who we were there to serve, curate, represent, or write about in the first place? Weren't they the ones whose works we were selling and promoting? The creators of the product for our businesses? All very fair questions. To answer that, I'll start with the ArtTable website mission statement:

"ArtTable is the foremost professional organization dedicated to advancing the *leadership* of women in the visual arts (emphasis mine)."

In my mind, the word leaders in the art world also included being the ones sticking our reputations and financial necks on the line to see to it that the women artists had viable markets, critics who would review their work, and dealers and representatives who would believe in them so deeply that, come hell or high water, they would carve out opportunities to exhibit or sell their work, get them museum exhibits, or other showings.

From day one, we leaders set out to create political, social, corporate, and cultural opportunities for women to advance in the art business and, by doing so, create bigger markets and greater exposure for the artists we served. We were a business networking organization, through and through. We were the voice of women's leadership in the arts. I like what Lowery Sims said in *ArtTable: Changing the Equation*: "We have a responsibility to be interpreters, intermediaries between the arts and society. I think it is important to air divergent ideas, facilitating encounters even among divergent ideas."

I look at my own mindset towards art, how I perceive the value of art, and the many facets of my career within it as agent, gallery owner, representative, curator, dealer, and historian. She nails it on the head: I have always been an interpreter, and God knows I've brought enough divergent ideas and pieces of art into my galleries and shows, shaking some trees and opening a lot of eyes in the process.

Our growth curve started almost immediately. By 1981, we had 36 committed members, and our dinners and lunches evolved into

20 programs and meetings. In September of that year, we also had our first formal membership meeting, at the American Federation for the Arts in New York. A month later, at our first evening program at the Tower Suite of the Time-Life Building, a member, art collector Clementine Brown, moderated a panel discussion focused on the problem of funding in the arts. There were 80 attendees and some prominent guests, including Corcoran Gallery of Art Director Peter Marzio and Lincoln Center for the Performing Arts Chairman Martin E. Segal, representatives of the United States State Department and Philip Morris, and former President Carter's art advisor. This group reflected exactly what we were trying to do: advocate in the areas of public affairs, the corporate world, galleries, and museums, as well as educate up-and-coming girls and young women who envisioned careers as artists or participants in the business of art. Finally, in December, our first president, Lila Hartnett, led a most important panel discussion entitled "The Future of Cable Programming: New Directions for the Visual Arts." We'd also grabbed the media's attention as well.

So let's fast forward a bit: By 1983, our founding group of 12 had grown to 225, now with women from 17 states and Canada, highlighted by a great November symposium entitled "Who Controls Museums?" with Grace Glueck moderating. And, for the first time, there was an ArtTable West event, with the members meeting at June Wayne's studio to discuss funding and development in the not-for-profit sector. Those attending included Dia Dorsey from the L.A. County Museum, Jackie Dubey from the L.A. Municipal Art Gallery, and Los Angeles *Times* art critic Barbara Isenberg, also the media coordinator of the 1984 L.A. Olympics. This establishment of ArtTable in Southern California would factor prominently in my future, when I worked and lived bi-coastally and then entirely in SoCal.

Of course, not everything was red wine, roses, and good tidings for our group. When you bring together 12 founding members who are all driven and forged their successes through many hard battles along the way, you have 12 Type-A personalities. Which increased in number as we took on more and more new members. We definitely tussled and had disagreements on certain aspects of what we were doing, how we would involve ourselves in certain advocacy programs—and who would do the heavy lifting and either receive credit or seize it for themselves. However, we'd all been through too much hell at times in our careers to let those disputes derail the overall goal to grow ArtTable and serve women now streaming into the business in greater numbers than ever. At least in the early years.

The 1980s ended with our 10th anniversary as a networking organization—during which we surpassed 400 active members. It also included a fete that would have been unthinkable in the early 1970s, or even when we formed ArtTable: the honoring of 53 women museum directors, 22 of which were ArtTable members. That included Association of Art Museum Directors Executive Director Mimi Gudieri, who noted women museum directors made up 19% of the total membership. In 1973, that number was 3%. A six-fold jump in 15 years? While the overall number was still very low, in my opinion, that certainly counted as progress. There were also more women who owned galleries in New York and other cities as well, and opportunities for women were growing in all directions, from the not-for-profit sector to media, from education to curating and exhibiting. But there was much work to do.

My involvement in ArtTable is divided into two time-distinct periods. I was very active as a Founding Member while owning the Hamilton Gallery, but then I stepped back for a while. In 1992, when I was working and living bi-coastally, I found ArtTable invaluable in establishing my network and fulfilling some of the larger goals I had, such as establishing summer internship programs. I also went much further in the organization than I had before, and put in another 13 years, a story in itself.

Now in its 44th year, ArtTable is without question one of the most important things to happen for women in the art business and for students, artists, and advocates of art in all public and private sectors making their way up the ladder. When I look back on my life and see decisions made that really made a difference, beyond what I envisioned at the time, this is one of them. Despite our lofty visions, I'm not sure any of the twelve of us who met at Peng's Restaurant could imagine so many thousand women throughout this country and world benefitting from our decision to form a networking organization. But that's what happened, and it feels great to know I was an integral part of it.

CHAPTER 10

The Last Picture Show: Closing Up Shop

As George Harrison famously sang, and we all know, all (good) things must pass. I just didn't expect Hamilton Gallery to pass from the heights of the art scene so rapidly, but when a dizzying string of personal and business events hits in quick succession, along with a recession, these things happen. Especially when your trusted associate turns out to be anything but.

My reputation in the art world, as both a tough-nosed seller of art and a welcoming gallery owner to a wide variety of expressions, could not have been better. Hamilton Gallery put on some of the best exhibits in the city, We always drew great press, and collectors and patrons alike raved over the creative diversity of our artists. I was now not only highly regarded for my eye for sculpture, but also for many art forms, and the new energy generated through our fledgling ArtTable networking organization just added to the good feeling. What could possibly go wrong?

Two things, both outside my control, got the snowball started down the hill: the crippling recession of 1981–82, which laid siege to the entire New York and national art scene among many economic hardships that resulted, and the news that my closest family member, my brother Rick, had cancer.

Rick was diagnosed in January 1982; he was just 37. During the Christmas season, he felt a pain in his chest and saw the doctor, who immediately admitted him to Massachusetts General Hospital in Boston for surgery. Rick was living outside of Boston, and he was a new father, as he and his wife, Dola, had just welcomed their baby. When surgeons operated, they found that cancer had already spread across his chest like melted cheese. They did a biopsy of the mass, diagnosed it as Hodgkin's Disease, and told Rick and Dola they could treat it with radiation.

Well, the radiation didn't work. They didn't waste any time looking for alternative solutions; in April, Rick flew to Northern California and went to Stanford University Hospital for another opinion. Unfortunately, the radiation and uncontrollable disease left him very weak, and he was hospitalized. One day later, on April 26th, he died just as they were about to tell him his cancer had become untreatable. Five months before, my brother seemed totally healthy.

I was devastated. It was so unexpected. It felt completely unreal to me that my older brother had died. One thing his death did accomplish, at the expense of incredible grief, was to get me to re-examine my life. I realized two things above all others. First, I had no personal life. None. Every waking moment was tied to work, making me a complete workaholic. What's the difference between a full-blown workaholic and a full-blown alcoholic? One substance is alcohol, and the other is the next job. That's about it. And secondly, I realize I was very unhappy, regardless of the successes my gallery and the artists I represented now enjoyed.

But before I dug more deeply into all of that, I had to get through Rick's funeral, which meant dealing again with my family at large. The thought alone left a giant knot in my stomach while the rest of my body and mind were fraught with tension. Naturally, it was an emotional nightmare that brought many of the old family nightmares back. The service was held in a Catholic church in Boston. All my brothers were to be pallbearers, and my sister Susan insisted on being one, too.

After the funeral, we traveled with Rick's body to a site outside of Wilmington, Delaware, where Dola's family lived. She wanted him buried there so that their son, Rylan, could visit his grave. He was just ten months old when Rick died, so this would be the closest he would ever get physically to his father for his entire growing-up years. It was all incredibly sad.

While I wasn't a pallbearer in Boston, I did give the eulogy in Wilmington. Later in the day, Rylan was christened. There wasn't a dry eye in the house. I would go on to remain friendly with Dola for the next 30 years, because I wanted Rylan to know his father's family, and I was the only sure, consistent connection she would have in our family.

After losing Rick, I needed time to regroup, figure out how to become a happy woman again, and how not to let work dominate my existence, but of course, life intervened to keep that snowball moving downhill. However, shortly after Rick died, my brother Peter's wife was hospitalized and nearly passed away.

At the same time Rick was diagnosed, my father also got some bad news: doctors found throat cancer. They say things happen in threes. Well, I get it. I was racing from one hospital to the next, unable to do anything about my grief over losing Rick except feel it fester inside my stomach.

In July of 1983, about fifteen months after Rick's passing, my father died. His funeral in New York turned into an alcoholic mess.

First, my older brother Bill was impossible when I accompanied him back to his Boston home after our dad's funeral. He was in constant touch with his psychiatrist, Dr. Frazier, at the funeral. He wasn't getting along with his wife and couldn't handle the drive back to Boston. Dr. Frazier met us at the airport in Boston and took him directly to McLean's, a state hospital about 15 miles away in Belmont. He was a mess. He was a complete mess. Then, my mother and sister ganged up on me yet again, expecting me to drop everything for my father—who I hated. They reasoned that since they were doing everything for him, why wasn't I? Susan proceeded to give the eulogy for my father—while drunk. While Dad was being treated for cancer, Susan let my parents live in her apartment, from where he would go down for therapy at St. Vincent's, and then stop by mine.

After all of this, I felt like I was going crazy. On top of that, my gallery was in the middle of a downward spiral.

. . .

As 1983 began, I realized I faced a lot of challenges with the gallery if I wanted to keep it open. I knew I would have to remove quite a few of the artists, and also deal with another growing problem under my roof—Jay. He was becoming more and more difficult to deal with in a way that was adversely affecting our business. Given my emotional state, grieving over the loss of Rick, and dealing with Dad's worsening condition from throat cancer, I didn't have a lot of reserves left in me to deal with a bunch of crap.

Besides my personal and family tragedies, the recession and hard times that had befallen the Hamilton Gallery, another major change swept across the New York art market. There was a glut of art students on the scene, and they weren't about to be shown in the fancy galleries. So, they promptly started their own market with curated shows and small storefront galleries. This turned out to be the beginning of the short-lived scene in the East Village.

The first dealer to open a gallery on the Lower East Side was Patty Astor, a film actress, with her friend Bill Stelling, whom she met at the Mudd Club. They were the first gallery to show graffiti artists Futura, Fab 5 Freddy, Kenny Scharff, and Keith Haring, who is now internationally renowned. Graffiti art was making the scene, and Haring drawings were everywhere—in the subway, on ads on telephone poles in SoHo—literally everywhere you looked.

Suddenly, Uptown collectors were mixing with graffiti artists in gritty Lower East Side storefronts. Peter Nagy opened Nature Morte. Soon after that, Civilian Warfare, International with Monument, and Gracie Mansion opened. A well-publicized group show at Times Square followed, including the work of Peter Nagy, Jane Dickson, Mike Bidlo, and John Ahearn. Annina Nosei had discovered a young hot artist who was making paintings in the basement of her gallery, Jean Michel Basquait.

The art business had traditionally been a mom-and-pop business. Your artists were like your family. You did everything with them: visited their vacation homes, had them for dinner, and were involved in their personal lives. When the art business changed, it became more corporate. Years after my gallery closed, Joan Snyder called me, complaining she had no personal relationship with her new gallery. "What kind of personal relationship do you have with your banker?" I asked. "Galleries are now like banks, and you shouldn't think of dealers in any other way."

The days of remaining encamped in New York, with possible trips up to Boston or out to California, suddenly felt like limited marketing. Going to Europe and all of the major art fairs became a necessity. Documenta, an international overview exhibition, happened every four years, and there was the Venice Biennale. Those were the top international shows you absolutely could not miss. Initially, I went to Europe alone and made contact with all the European dealers. Later, Jay bugged me and insisted he go as well. After ten months of art fairs and exhibitions, we wanted a vacation. I was studying Italian at the time and asked my Italian teacher for the most glamorous place to stay. She said, without hesitation, the Villa d'Este on Lake Como, the summer home of Isabella d'Este, a major cultural figure during the Renaissance. It was as elegant as it could be, but we were the youngest guests there by about 30 years.

We spotted a group of American models being photographed by *Vogue*. We all became friendly. One morning, by the pool, a bunch of the male models approached us and talked to Jay. They told him he reminded him of a movie star. Jay puffed up like a peacock. "Who?" Jay asked, in rapt attention. When they told him the star was John Belushi, I almost fell off my chair. Jay was mortified.

Along with the change in the art market came an equally profound change in the way artists were promoted. Julian Schnabel had his first exhibition of plate paintings in 1979 at the Mary Boone Gallery. It was the talk of the town. Mary hired a publicist who helped get herself on the cover of *New York Magazine* as "Queen of The New York Art Scene." She also showed David Salle at the time and claimed that every show she mounted in her gallery was sold out. No one actually believed that, but word got around, and perception often trumps reality, especially when it comes to publicity.

One of Mary's big collectors was the English ad genius, Charles Saatchi. He had an enormous collection and bought many of Mary's artists. His idea was to promote her artists' work internationally, so he helped her establish relationships with dealers in London, Paris, Zurich, and Milan. Who better to have promoted your artists than Charles Saatchi? One of the most important dealers with whom she connected was Bruno Bischofsberger. The kind of work Mary was showing was called "Neo Expressionism," and it launched like a rocket. You'd go to art fairs and see all the same artists represented by a handful of galleries.

Meanwhile, a year or two after Julian Schnabel was with Mary

Boone, he approached Leo Castelli and told him he wanted to leave Mary to join Castelli's gallery. But to Schnabel's chagrin, Leo was a world-class gentleman and would not do this to Mary. He knew it would break her heart. He decided to meet Julian in the middle and, with Mary, co-represent him.

Since Mary and I were approximately the same age, we became friendly. She was really a piece of work. Her mood swings were enormous, but she sure did like to party. She told me specifically about "my personal life and all the men I'm involved with." At one point, she told me, in what sounded like indirect financial advice, "I wrote off all my clothes, shoes, jewelry, hairdressers, and even my rent" as gallery expenses.

I immediately called my accountant and asked him if I could do that. "Well, that's not a tax return I would sign," he said. "You will go to jail." That answer stunned me, but I didn't fight him on it.

Sure enough, my accountant proved to know what he was talking about. Mary rode through all the recessions and hung in there until the mid-2010s, when things really began to fall apart. In 2017, the actor Alec Baldwin went to Mary and told her he wanted to buy Ross Bleckner's *Sea and Mirror*. It had come up for auction in 2007, but Baldwin got outbid and asked her to find it for him. Mary did her due diligence, located the painting, and went to the collector. He refused to sell.

Rather than tell Baldwin the painting was unavailable, though, Mary had Bleckner paint a "copy." He signed and dated it 1996, the date of its original creation. Bleckner even stamped it with the same inventory number as the original. When the painting arrived, Baldwin, who has an astute eye himself, noticed that the colors seemed off. When he complained to Mary, she told him that it had been cleaned as a courtesy. That didn't satisfy Baldwin, so he went to Sotheby's, and they tested the painting. They told him the painting was more recent, not created in 1996. He confronted Mary, who admitted what she did and offered to refund the painting and pay interest.

However, Baldwin wanted to make an example of her, so he sued her. Later, a $1 million settlement was reached. He was also allowed to keep the copy and received a new work by Bleckner. The artist also apologized to Baldwin.

Everything finally caught up with Mary in 2018—as in the IRS caught up. She was busted for the very things my accountant in New York had predicted. Mind you, when she first started out at the Bykert Gallery, she was the bookkeeper. So she knew what she was doing. In 2012, she reported that the gallery lost $52,000 in their income tax returns. Not quite right: the gallery actually made a profit of $3.7 million. To close that rather large numbers gap, she wrote off $1.6 million of personal expenses as gallery expenses, including renovating her apartment, plus her clothes, shoes, jewelry, and other items.

The IRS dug deeper. Her 2009, 2010, and 2011 taxes were carefully scrutinized, and she ended up paying $3 million.

You would think taking a $3 million hit would make you start toeing the straight-and-narrow. But not Mary. In 2018, she broke the law again, writing off personal expenses as business expenses. *The same thing as before!* She went to court and was subsequently sentenced to 30 months in prison. Her lawyers argued that she had a troubled childhood that led to mental health issues and drug and alcohol abuse and that, somehow, that made her write down fraudulent numbers on tax returns.

The judge was unmoved.

• • •

No longer was it enough to simply sell out a show at Hamilton Gallery, or any other gallery, and get great reviews at Hamilton Gallery. Selling art had evolved into a worldwide network. Subsequently, the artists that were promoted by all the right galleries became not just high-flying artists, but "rock stars." After a decade of watching the real rock stars dress up in amazing outfits at their concerts and vault into the center of pop culture consciousness and the media stratosphere, everyone younger than 50 was taking firm notice. No longer were artists photographed in paint-splattered jeans. Suddenly they were in Armani suits, taking limousines, and drinking French champagne—living the lives of their collectors.

Amidst all of this, I soldiered on for the first part of the year. In April 1983, I let Jay curate a show called "The New Biomorphism and New Automatism." It featured Carroll Dunham, John Newman, and Mel Kendrick, among others, and earned Jay a write-up in *New York Magazine*. Then, in a sign of things to come and paying homage to his own ability to spot good art, he said, "My eyes should be insured by Lloyd's of London."

I almost puked.

A month later, we were putting together a group show called the "New Sculpture," featuring young experimental sculptors, when I got into a discussion with *Artforum* editor Ingrid Sischy. She was smart and savvy; I liked her a lot. At Ingrid's suggestion, I wanted to add Peter Gourfain to the show, and possibly represent him.

I decided to head out to Peter's studio, which was in Red Hook, Brooklyn. In 1983, Red Hook felt like a quick right turn away from the end of the world. Peter was a ceramic artist and made incredible figurative large pots at Kent State during the time of the riots, in 1970, when National Guardsmen shot four anti-Vietnam War protestors dead. He was politically far left and a real throwback to the '60s. He was also very volatile when he drank, and his bad temper would come out. I loved his work but grew to become afraid that I could not control him. Plus, the last thing I needed in my life was another alcoholic to deal with. I urged Sidney Singer, a collector I knew, to buy all the pots and consign them to the gallery. Sid lived in Mamaroneck and, unfortunately, didn't want anyone to make money on this or any other deal but himself. He was the biggest bottom feeder I have ever met and beyond cheap, but he agreed to buy the pots.

However, the timing didn't work so well between Peter and me. My gallery closed before I could give Peter a show, but I managed to get Charlotta Kotik of the Brooklyn Museum to curate a show of his pots in 1986, since Peter was a Brooklyn resident. And I also did a show at a pop-up space at 112 Greene Street in SoHo at the same time. At the opening at Greene Street, he invited everyone he ever drank with at Finelli's to the dinner, which I originally intended to host. When I saw the cast of characters before me, though, I stood up before anyone ordered "This dinner is a Dutch treat," I announced. I was not picking up the tab for 20 of Peter's drunk friends.

Two months later, on July 17, my father died. By this point, the constant stressors of grief and gallery struggles, which I was not properly dealing with, had manifested in another way: I was throwing up blood every morning from what turned out to be a bleeding ulcer. My family, the death of my brother, and the business were literally consuming me.

After Dad's funeral, I went to the Women's Bank and secured a loan for the fall. Not a problem; the bank officer knew me, loved what I'd done with the Hamilton Gallery and for the New York art scene in general, and promised its approval. With that sense of security in mind, knowing I would be okay for the opening of the new art season, I headed off to England and Scotland for six weeks of rest and recuperation, and to drop in on some artists and their work. However, the whole time I was over there, I could tell my heart was not into it. I am very passionate in everything I do, and if the passion and fire aren't there, it becomes quite a challenge for me.

In September, I came home in time to prepare for the new season and to sign the loan papers. When I arrived at the bank, another bomb fell right onto my head: the bank officer who worked with me had been fired. And just like that, my loan was turned down.

That crushing news came at a terrible time, and not just for the gallery at large. On top of that, I owed a collector money for a Joan Snyder painting of his that I'd sold. He paid $5,000 for the painting, and I promised him $20,000 to sell it. I spent the money thinking I could pay him back with the bank loan.

When I didn't have the money to pay him, he pressed me hard. He even tried to persuade me to pay him before I took care of the taxes on the painting with the IRS. My accountant squashed that notion in a second.

Finally, I spoke to the collector. "Look," I said, the truth pouring from my mouth, my bleeding ulcer gripping me with pain. "I spent the money thinking I had the bank loan from the Women's Bank. A third of my family just died of cancer." I was a wreck, which he could clearly see.

Maybe a little show of empathy might be forthcoming? *No.* That afternoon, he sent a lawyer to my gallery, and promptly sued me. I was able to settle his suit satisfactorily.

At this point, I was burned out. I knew I was done. It was time to close the gallery.

With that cloud looming over my head, I opened the Fall 1983 art season with John Torreano, who made very experimental works that he later destroyed. They were Pop explorations of jewels without the jewels. He got creamed by the critics, and we didn't sell a thing. That dropped another dark cloud over our prospects of keeping the door open.

What kept the Hamilton Gallery through the remainder of the year was largely Michael David, who we took on in the spring and then showed throughout the fall. Also, Peter Gourfain's works were selling. Formerly with the Janis Gallery, Michael wanted to be with a more relevant dealer who showed younger artists. I was definitely his girl. He had appeared in the National Academy of Design show and made very minimal work with encaustic wax. His work knocked me out.

Michael was smart and loved painting, but his problem, a rather unique one in my experience, was that he turned *to me* for ideas for his next compositions. He literally didn't know what to paint. At first, I told him to go to The Met and MoMA for inspiration. A dealer can do a lot of things for an artist, but not tell them what to paint. Michael's other problem was that he had a very strong but confusing personality, his moods switching suddenly and dramatically, which I realized was a mental problem. Not a winning combination in life. Nor in dealing with gallery owners who are representing you. Sometimes, he was beyond sweet; at other times, he was a raving lunatic. He called me every day, like four times a day, always unhinged. I even invented a few sentences and expressions whenever Michael acted out.

One time, he called in a raging fit. "There's a landscape show at Diana Fuller Gallery in San Francisco, and I'm not included because you have such a nowhere gallery that Diana hasn't seen my work," he yelled.

"*Au contraire*, Michael," I responded. "She did see your work and didn't like it." Then I used my great line: "All behavior is explainable, but not all behavior is acceptable. Ax murderers always have a great reason for killing their spouse, but they still get the electric chair. Your behavior is completely unacceptable."

He calmed down—for about a minute. Then he was off the rails again. But his work sold well, and I needed that to keep the doors open, so I tolerated him.

When the gallery closed, Michael turned into the best side of himself. He was a real *mensch*, just wonderful. I introduced him to the collector Sid Singer, who bought a lot of work from him. That paid off my account with him in no time. Sid proceeded to call Ann

Freedman from Knoedler Gallery, who ended up taking Michael to the gallery. Knoedler was one of the oldest and most respected galleries in New York. They showed artists from another generation, on the caliber of Frank Stella and Nancy Graves. Michael was the youngest artist in the gallery. He'd come to me to be in a gallery known for showing younger artists, but in the end, being the youngest artist at Knoedler served him very well.

After that, Richard Hennessy came in and did a large show, which received a great review in the *New York Times*; I had good success selling his paintings. Unfortunately, his and Jay's relationship was so at odds that Jay wouldn't have anything to do with him, part of a behavior in my associate that concerned me.

We couldn't keep lurching from artist to artist. Every gallery owner hopes their artists sell well, of course; that's what keeps doors open. However, when do you have to *count on* each and every artist to have a great show financially? I was now in that position, and it was most uncomfortable—and not doing my health any good, either.

Plus, Jay had become intolerable—my associate for all seven years of the gallery needed to go.

. . .

I'd known Jay since our days at the Crispo Gallery. I'd trusted him and his keen eye for art, and also as a person. After all, he was my number two at the gallery, and I really wanted him to experience the same success as the other financial partners. But now, he was causing major problems. Jay was an absolute pain in the ass, and as time went on, it became clear I couldn't work with him anymore. I also knew that I would have to let go of many of the gallery artists whose work was not selling, but these people were my friends, and I didn't have the emotional strength to go through it.

Jay was losing his power base and completely freaked out about closing the gallery. He had this habit of repeating stories that showed how smart he was. It drove me nuts. A future partner of Jay's, John Post Lee, came up with a solution to this. He would say "broccoli," and Jay understood he had repeated the story. Jay was very bright but had a real personality disorder. I often wondered how much better he might work with others had he gone on medication.

I also knew Jay never signed the partnership papers we'd drawn up; I personally thought the reason was that he was too cheap to hire a lawyer. I never guessed his real intentions, that he never wanted to own a piece of the gallery, even though he sure acted like the co-owner when he talked with people.

The final downfall began in the Fall of 1983. Jay would come into the gallery late, close himself in his office, and talk on the phone with all his friends. One day, a client showed up with $1,000 in cash. Jay was owed two weeks' back salary. He grabbed the money and took all but $20. I hadn't paid myself in weeks and was so broke I was walking 47 blocks to work every day. I even borrowed some money from a friend to pay my apartment rent. Imagine that! I knew Jay had to leave but didn't know quite how to break the news. Once again, I was in a situation where I should have ended his employment at the gallery years before, but my overly loyal nature won out, and I paid the price.

Well, he solved the problem for me. I was sitting in my office, worrying, and said to Jay, "Gee, Jay, if we don't sell the lease, we are fucked."

Without missing a beat, he replied, "No Patty, you're fucked. I never signed the partnership papers."

That comment sent me over the edge. "Get the fuck out!" I yelled. "You're fired." I didn't allow him to take a thing. Later, I shipped his rolodex to him. He could take his Lloyd's of London "eye" with him, too.

Meantime, I needed to sell the lease, which still had three years remaining on it. I knew my best chance at paying off the debts was to sell the lease by saying I was moving to SoHo. It was important that the new tenant did not know I was going out of business, because I would not get the best deal. Also, the lease was in my name, but I planned on paying debts with every nickel.

Thankfully, I found a buyer quickly.

. . .

All the changes in the art market changed the way I felt about dealing with it. I never made much money when I worked at the gallery. I took a salary, and that was it. All the travel was hard work. What kept me going were the personal relationships with the artists. I really enjoyed them. When an artist would tell me they didn't have enough money to pay the rent, I understood. I had been in that position myself many times.

Now, many of the new dealers were simply rich. They bought lots of work and collected it personally. They made their real money by holding onto the work they bought early in the artist's career. Certainly, running a contemporary gallery was a losing proposition unless you sold blue-chip art out of the back room and work that the gallery owned. My gallery was never in a position to buy inventory, and I didn't have experience selling blue-chip work. To exist on selling work from one month to another was not going to make it in the '80s when everything became about money. This situation reminded me of a great old joke about owning an art gallery: "How do you make a million dollars in the contemporary art business? Start out with two million."

The fact that I was able to keep Hamilton Gallery open for seven years was somewhat of a miracle, but it took all of my time and energy. And my health. I worked seven days a week, always on the lookout for new artists and new clients.

But I didn't have it in me anymore. I was exhausted, sick, and tired of the gallery. Still, despite every primal instinct telling me to GO, I wanted to close with as much class as possible and pay off every nickel I owed my artists. In the gallery world, that was probably a first. Most galleries close and walk away from their artists, no matter how high the debts. That sentiment leaked into attorney's offices as well. I even had a lawyer who told me to cash the check for the lease and walk away from the debts. I fired him.

I was only 36, and I wanted to stay in the business. I knew I had to pay off the artists.

My lease buyer was AAA Gallery, a well-known print dealer. It was run by Sylvan Cole. Of course, Cole's idea of buying the lease included everything from the lights to the water fountain to the copy machine. It proved to be a struggle getting out of there. The weekend before we packed up the gallery, I went to the Gurney Inn in Montauk with Dick Sage to get pampered. Jay went to the gallery, fired or not, and someone from the Hammer Gallery stopped by, and Jay showed him around the space like the proprietor. (He had no knowledge that I had already sold the lease.) Fortunately, I had locked my desk with the checkbook that he repeatedly tried to break into.

My secretary called me and told me what was going on, and I asked to speak to Jay. "Get the fuck out," I said.

"Well, I want the chairs and the Le Corbusier coffee table," he said.

"They are gallery assets. How much would you pay for them?"

"Nothing."

My blood boiled over. "Get the fuck out of there. If you don't leave immediately, I will call the cops."

The night before, I had dinner with John Torreano to announce the gallery was closing. He suggested something for which I'll be forever thankful: that I do a "Last Picture Show" through December and feature all the gallery artists, past and present. Anyone with a beating pop culture heart in 1983 who was over 30 well knew that namesake, an epic black and white film starring Cybill Shepherd, Peter Bogdanovich, Cloris Leachman, Timothy Bottoms, and Jeff Bridges. The name alone would draw attention.

Not surprisingly, my version of The Last Picture Show did well. Many artists, from Isaac Witkin on through many others during our seven-year history, gave us works to sell. While Isaac took his share, which I gratefully gave him for helping us out, many artists donated entirely, allowing me to keep 100% of the commissions. I will forever appreciate their generosity and kindness. Even old secretaries of mine volunteered to work to help put The Last Picture Show together. We were all able to put some smiles on our faces. The Last Picture Show netted me several sales that made a big difference moving forward.

Of the $150,000 lease sale to AAA Gallery, the first $50,000 went to bank loans, the collector I owed money to, and other immediate things, and the next $50,000 went to debts. My agreement with AAA was for them to pay over time, so I saw nothing until the last $50,000. I stopped paying myself a salary in October 1983 and borrowed money from friends to stay afloat. Thankfully, I had a rent-controlled apartment. Imagine doing that today.

. . .

There was one last thing I wanted to do: find new homes for my artists. I went right to work on that. I placed Loren Calaway into Jeffrey Hoffeld, David Hare with Grunebaum, Robert Murray found a home at Green Gallery, and I got Michael David into Knoedler. I landed Peter Gourfain a show at the Brooklyn Museum and, as mentioned, gave him a show at 112 Greene Street at the same time. I ended up on friendly terms with most of the artists. I still get Christmas Cards from most of the artists. Many continue to tell me I was the best dealer they ever had, which is a wonderful sentiment. Because, for all the difficulty and heartache and financial struggle at the end, my seven-year run at the Hamilton Gallery was great in so many ways.

By April 1, 1984, just three months after closing, I had paid off all the debts. I was out from under the Hamilton Gallery, and had to figure out what I would do with my next chapter. I wasn't speaking to Jay, and sadly, we have remained enemies since. But Jay certainly wasn't done behaving badly. One day, I took an old boyfriend of mine, the art collector Dick Sage, to Jay's Lower East Side gallery. Jay wanted to show Dick his office. When Jay saw me, he grabbed Dick, pulled him inside—and slammed the door in my face.

"Jay, I'm embarrassed for you," Dick simply said. We promptly left.

Not only did my debt clear in 90 days—but so did my health. When I wrote my final check pertaining to the Hamilton Gallery, I realized something else: my bleeding ulcer was gone.

I was off to another new chapter—and a new career within the art world.

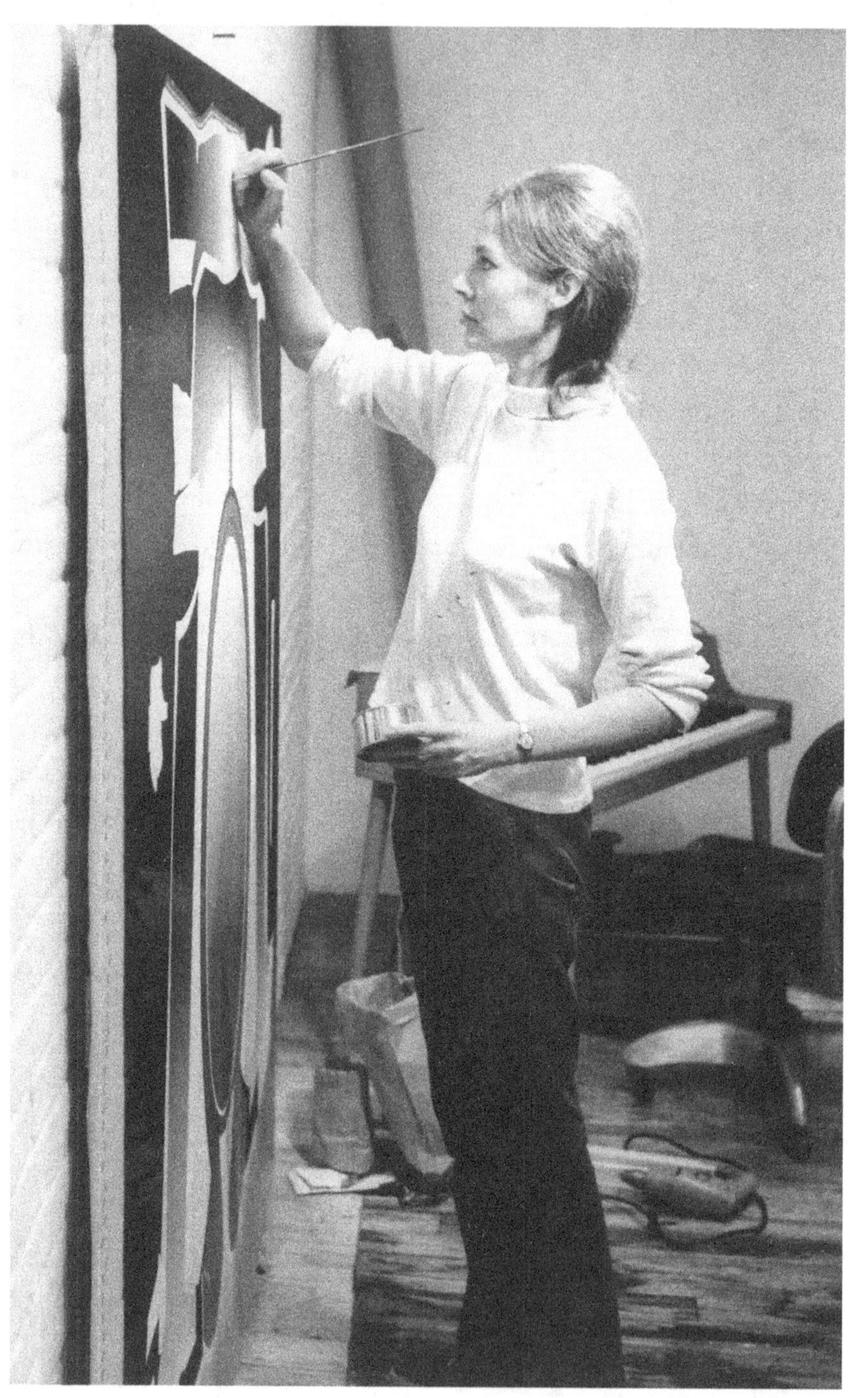

Deborah Remington in her studio at 309 West Broadway, New York, NY, 1974. Image © 2024 The Deborah Remington Charitable Trust for the Visual Arts / Licensed by Artists Rights Society (ARS), NY

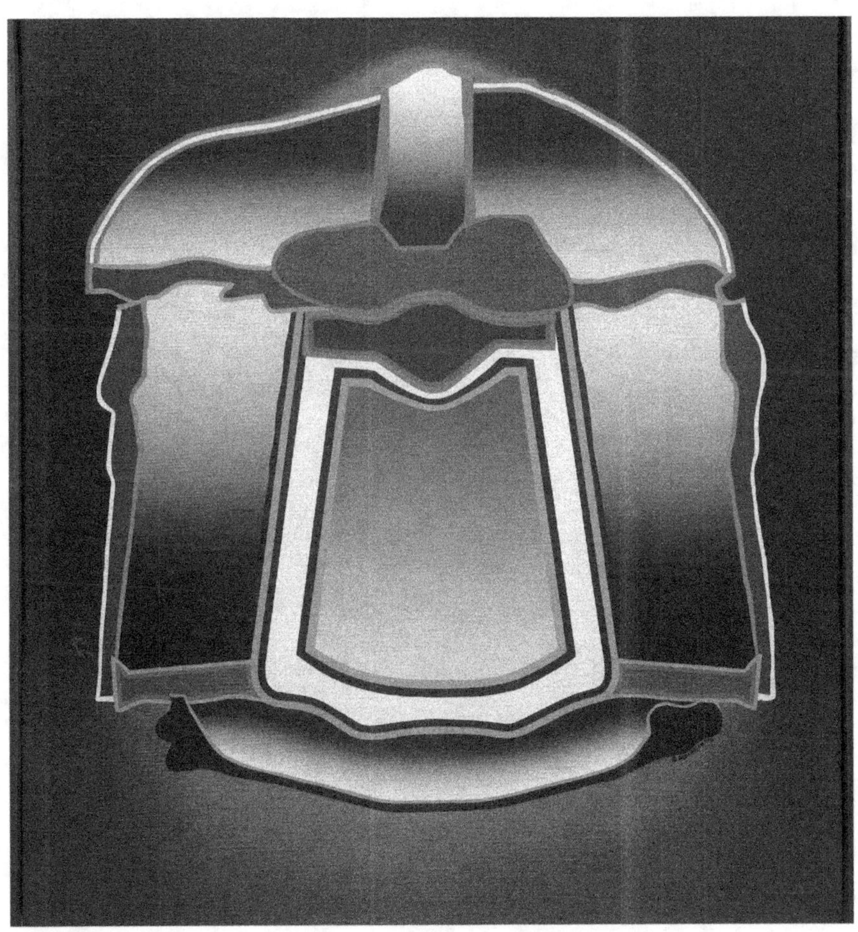

Deborah Remington
Tay, 1976
Oil on canvas
20 x 18 in (50.8 x 45.7 cm)
Private Collection of Dr. Peter Dallos
Image © 2024 The Deborah Remington Charitable Trust for the Visual Arts /
Licensed by Artists Rights Society (ARS), NY. Photo: April Tracey

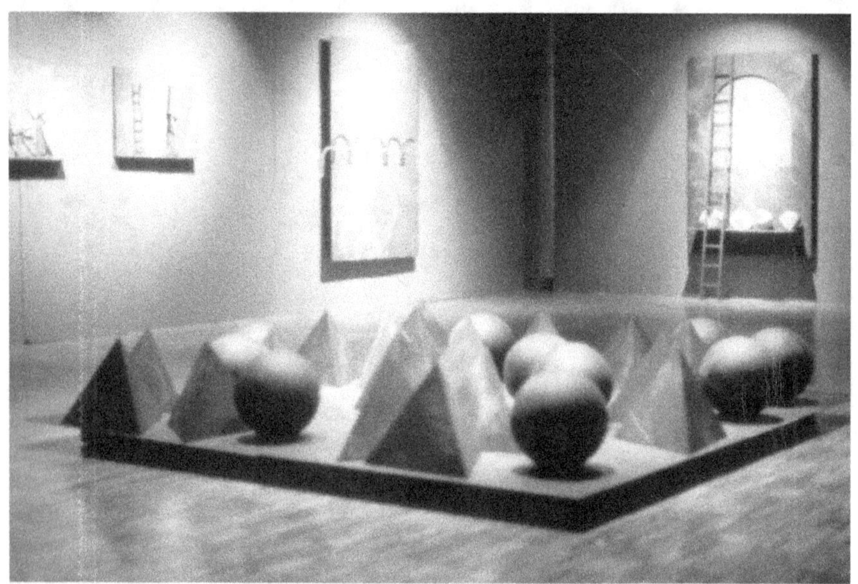

Allentown Art Museum, 1979—one-man show of John Willenbecher

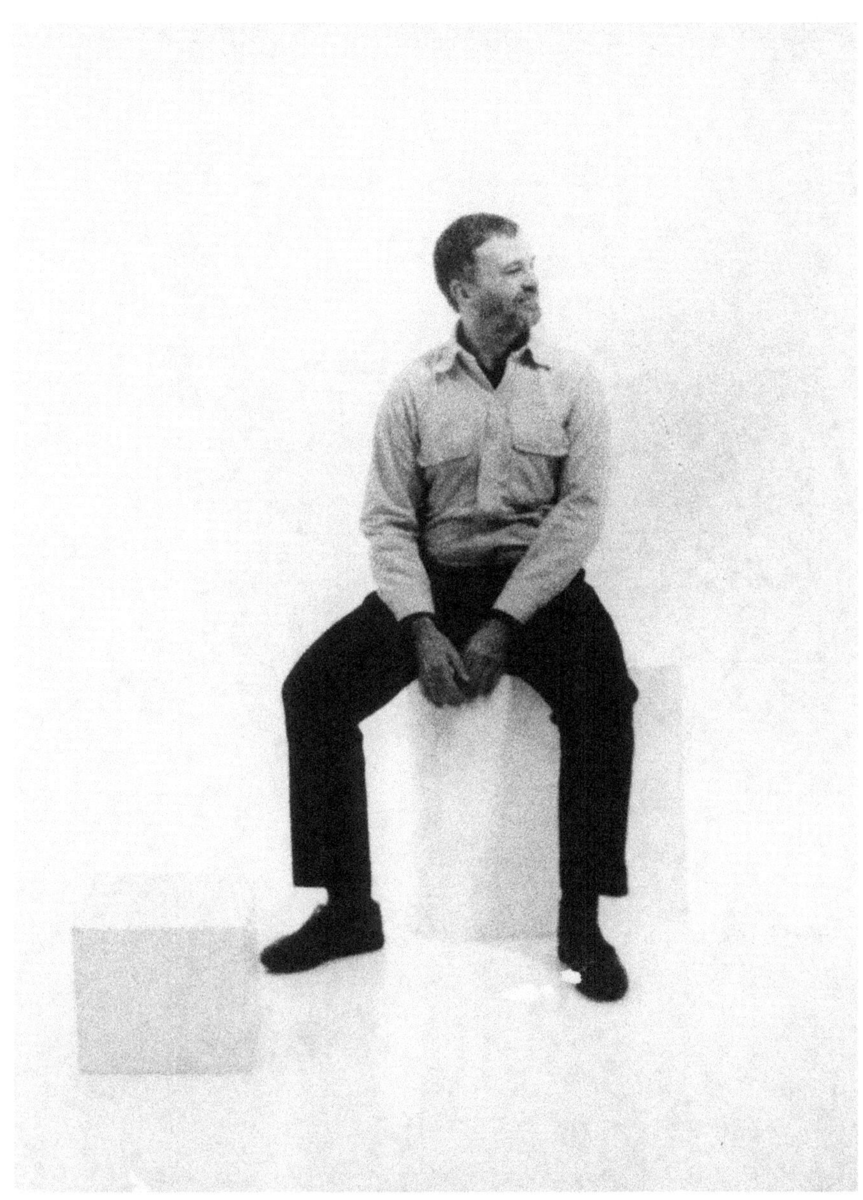

John Willenbecher 1982, photo by Denise Browne Hare

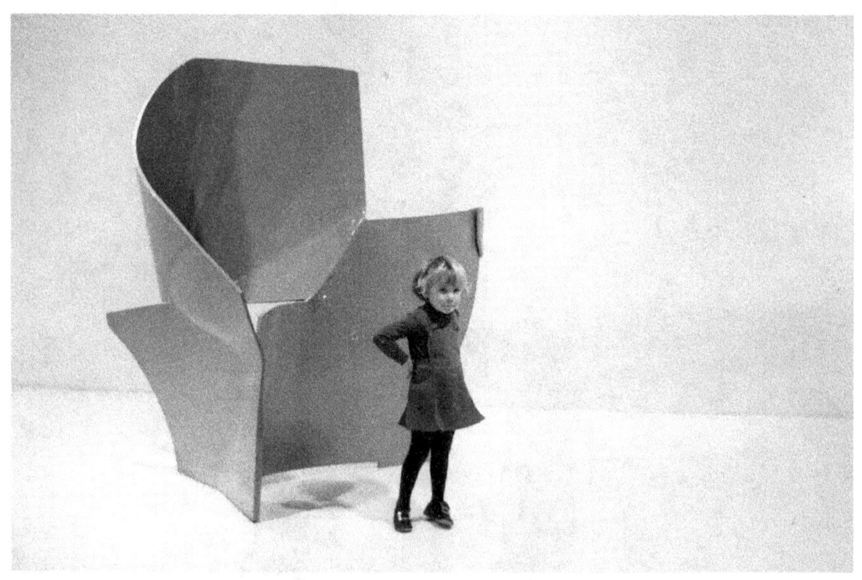

Claire Murray in front of one of Robert Murray's sculptures, 1977

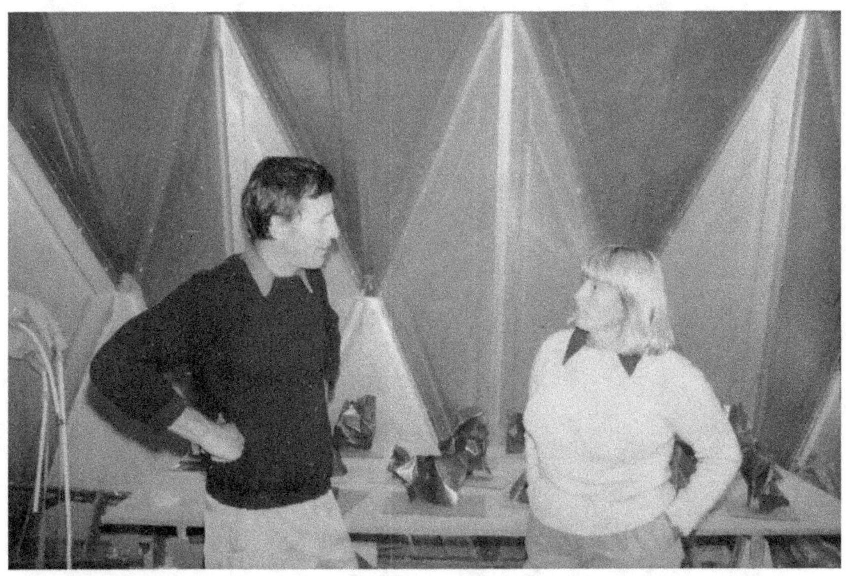

Robert Murray studio visit Pointe au Baril, Canada

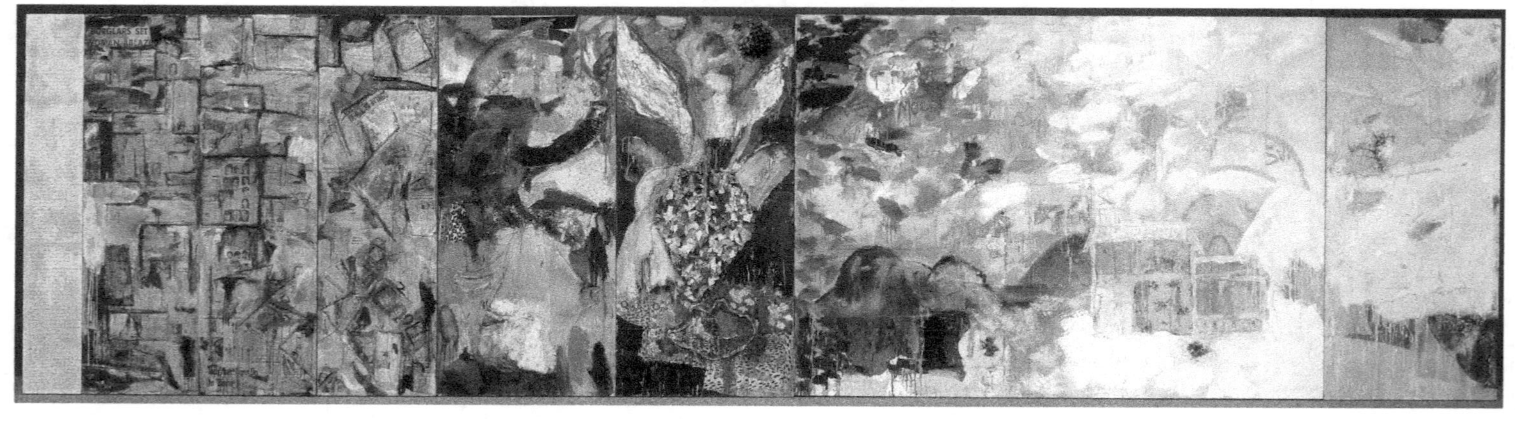

Joan Snyder
Resurrection, 1977
Oil, acrylic, fabric, wallpaper, newspaper, tissue paper, gold paint, paper mache, graphite on canvas
78 x 312 in
Collection of The Museum of Fine Arts, Boston
Gift of Sidney Singer, 1986
Photograph © Museum of Fine Arts, Boston

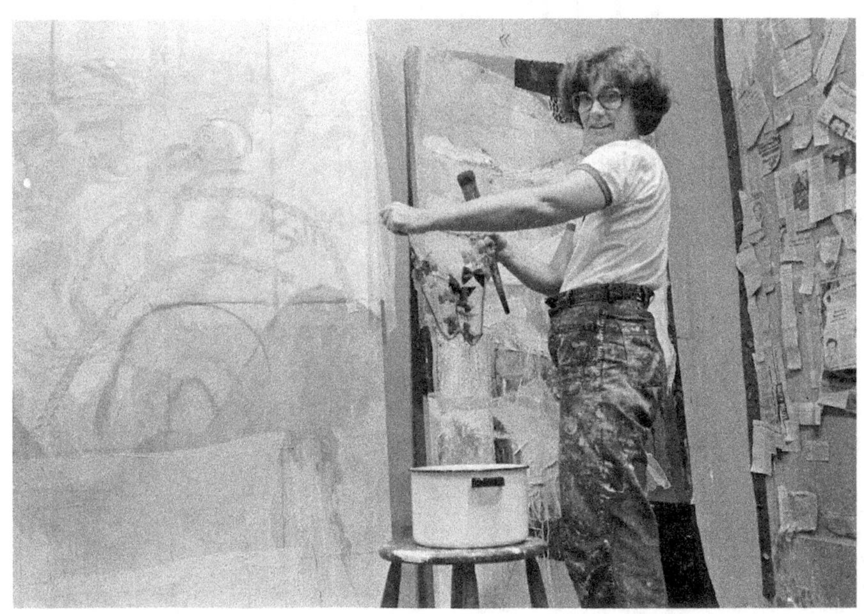

Joan Snyder working on *Resurrection*, 1977

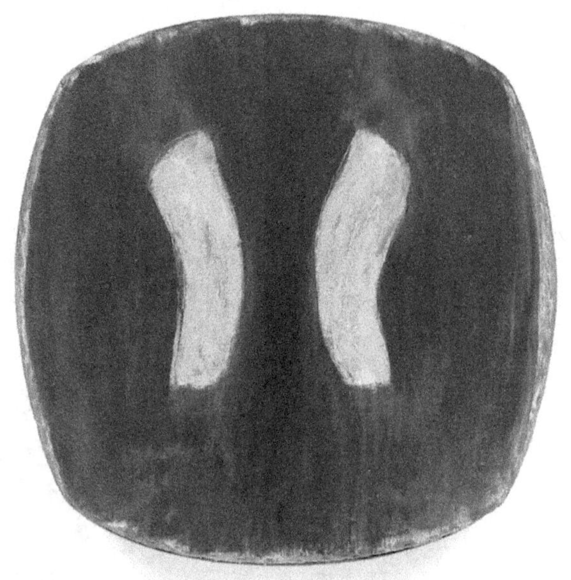

Ron Gorchov
Diver, 1978
Oil on linen
31 1/2 x 31 1/2 x 12 inches (80 x 80 x 30.5 cm)
© 2023 Estate of Ron Gorchov / Artists Rights Society (ARS), New York.
Photo by Argenis Apolinario; Courtesy Vito Schnabel Gallery. Courtesy of the
Artist Rights Society, New York.

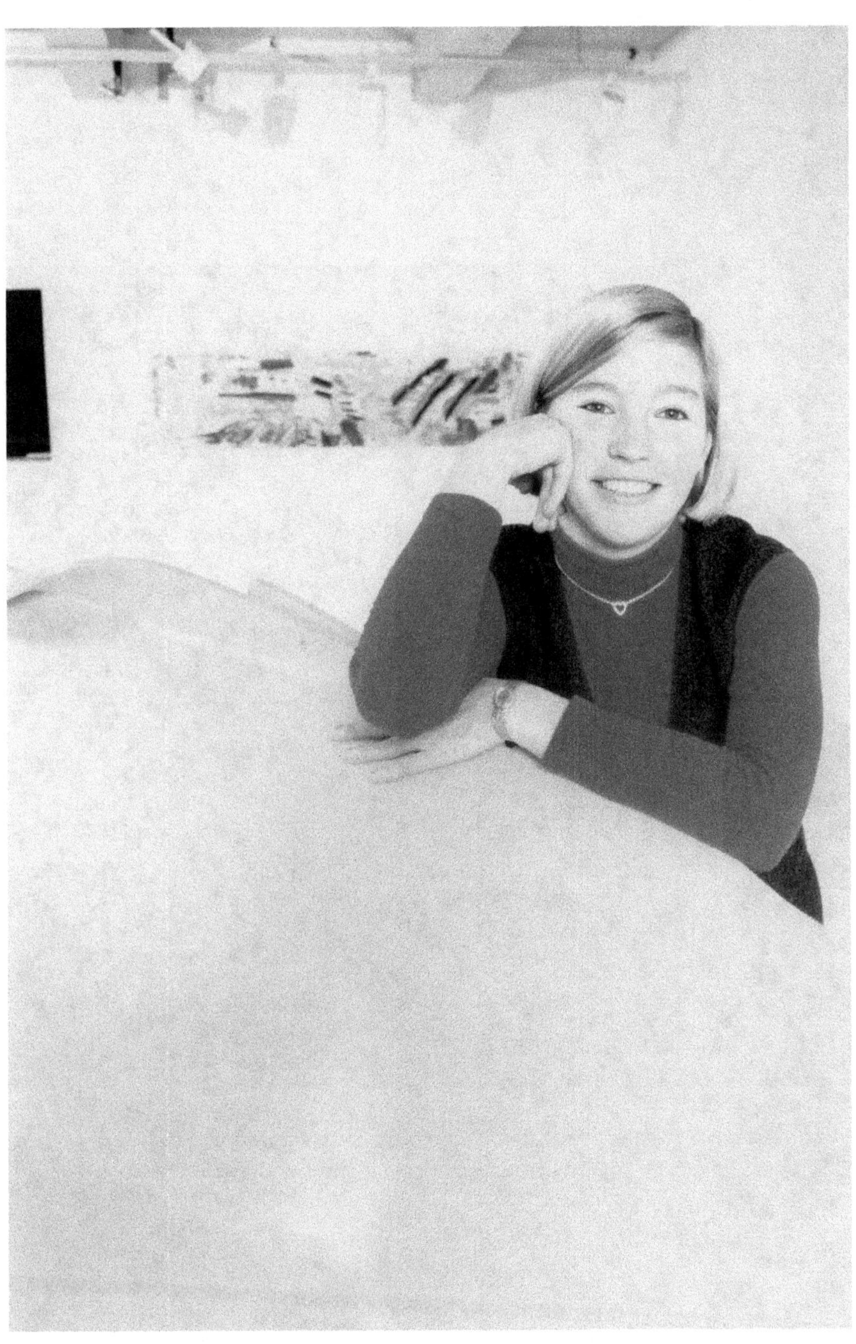

Portrait of me, 1979, photo by Bob Day

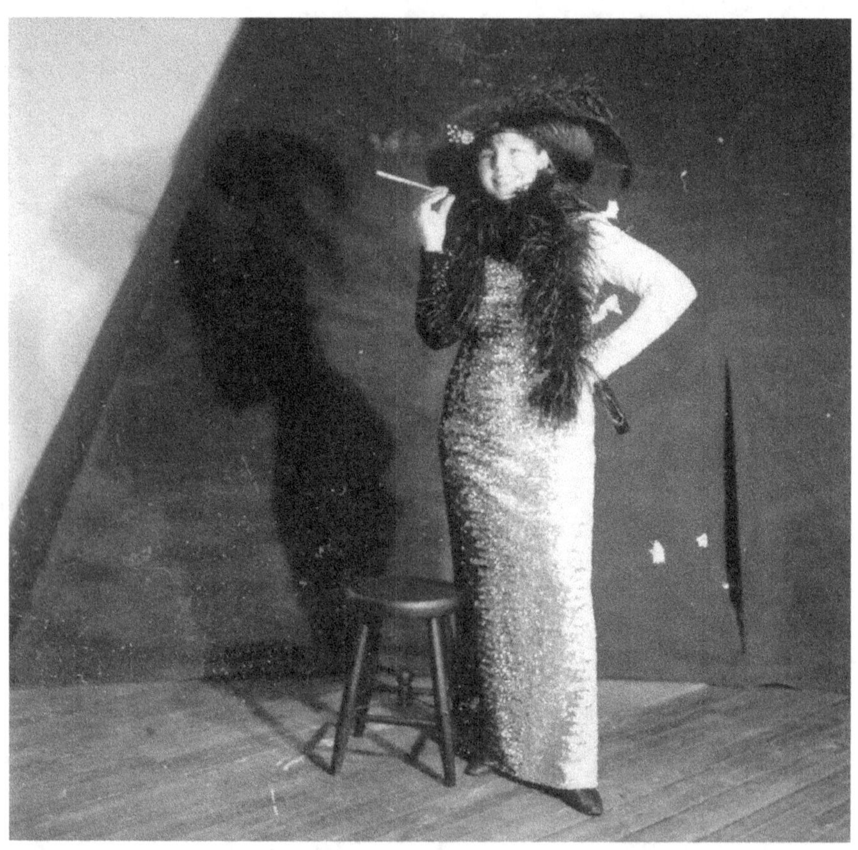

Me dressed up as Mae West, photo by Mary Beth Edelson, in honor of Louise Bourgeois, in honor of Judy Chicago show at the Brooklyn Museum

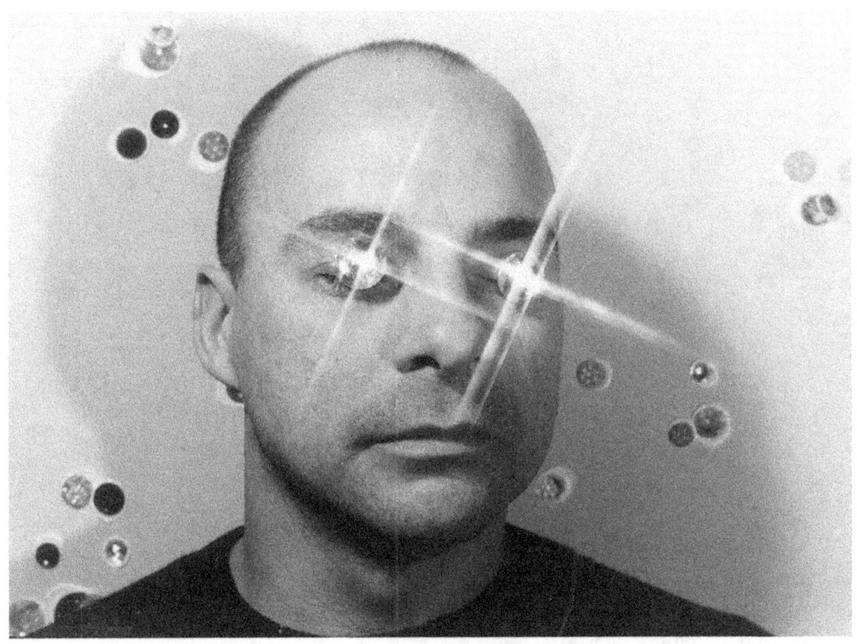

Portrait of John Torreano, photo credit © 1980 Ellen Carey

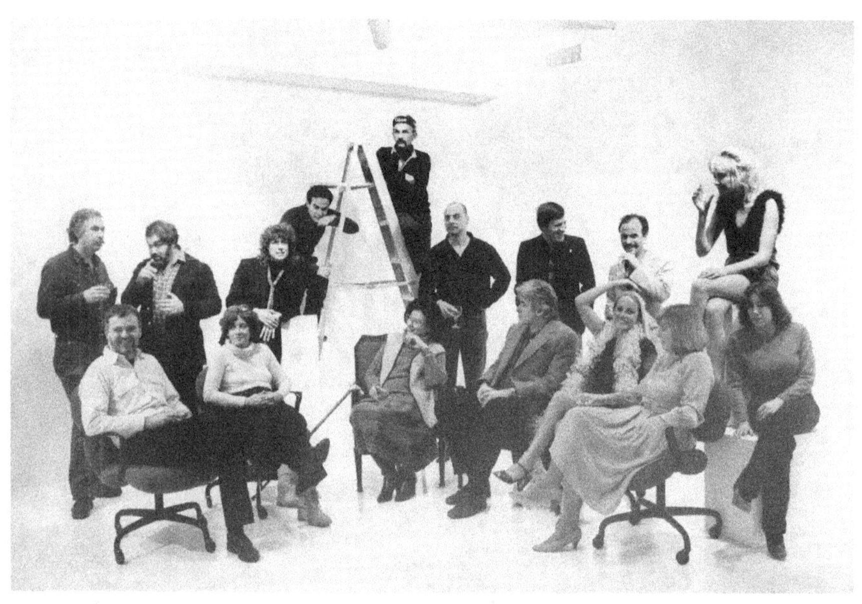

5th Anniversary of gallery 1982
1st Row: John Willenbecher, John Snyder, Grace Hartigan, Ron Gorchov,
Susan Hall, me, Linda Dukkess
2nd row: Walter Dusenbery, Isaac Witkin, Janet Stayton, John Torreano,
Richard Hennessy, Auste
3rd row: Jay Gorney, Rafi Ferrer

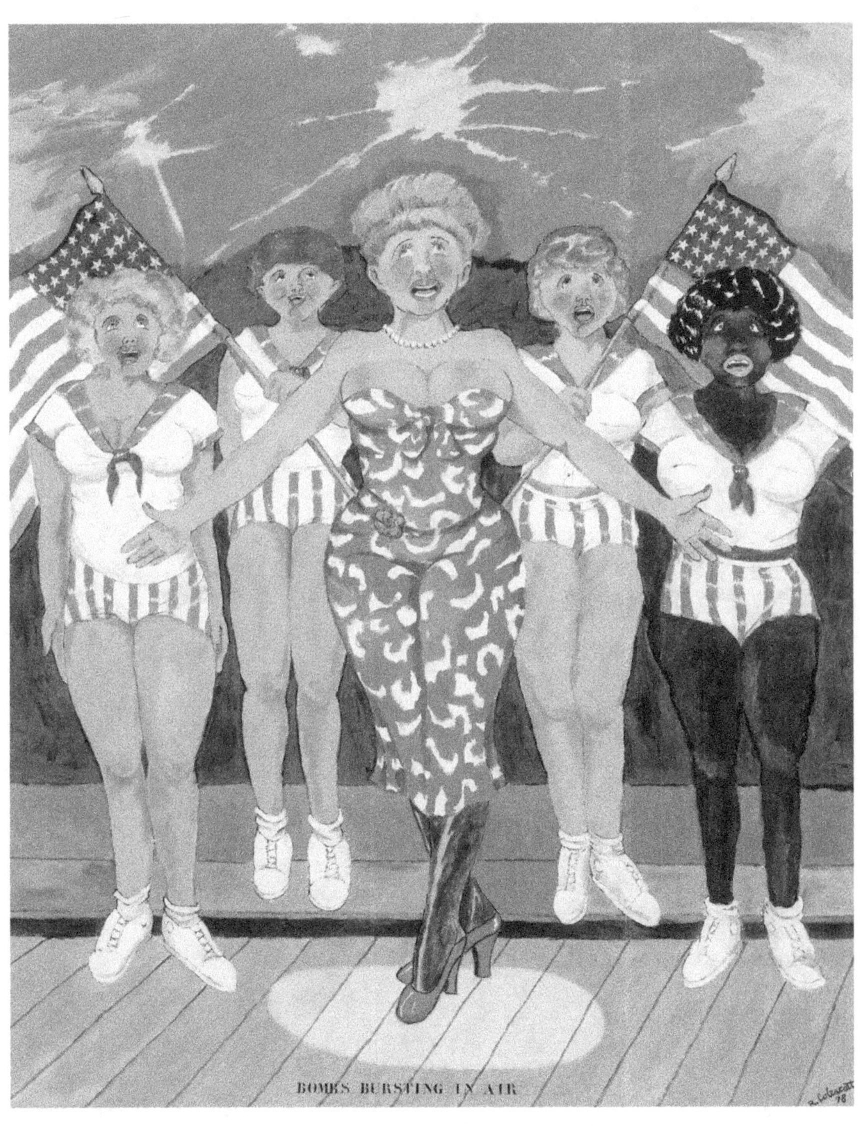

Robert Colescott
Bombs Bursting in Air, 1978
Acrylic on canvas
83 3/4 x 65 7/8 x 1 5/8 inches (212.7 x 167.3 x 4.1 centimeters)
© The Robert H. Colescott Separate Property Trust / Artists Rights Society
(ARS), New York; Courtesy of the Trust and BLUM Los Angeles, Tokyo, New
York. Photo: Joshua White (Filename for internal reference: RCO 16)
Courtesy of the Artist Rights Society, New York

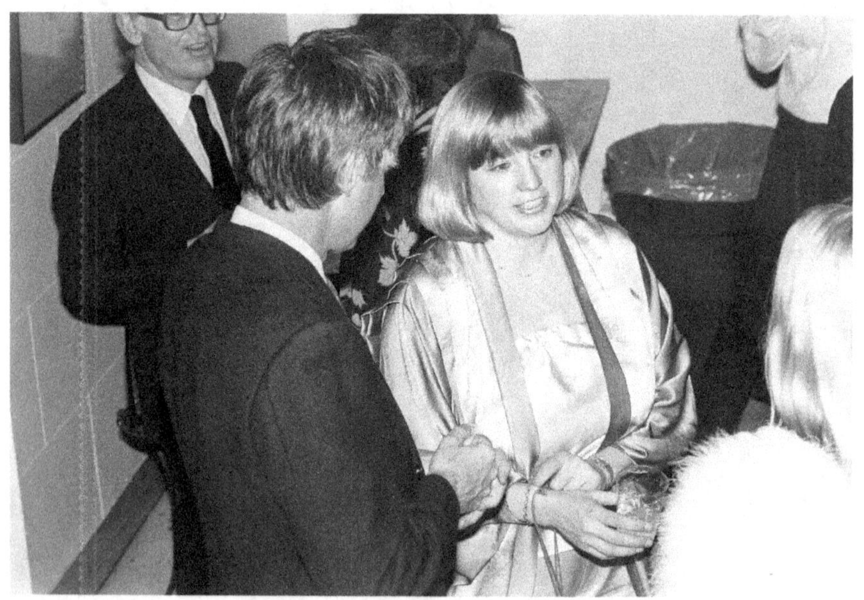

Portrait of me, 1982

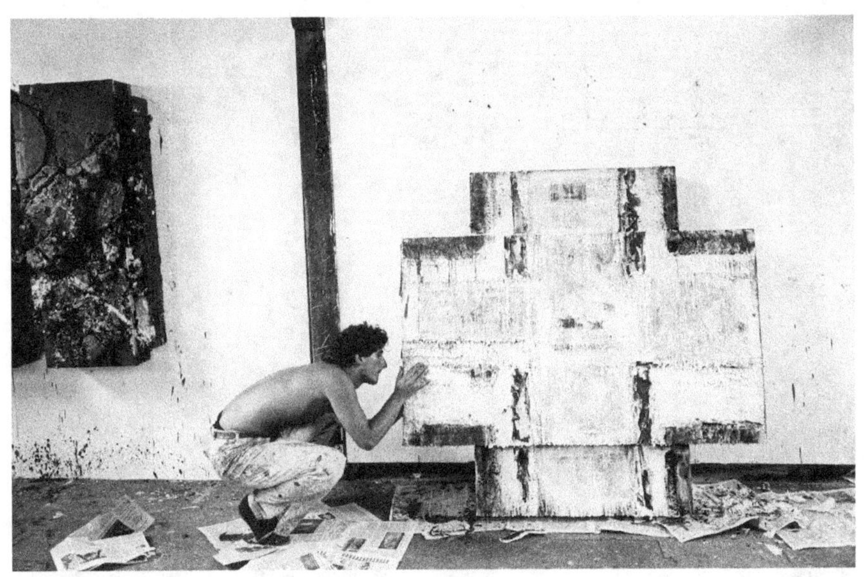

Michael David at Montauk working on painting summer 1983
© Michael Ackerman Ulick 198—all rights reserved

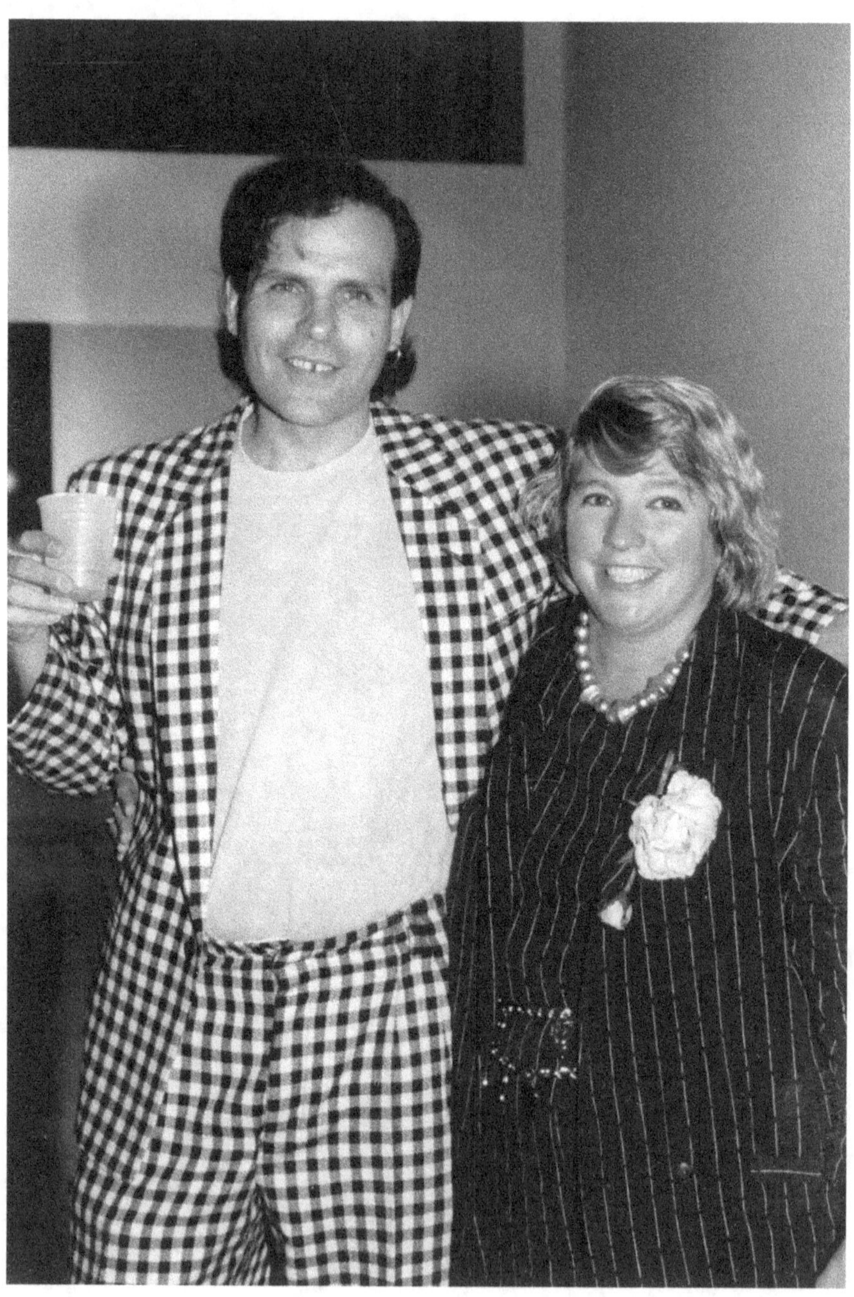

Rob Wynne + Patty at his show at 112 Greene St, 1988

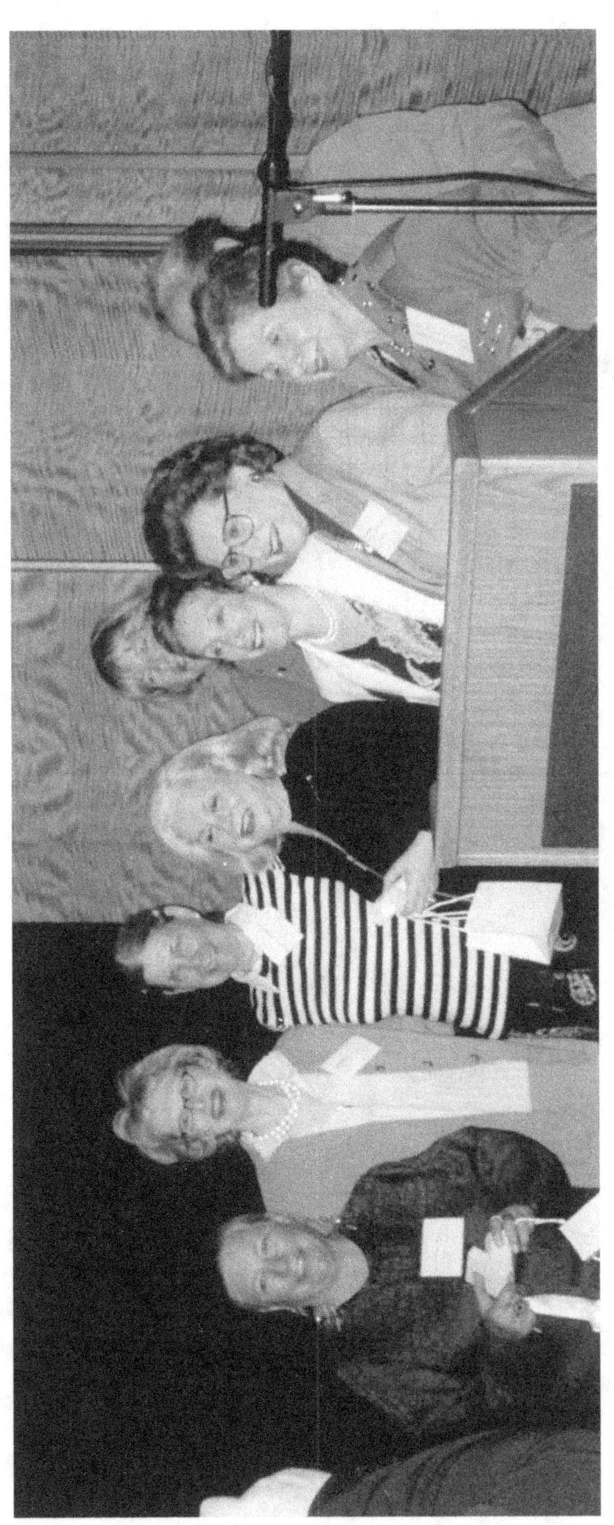

Founding members of Art Table at 25th anniversary, Me, Liz Robbins, Ali Anderson, Mimi Poser, Diane Frankel, Lila Harnett, Liz Pomeroy Schwartz, Lowery Sims

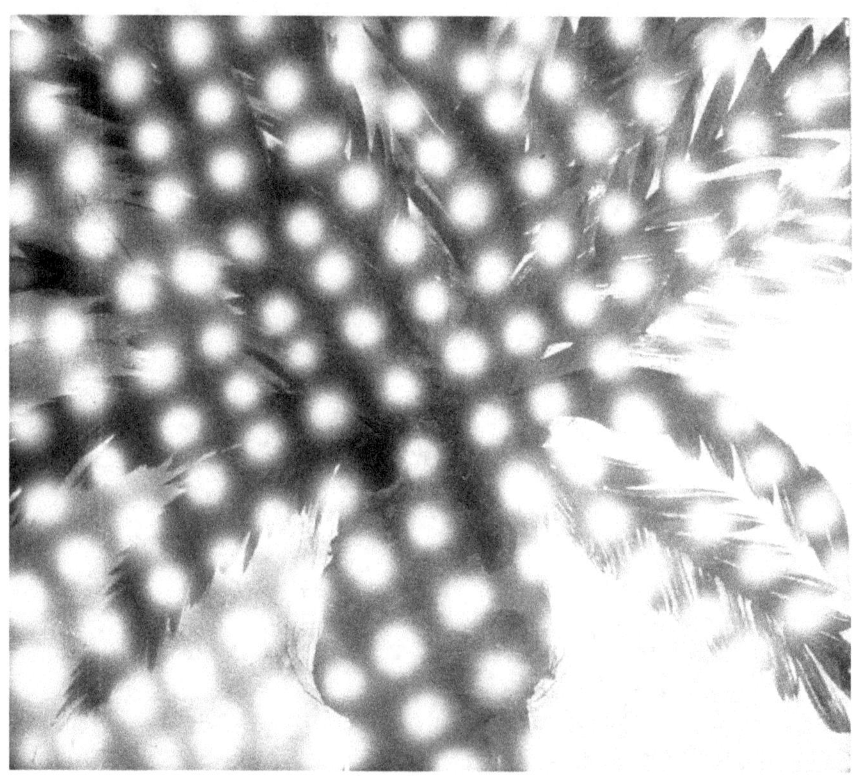

Peter Alexander
Stardust, 1993
Acrylic on canvas
48 x 53 inches
Courtesy of The Estate of Peter Alexander

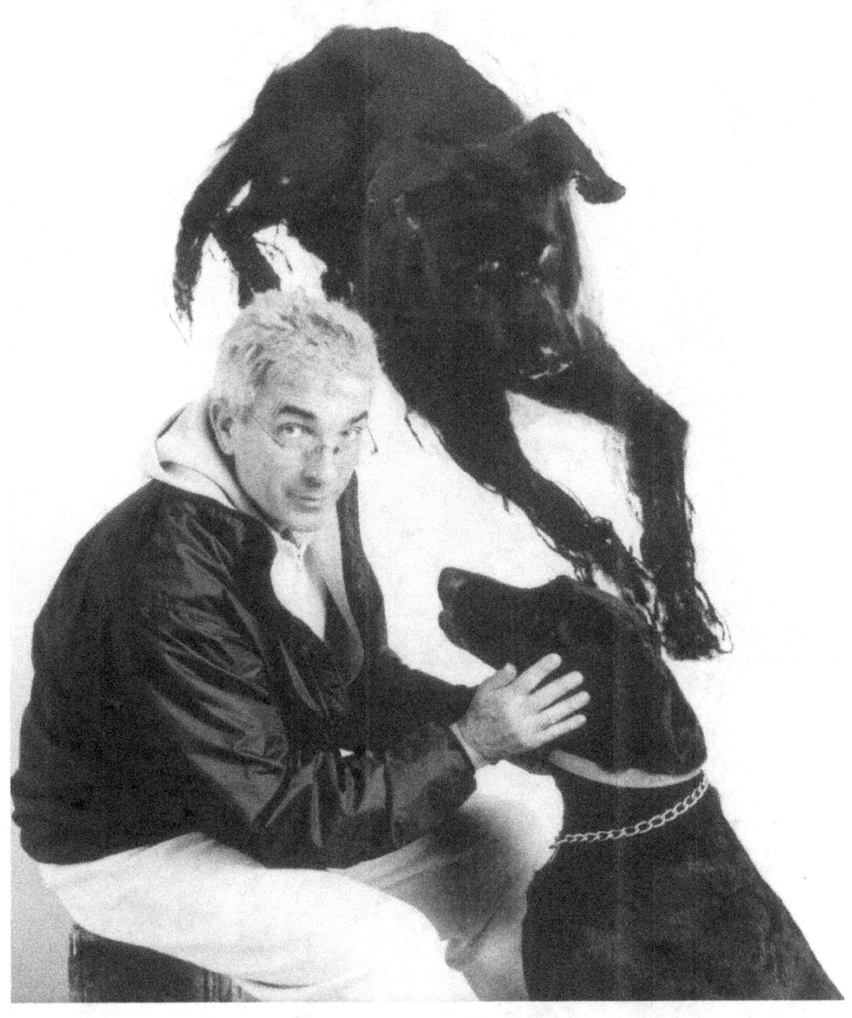

Peter Alexander 2002, photo by Michael Childers
Courtesy of The Estate of Peter Alexander

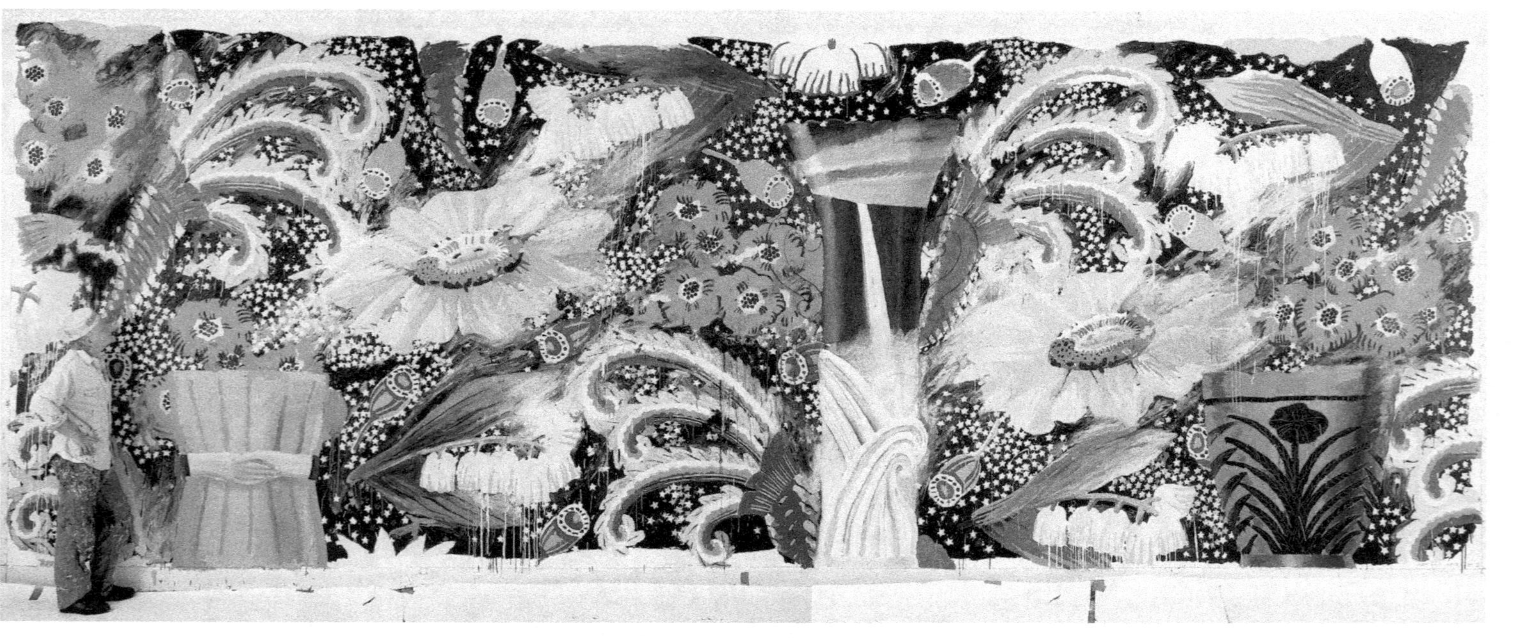

Robert Zakanitch
Big Bungalow Suite IV—Artist self-portrait, 1993

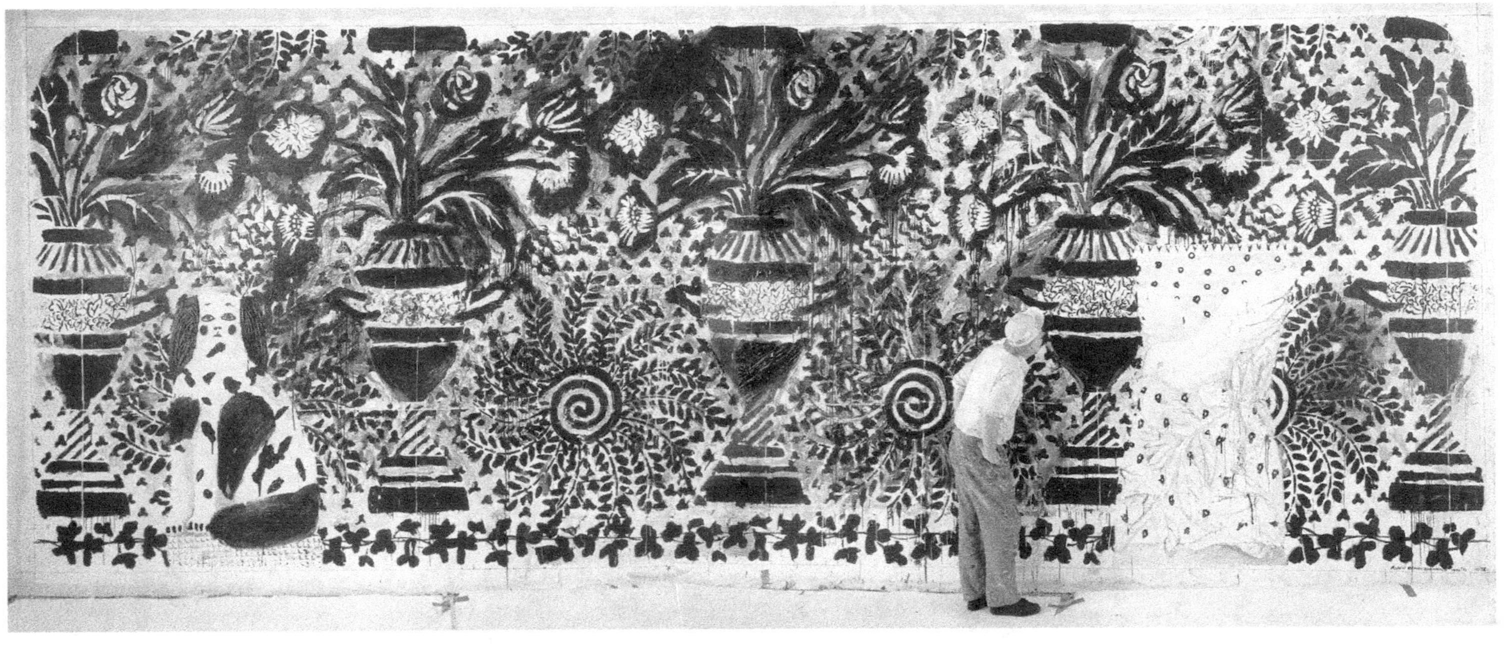

Robert Zakanitch
Big Bungalow Suite I—Artist self-portrait, 1991

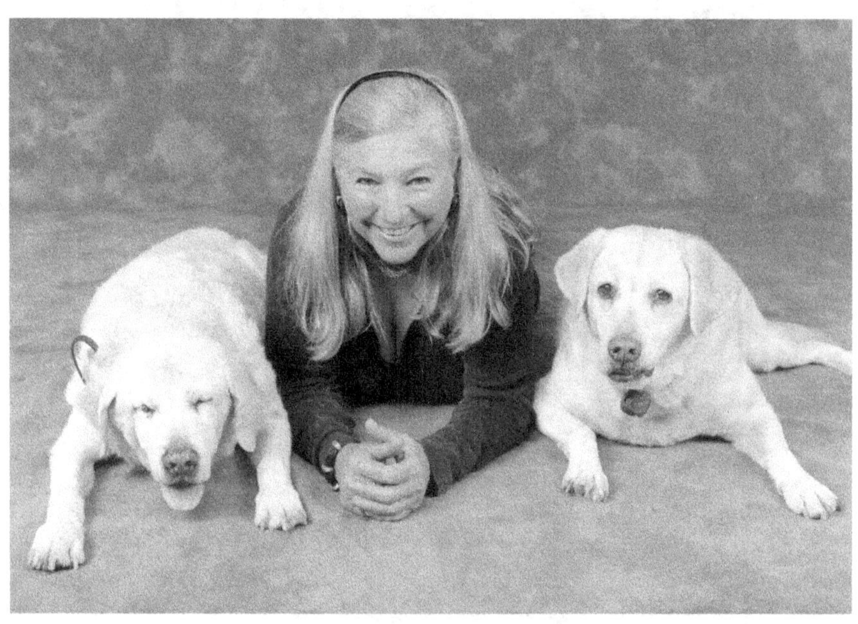

Me with the dogs in Whitley Heights, 2018

CHAPTER 11

Reinventing Myself as an Artist's Agent

Losing a job is always tough, no matter who you are. Even if it's a job you don't like. Worries about paying bills and rent come tumbling in—and as many of us know and have experienced at some point in our lives, there's nothing quite like the stress of mounting bills with no means to pay them.

But what do you do when you pour *your entire life* into a single endeavor? One that you held and cherished like the finest love? One so attached to who you are that your name is literally on it? Along with your finances, reputation, dreams, and just about everything else into which you poured your entire knowledge and experience? What can come next after spending hours each day crying and dealing with the resulting $180,000 mountain of debt? And feeling lost and without purpose, with no visible direction to go for the first time since showing up in New York 13 years before as a 22-year-old?

Well, after I scaled the mountain of debt within 90 days of closing the Hamilton Gallery and found the collective burden of the gallery, debt, and my bleeding ulcer all cleared up, the answer came to me quite clearly: *Get a life, Patty!* Which meant enjoying my leisure time, getting a new boyfriend and a social life, and exercising myself back into shape with tennis. And keeping my toes in the water, selling art here and there.

In the aftermath of the closing of the Hamilton Gallery, I found out just how narrowly focused my life and attention had been on keeping the gallery alive. It came in the form of something I never expected: an outpouring of people who not only appreciated my contributions to the art community, but also saw me as a *friend.* They were so nice and supportive. I realized that all along, I had friends I never realized were there, including versatile art critic and ArtTable member Phyllis Tuchman, artists Karen Gunderson and Graham Nickson, and my regular tennis partner, the private art dealer Mark Kelman. I was so hyper-focused on business that I saw them for their respective roles in my life: Phyllis through the *Artnews* and other pieces she wrote, Karen and Graham as artists, and Mark as the guy who batted tennis balls back to me. Mark specialized in Surrealism and photography, so he, too, knew what he was doing. Now, I saw who they really were as they listened to me during my most downtrodden period. More importantly, as I struggled to find my new place, like a drowning person fighting for breath, they assured me and flatly me that I would find my new *métier.* They assured me that I had "a vision," that the gallery would be remembered, and my vision and gallery experience would lead to a very good future somewhere in the art world.

Sure enough, as spring blossoms and leaves started spreading across the flowers and trees of Central Park again, the tides began turning my way. One day, I was waiting for my Mark on the Central Park tennis courts when I met a young German who worked at the German Embassy. His name was Toni Hamberger, and he, too, played tennis. So we started playing tennis, and before long, began dating. A new boyfriend! Even better, he was ten years younger than me. What a refreshing change from my former boyfriends, who were a generation older! I immediately noticed he had more energy than me, which is saying a lot. And he did the things about which the other guys had no clue, such as cooking. Toni was a wonderful cook and companion. I loved taking him on tours to see the sites in New York. Perhaps best of all? He wasn't a heavy drinker.

Toni was also a great athlete, an Olympic-level athlete, to be more specific. Imagine going from two alcoholic, self-indulgent men in Chuck and Tom to a *fucking Olympic-level athlete who cared about my feelings!* Besides his job at the Embassy, Toni was in the United States, in part, to attend the long-anticipated 1984 Summer Olympics in Los Angeles, the first Summer Games hosted in L.A. since 1932. The whole country was buzzing about the games since the United States had boycotted the 1980 Moscow Olympics over Russia's invasion of Afghanistan (sounds eerie when you think about the sports world's boycott of Russia after their 2022 invasion of Ukraine, doesn't it?). Americans hadn't been in the Summer Olympics since 1976; we had a great team—and my boyfriend was on his way, not as an official participant, but to compete in an exhibition of the team sport. (Orienteering was then being considered as a future Olympic sport). The sport combined archery with mapping, reading compasses, and doing so while moving on a course as fast as you could. It took about 90 minutes. More than anything, it involved having a great sense of direction. Considering that I have absolutely no sense of direction, we made quite an interesting partnership.

While I didn't make it to L.A. to see Toni compete in the Olympic exhibition, I did go to the Orienteering World Cup, held later that year in Boston. We stayed at my brother Bill's house and watched him compete. That was quite a thrill. Sadly, he only remained in New York for a year; our relationship ended when he moved back to Germany.

When summer arrived, I was back in shape, happy in my personal life, and ready to set out on my next path in the art world. Thanks to Phyllis Tuchman, I went to Peter Reginato's studio to see his new sculpture. Peter was originally from Oakland, California, and Phyllis had been friends with him for years. I knew Peter's work, since he had been exhibiting regularly in New York, usually at the Tibor de Nagy Gallery. He made formalist steel abstract sculptures but was now painting those sculptures in lively, catchy colors. They were clearly influenced by the sculpture of Robert Hudson, a California artist who I thought was underrated.

I found Peter's new work to be terrific. "If I still had the gallery," I told him, "I would have shown them."

That was enough for Peter to ask me to represent him and curate a show. He told me he had a friend, Stephen Montefiore, who might pay for an exhibition in a rental space. We promptly began planning a pop-up show, an event that "pops up" for a short period of time to achieve a specific goal. Today, they're a dime a dozen, spread across the spectrum of art and merchandising. Then? Unheard of. Peter suggested the space at 112 Greene Street, down the street from his loft in SoHo. You could rent it from owner Jeffrey Lew on a monthly basis, and it was already set up as a gallery. I met with Stephen Montefiore, and he was amenable to financially assisting Peter, so we crunched the numbers. Peter, quite the entrepreneur (not so often the case with working artists), even managed to find someone to underwrite a catalogue.

Our show opened in February 1985, almost one year to the day after I closed the gallery. This was my first big splash since that time. The opening was unbelievably packed, with around 700 people turning up to see ten of Peter's pieces. The show sold out, and everyone was talking about it. Interestingly, most of the work sold to clients was not from New York but from Los Angeles. This was not surprising given its whimsical, colorful, and joyous nature.

• • •

After Peter made his artistic breakthrough on Greene Street, I suddenly found myself representing artists without a gallery or a stable home base of any kind to exhibit their work. In other words, I was an artist's agent. Why did the artist need a freelancer like me? Simple: no artist could successfully sell their own work without the stamp of a dealer to validate it. I was that validating stamp, and as a former gallery owner, I knew all the important art dealers in the city very well. Even though I no longer had a gallery, I could still communicate with them on a dealer-to-dealer basis. It is considered very tacky for an artist to represent themselves, and in Peter's case, it would not have been good. Left to his own devices, he would make any deal he could for any amount of money. While it might put quick cash in his pocket, the damage would outweigh the benefit: such discounting would invalidate the established prices. Why would anyone pay retail if they could go to Peter's studio and get it for 50% off?

It didn't take a great intellect to figure out that the overhead of a gallery was very high, and if you continued to show work that did not sell, you would never make money. Now, I saw a new opportunity without the heavy lifting and financial burden: I could commit myself to the artists I liked and wanted to represent and help promote their careers without spending the huge amount of money it took to show the work. When I owned Hamilton Gallery, there were only two or three artists whose work sold well; all of the other artists were supported through those sales. Since I wasn't involved in the resale market, that put a lot of pressure on me every month; as the *New York Times* later noted, my annual overhead fell from about $300,000 to $60,000 by agenting. I would soon be earning six figures, beyond what I'd ever put in my pocket as a gallery owner. By only mounting exhibitions that I knew would be profitable, I cut out a lot of the headaches.

In addition, my market was now expanded beyond the closed-circuit world of my gallery and the pressure to continually produce successful shows to pay the overhead. The art market was growing quickly on an international basis, a sea change from the more insular gallery-oriented scene before that. Now, I could take the artists I represented into those markets. Shows were getting big in Los Angeles, Chicago, San Francisco, and Europe, and I wanted my artists and their works to gain exposure in all of those places.

In 1985, agenting artists was a new concept. Only two other people I knew were working as "artist's agents," Michael Klein and Karen Amiel. Michael, an extremely bright and funny guy, represented Pat Steir, Robin Winters, and Vito Acconci, among others. He enjoyed great connections in Europe and arranged many museum exhibitions. Karen had worked for a few dealers in town and was representing Italo Scanga and James Surls.

It was good to see my knack for forging new ground hadn't deserted me as my morale sank in the final year of Hamilton Gallery. While I will never be accused of jumping on or following a trend—definitely not my approach—I did gain a reputation as a person who took on new challenges, like curating major shows in my early 20s or becoming the woman in New York known for her risky (and successful) sculpture exhibits. Now I guess I could add pop-up shows and agenting artists to the mix.

One night in early 1986, Michael, Karen and I got together for dinner and tried to outline some common parameters of working as artist's agents. My lawyer, Jane Gregory Rubin, tried to get me to form an association of artists' agents, but with only three of us, it seemed premature. I had lunch with Douglas McGill from the *New York Times* and urged him to write an article about artist's agents, which appeared in the March 5, 1986 edition.

"The entire art world has expanded on a worldwide basis," I told Douglas. "There are more galleries, more artists, and more dealers.

It seems to me that the art business has become like the movie industry, with the galleries like the producers. Sometimes, they never show an artist more than one time. The agent has a broader commitment to the promotion of the work."

Douglas also interviewed Michael, Karen and Pam Adler, who by that point had begun agenting. All of us were former art dealers who came upon a similar realization: we could get beyond our galleries, their overhead, and the limitations they presented, keep working with artists, and take their works into the world while simultaneously helping them further develop and grow their careers.

Boy, did the phone start ringing after the *Times* article came out!

. . .

Prior to the article's appearance, my next project for Peter was to get him shown in a few Los Angeles galleries. After picking up the phone and trying to place him in a few, I decided to take the Patricia Hamilton direct approach—fly out to L.A. and do the exhibition myself. I found another pop-up space on La Brea and Melrose in Jerry Solomon's building that he allowed me to rent for a month. Next door was the Fiona Whitney Gallery, and next to that, the Burnett Miller Gallery. I became friendly with Burnett Miller. He had very good taste and was a real visionary. He was showing a lot of European artists, specifically German artists. He had been a curator at the La Jolla Museum and then opened a gallery. He was getting married to a wonderful mortgage banker named Tara Guizot that summer and invited me to the wedding. There was also available parking, an essential in Los Angeles but a foreign concept in New York.

Once again, Peter's entrepreneurial spirit came in. He traded sculptures with Arnold Ashkenazy, who owned a chain of hotels all over Los Angeles. In exchange for a large sculpture, Peter received a credit with these hotels, which he extended to me. If I did a show in

L.A., I could stay in one of the residential hotels in West Hollywood.

I scheduled a sculpture exhibition by Peter for February 1986, a year after our successful Greene Street pop-up. During that six-week show, I met not only the California collectors, but also some of their friends and colleagues who had begun collecting art themselves. I also sold all eight of Peter's sculptures for an average of $20,000 apiece. That promptly began my working relationship with the L.A. art scene.

There was one other thing working in Los Angeles required: learning how to drive a car. An odd skill for a person in the United States to be picking up at age 36, but New York was (and still is) full of residents who don't have or need cars. Greater Los Angeles and its many surrounding communities, the 50-mile-wide, 50-mile-long L.A. Basin, are so spread out, and the public transportation so inferior to New York, Chicago, and other big cities that you must own a car.

I began my driving lessons on 14th Street. It's a daring place to start, for sure. There was a reason I did not drive: I had been in a number of accidents when I was a teenager and was scared to death. Unsurprisingly, I started out as a terrible driver, cautious and scared. When I first took my driver's exam, one of the tests involved the skill that sends any typical 16- or 17-year-old candidate into fits of anxiety, especially when the stone-faced person sitting in your passenger seat is holding that scoresheet and clipboard—parallel parking. Imagine how I felt. And I'm still bad at it. I failed on the first try. The day before I left California, though, I retook the driver's exam and passed. On my learner's permit, it was stamped "Failed" then "Passed."

When I finally rented my first car in LA, and I showed my permit, the owner of the rental agency asked, with a bemused look on his face, "Are you like all those New Yorkers who drove for years but let their license expire?"

"No."

His bemused look switched to one of concern very quickly. He made me drive with him in the car to make sure I was not a reckless driver. He needn't have worried; I drove more like an 80-year-old woman.

Before I knew it, my month-long scheduled trip to L.A. had turned into six glorious weeks. Time slips away when you fall in love, and I really did fall in love with the city, the sparkling weather, and a lifestyle that seemed so much more relaxed than New York. Plus, I could swim, play tennis, and do other exercise outside year-round, which I quickly realized by doing all of these things in January and early February. It was so much better than waking up every morning to gray, bleary skies and freezing temperatures. I thought more and more about how great it would be to live and do business bi-coastally. I even had dinner with the dealer Christopher Ford, director of the Pence Gallery in Santa Monica and a former New York resident. He told me, "If you want to make money, you have to stay in New York. If you want a nice lifestyle, you move to LA."

When my brain processed Christopher's observation, it arrived at this conclusion: *I needed to figure out a way to do both.*

On the last day I was in Los Angeles, the Douglas McGill article came out in *The New York Times.*

. . .

One of the most important aspects of being an artist agent is to work year-round on their career. I could finally embark on long-term projects I often thought about engaging, but I never had time to work on with Hamilton Gallery. I could work on big museum and gallery shows for my artists, articles, and books. I always loved promoting the work of artists the best, going back to my early days as a curator for Crispo Gallery, and that was now a specific part of my job as an agent. Also, as mentioned, it was important to show it all over the United States and Europe.

I represented younger artists and tried to get them into galleries. With older artists, I tried to revive their careers, but I also worked with artists in their 40s or 50s whose careers had once been strong but then stalled for one reason or another. This was the same category with which I'd succeeded at the Gallery, beginning with reviving Louise Bourgeois after her 20-year absence from contemporary art galleries and helping launch her eventual blue-chip career late in life.

I met one of the younger artists, Glenn Goldberg, through Michael David. When Glenn and I first became acquainted, he made beautiful abstract paintings with a symbol in the middle of each work. They were either very small or very large. At one point, he started making all white paintings except for one single-colored symbol. They were compelling, unforgettable, and, in a word, terrific.

I brought the dealer Rebecca Donelson from the Dart Gallery in Chicago to his studio, and she immediately scheduled a show. She recommended I also show the work to Miani Johnson at the Willard Gallery in New York; Miani had been one of the gallery owners featured with me in the book *The Art Dealers*, another trailblazer among feminist women becoming gallery owners in the 1970s. I brought Miani in, and she bought two paintings on the spot. Then we planned a show. Generally, gallery exhibitions are scheduled a year in advance, so the Dart and Willard Gallery show was to happen in a year.

Glenn's show at the Willard took place in the Fall of 1987 and earned a piece from Amei Wallach in *Newsday*, one of New York's three biggest newspapers. My friend Lowery Sims from The Met, whom I'd brought into ArtTable when we formed the group in 1979, bought a work. Scott Spiegel, a major collector from Los Angeles, also bought a painting—and then he convinced the L.A. County Museum of Art to purchase a piece.

Suddenly, Glenn was hot—which, as he learned, can certainly feel like a double-edged sword. You can soar to the heavens with a career (and artist) with a strong foundation, but artists can also be consumed by instant success and fall quickly back to earth, like Icarus in the Greek myth of flying too close to the sun with waxen wings. Different artists handle sell-out shows in different ways. Some show humility, dignity, and grace, fully appreciating those who buy their works, and see the show as a great step in the process, but still a step. Or, they let the success go to their heads.

Unfortunately, Glenn handled the success very badly. It went right to his head. "Many people are comparing me to Jasper Johns," he said at one point.

That's not the thing you want to hear from a young artist. "Those are the kinds of things you whisper to your wife late at night," I advised, "not the kinds of things you say out loud."

Later, Miani decided that she and Willard could handle Glenn's career by herself and would just cut me out of the picture. Besides feeling insulted, that threw up a big red flag right in my face and career aspirations. It became clear that my role as an agent was a vulnerable one.

I immediately saw Harriet Dorsen, a litigator, in my attorney Jane Gregory Rubin's office. Harriet told me that Glenn could fire me as his agent anytime he wanted. However, she added that if he did, he could not continue to do business with anyone to whom I introduced him. Harriet told me I absolutely had a case against Miani Johnson and Glenn.

Shortly after that, Miani invited me for dinner with Glenn, set in her purpose of cutting me out of his career. I replied, "If you try to do that, I will sue you." I needed to set a precedent. "Glenn can fire me as his agent at any time, but he cannot continue to do business with anyone I have set him up with, past or present."

"According to who?" Miani asked.

"According to the law."

I promptly left the restaurant, my appetite ruined and my course of action already determined.

The next day, I served Miani with papers. She was notoriously cheap, so I knew she would settle before ever fighting a lawsuit. She hired an attorney who was friendly with my attorney. Furthermore, Miani said that Glenn was "no Susan Rothenberg," and she did not intend to spend much money on a lawsuit. That's a rather cutting remark to make about someone you're supposedly representing and promoting.

Ironically, Glenn's show at the Willard Gallery was Miani's last. Her lease was up on the space, and had she re-upped, the rent increase would have been astronomical. She chose not to remain open. She tried to be an artist's agent after she closed the gallery, and of course, wanted Glenn as her first client.

It didn't quite work out according to Miani's grand scheme. Soon after she left for Mexico on vacation, Glenn was wooed by Knoedler Gallery, the cream of the crop. He promptly cut Miani out as quickly as he cut me out. Tigers truly don't change their stripes. And what a surprise: it turns out Glenn was not the next Jasper Johns. He later showed up with Charlie Cowles, then with Jason McCoy, and more recently, with Betty Cunningham. Betty endured the exact same experience with Glenn as I did and quickly ended the relationship.

What Glenn Goldberg didn't realize is that sometimes, to reprise Andy Warhol's iconic saying, artists only have 15 minutes of fame.

Another young artist I met was the California sculptor Stephen Whisler, who made large Surrealist sculptures and gorgeous drawings. He was also a nice guy. I was able to sell quite a few of his works from his studio and arranged for a one-person show with new young dealers Max Lang and Jonathan O'Hara. Also, I rented Jerry

Solomon's space again in California and did a show for Stephen in L.A. After his first show at Lang/O'Hara, they wanted to cut me out like Willard did, but Stephen's work was more difficult to sell than Glenn's. Seems the gallery owners didn't understand the middle-man concept of agenting, nor that had I not presented Stephen to them, they likely still wouldn't know who he is. Also, Stephen was aware of the trouble that Glenn had caused and didn't want to burn that bridge with me. I paid to fabricate one of the bronzes in his show, and he told me to keep it without paying him a commission.

Still, he left me. Years later, we got together for dinner in California. "Leaving you was one of the biggest mistakes I've ever made," he admitted.

How right he was. Lang/O'Hara was unable to sell the work and, besides, was more interested in resale marketing than trying to sell young artists' work. They never set him up with galleries outside of New York and did very little for him. Too bad. He did fine work and had a lot of potential.

Another artist I showed in New York was the California artist Michael McMillen. Michael made a name for himself in Hollywood doing sets for movies in miniature. In 1983, he won an Academy Award for Best Technical Achievement in *Blade Runner*. His art was related to his movie work. He made miniature dilapidated buildings, warehouses, and entire cities and built incredible installations and environments. I put together and curated two shows for Michael at 112 Greene Street, and landed a big *New York Times* review. The first show featured a wrecked ship that looked as fresh as if pirates had just deserted it. Mobs of people came to the gallery; pirates always seem to be an attraction, and this was a good 15 years before Johnny Depp and Disney re-energized the whole concept with the *Pirates of the Caribbean* movies. Kids especially wanted to see the wrecked ship, and I was constantly holding kids up to view the ship in detail on its three-foot pedestal.

During Michael's show, veteran art dealer and gallerist Ivan Karp walked in. Ivan had established a lofty reputation in the '60s for helping develop the SoHo gallery district and participating in the emergence of pop art. Well, as I realized, being a very big scene-setter of the '60s doesn't necessarily mean you're up with the direction of things in the '80s. Ivan couldn't understand what I was doing with Michael and why he didn't have a real dealer. He also didn't understand the concept of a pop-up show. He was truly old-fashioned.

. . .

I really enjoyed direct agenting and putting together shows, but both could be very time-consuming and taxing. So, in my way of continuously evolving myself and creating new roles or wrinkles I could fulfill in the art world, I also found a way to work with artists that did not involve mounting an exhibition or direct representation.

This began with a call from Ursula von Rydingsvard, who was about to have her first show at Exit Art, a nonprofit space on Broadway run by Jeannette Ingerman. I went to the studio and was knocked out. Rarely had I seen someone who works in wood, and in her case, cedar in particular. She made predominantly large-scale abstract work, carved into the cedar, and then laminated it. Some of her frequently used themes were shovels, bowls, and vessels. It felt as if she was bringing her own emotion into the wood and humanizing it. The work was mature and extremely moving. I told Rebecca Donelson about the work; she came over and looked at it and was also blown away. Between the two of us, we managed to introduce Martin Friedman, director of the Walker Art Center, and Jim Demetrion, director of the Hirschhorn Museum, to the work. We also sold quite a bit of it.

Soon thereafter, Ed Leffingwell, a curator at PS1, recommended an interesting painter named Rob Wynne. Rob made really beautiful abstract paintings and a series of works about the four elements: earth, fire, wind, and water. We did a gorgeous and well-received show at 112 Greene Street. Our rich and fulfilling relationship led both of us forward. Now, Rob is with Sara Gavlak Gallery, both in L.A. and in Palm Beach, Florida. He's doing well.

My long-held reputation in the industry and my network continued to serve me well. The critic Carter Ratcliff recommended the Japanese American Artist Nobu Fukui. After being with Max Hutchinson for years, he hadn't shown in a very long time. His works were complicated abstract paintings, such as landscapes. Technically, they were gorgeous. I fell in love with his work—and also with his family. His wife, Kwisoon, was a beautiful Korean woman, and they had an incredibly bright small child, Tomo. They lived in a wonderful loft in Chelsea, and Kwisoon was an extraordinary cook. I showed his work twice in New York at 112 Greene Street and again in Los Angeles. It was difficult to sell, but I believed in it and would continue to represent him even, though I was not really making any money.

In the Fall of 1988, I did an exhibition for Nobu at 112 Greene Street, right around the time I turned 40. The renowned British artist Howard Hodgkin came to see the show. I met Howard through Terry McInerney and knew of him not only as an artist, but also as a serious collector of Indian paintings. Howard was probably the second most famous painter in Britain and was knighted by the Queen. When Howard walked into 112 Greene Street, I was reading a book called *How to Buy a Mink Coat,* as I planned to buy myself a coat for my birthday. Howard picked up the book and immediately selected the coat I was to buy. He had fabulous taste.

A few years earlier, Howard's work was the British entry to the Venice Biennale, one of the most prestigious shows in the work. It started in 1895 and, true to its name, occurs once every two years. It is pretty much the *Carnevale* of the art world; today, about 500,000 people attend each Biennale. To have your work selected is both a huge honor and a boon for an artist's career.

Terry and I were overseas in Venice when Howard's work was shown. Howard and Terry wanted to see shows and spend time together, and then the three of us would convene for dinner at Harry's Bar. I was sitting at Harry's, waiting for them, when an Italian man approached me and said, "You are the empress of my eyes."

I had never heard of a better pickup line in my life. "I'm busy for dinner," I said while inwardly warming to that wonderful line.

When Howard and Terry arrived, I told them the story."What a great title for a painting," Howard said.

"If you use the title for the painting," I responded, "you have to tell the story."

Years later, at Brooke Alexander's gallery, I met a British painter. When I introduced myself, he said, "Ah, the empress of my eyes."

CHAPTER 12

Interventions

Life really felt good again. My agenting career continued to grow, and with it, my personal horizons: not only was I doing business in New York, but more and more so in California. Like the Mamas and Papas sang a generation before, I was "California Dreamin'" and not only dreaming, but also beginning to live the West Coast life. Every bit of it appealed to me—the sun-splashed days, the more casual lifestyle, the mild winters where I could play tennis and swim instead of being blasted by icy winds every time I walked out of my apartment, and the nascent art scene that was really taking shape. My artists loved it, I loved it, and I spent more and more time there. If I wanted to play in cold weather, I went skiing in Aspen.

Then, in the summers, I'd rent houses in the Hamptons and enjoy that particular upscale beach life culture. More and more, the good memories of Hamilton Gallery filled my mind, and the severe stress at the end and subsequent health issues faded further into the background. It felt great to be alive, and I went to bed already, looking forward to the next day and the deals and adventures it might bring along.

One day, the phone rang. I had just returned from Aspen, where I'd dug further and harder into one of those beautiful, steep, powdery slopes than my left knee permitted, proceeding to tear my ACL.

It is not an injury an athletic person wants; even the top professional athletes require a year of recovery and treatment to return to full performance capacity. I hobbled over to the phone on crutches, my body sore but otherwise delighted with the course of my life.

It was Father Bert Draesel, my sister Susan's parish priest. "Can you intervene to help Susan seek treatment?" he asked. "I'm worried about her alcoholism."

I listened, though it was the last thing I wanted to hear or deal with. His voice was etched with concern. He was definitely worried.

Great. Right in the middle of this Renaissance of well-being in my life and career, my sister Susan and her rampant alcoholism and associated problems plopped headlong into my life. Again. *It figures.*

Susan's life was a headlong mess, and much as I didn't want anything to do with her at times, she was still my sister, and I still interacted with her. Prior to Bert Draesel's call, she lost one job after another on Wall Street and finally ended up in Boca Raton, Florida. She was dating losers at this point because no one in their right mind would date her. She was a mess—a mess who was receiving plenty of enabling from my mother, who moved to Florida to be with her. They were tied at the hip, which had caused me so many problems throughout my life—and would again.

Soon, Susan lost her job in Florida and moved back to New York City. She then moved out of Brooklyn and into the 91st Street apartment shared with her alcoholic boyfriend, who was beyond a loser. Eventually, she moved away from her boyfriend and back into her old place.

That's when Bert called for the Intervention.

This was my second attempt to intervene to help my sister stop drinking and get some real help for the many deeper issues that created her desire to drink. Our first attempt was an utter disaster. My brother Bill, also a screaming alcoholic, called from Boston and demanded my presence to stage an intervention. The request itself was surreal: *you're an alcoholic, and you want to intervene on another alco-holic—thought of looking in the mirror, Bill?* In a way, he *was* looking in the mirror, just not recognizing or admitting that in Susan, he was also staring at himself. For him, it was a classic deflection. For me, despite my love-hate relationship with my sister, it was a serious concern.

I promptly called Smithers, only to be told this was not the way to do an intervention. In a structured intervention, a rehabilitation professional sits in the room with concerned family members or friends, facilitating a process in which each person shows their concern, love, and support while simultaneously holding a tight line: *we are here to help you help yourself, but it's time for you to help yourself. Now.* If the recipient is worn out, done drinking their life, relationships, and friendships to ruins, "sick and tired of being sick and tired," as they say in AA, then the time really is *now*—and that person will be more receptive to entering a treatment program or, at the very least, a solid 12-Step program like AA.

However, the person has to be ready—and having our alcoholic brother dumping on Susan, without a professional in the room, was going to enhance her state of readiness about as much as humid weather repels mosquitoes. We did convince her to enter a treatment program in New Hampshire that Bill found, but the second she got out, she did the predictable for someone who truly isn't ready for sober living: stop at a 7/11 and buy a six-pack. She then lived with my mother and worked as a substitute teacher, continuing the disaster that was her life at that point.

While Bert and I talked, so many feelings, memories, and moments raced through my mind, images, and emotions that took me all the way back to our births.

. . .

My relationship with Susan was complex, to say the least. My mother had five children in a seven-year span; Susan was the fourth, and ten months later, I was the fifth. Our baby brother followed, five years after me. There's a term for Susan and me: Irish Twins. While emotionally balanced parents would view us as their two baby daughters, equally loved and beheld in all ways, our family was not emotionally balanced. Susan became my parents' "chosen one." She could do no wrong. Even though she had the attention span of a small gnat, she was the perfect, spoiled one my mother doted upon. It began early. When we were little, my mother used to take us into the yard to play on sunny days, a normal childhood activity. It drove Susan nuts. She could not be satisfied with anything—not dolls, toys, a normal amount of attention—nothing appeased her. So she stirred up attention-seeking trouble, often directed at me. On the other hand, I was a doll collector and would escape for hours, happy in myself, happy to be convening with my dolls. She couldn't do that.

I also loved the outdoors in a way she never did. I was an athletic tomboy, wearing guns, climbing trees, riding horses, and many other activities that would keep me outside of our house. Inside, my mother was being constantly put down by my father, and two of my three brothers only added to the toxic male energy. Then and there, I wanted to be anything but a girl expected to keep a house, or remain indoors in any other way. Also, my father was a major male chauvinist and would say things like, "Women can't do anything but have children." I fought back against these assertions, in a way that later fed into my life as a feminist and no-nonsense businesswoman, but Susan internalized his messages and toxic behavior while being, in essence, a besieged comrade-in-arms with my mother, who favored her even more.

Not good.

Susan's alcoholism first became apparent when we were in high school. On one occasion, she went to New York City with the staff of our high school newspaper, *The Acorn,* and convinced all of the fledgling reporters, editors, and photographers to drink beer and get drunk. I guess she already knew the favorite post-deadline pastime of many an editorial department in those days! School officials found out about it and came down on her hard. They kicked her off the May Queen's Court and threatened to call the University of Pennsylvania, where she had achieved early admission by virtue of her glowing grades.

What is the reason for the harsh, potentially life-changing threat? My parents protested the school, kicking her off the Queen's court! Rather than really look at the problem with Susan and her emerging alcoholism, my parents decided *their* daughter was beyond such trivial nonsense and erupted like a couple of irate prudes, what today we would call *major denial*. Not knowing what to do, I went along with them, thus unknowingly enabling the situation.

Susan got through this episode and entered the University of Pennsylvania. She joined the best sorority there, Kappa Kappa Gamma, while commuting to and from campus. Among the members was a California girl and the reigning Miss University and Homecoming Queen, Candice Bergen, who would soon star in *Carnal Knowledge*, the movie that launched her as a major film star. Susan was a striking girl herself, and when later nominated for University Homecoming Queen, she won—quite an honor. She looked a bit like the gorgeous Olivia Hussey in Zeffirelli's Golden Globe-winning *Romeo & Juliet*, then blanketing theaters across America. When Susan became a senior, with scholarships and jobs lined up left and right, she was able to rent an apartment in Philadelphia.

Sadly, like some of those kids in *American Graffiti*, Susan's life highlight happened in school: being the University of Pennsylvania's Homecoming Queen.

By this point, Susan considered me an embarrassment of a sister, because I was at "lowly" Temple University and "not cool." When I look back at that characterization, I always remember one thing: she was drinking like a fish.

Later that summer, while I was lifeguarding at the Chatham Bars Inn on Cape Cod, my parents called to say she was getting married. Being the naturally protective little sister, I felt she was pushed into getting married, and I could already see her throwing her life down the drain. In this case, she'd literally made a choice between the two guys she was dating. Or so I thought. As it turned out, she never let go of the first guy she was dating and had an affair with him while she was married. Meanwhile, her new husband had signed up as a pilot in the Navy, which meant she would need to leave the East Coast for Pensacola, Florida, an entirely different world culturally and otherwise.

Not surprisingly, her marriage was a disaster. She continued drinking but found that alcohol didn't give her enough zip in her life, so she became addicted to Black Beauties, the version of speed preferred by many in the '70s. She also grew thinner and thinner, exhibiting anorexic tendencies. Was her husband nagging her about her already lightweight? Doubtful. I traced it right back to my parents and the shit they always gave me for my weight. She observed many of those moments and wanted no part of the abuse. She stopped eating, which in her state amounted to a problem called Drunkorexia.

After some time in Pensacola, her husband was stationed in Europe. She wanted to get closer to home, so she rented an apartment in Boston, waited tables—and found a stateside boyfriend to keep her warm and comforted. Her ex-boyfriend. I visited her and witnessed all of this drunken, college-like behavior. I thought it was strange. She also traveled overseas to visit her husband, during which she lined her clothes with black beauties to avoid detection at customs; otherwise, she was completely oblivious to the risk involved. I think her boyfriend thought she was going to end the relationship with her husband. She didn't—but her husband sure did. After he returned to the States, he divorced her.

By this point, my career in New York had begun. I was a senior editor at *Art in America,* and I'd started dating Chuck. When Chuck and I moved in together, he made it very clear he wanted nothing to do with Susan. They did not get along. He felt she was irresponsible and impossible and couldn't understand why I put up with her. *Well, Chuck, for one thing, she's my sister, and despite the problems, I still do care about my family and my sister.* And, in retrospect, knowing how things turned out with Chuck, it's ironic he would see those very undesirable qualities in her, don't you think? Still, in deference to him, I didn't see Susan much in the mid- and late 1970s.

In 1977 or 1978, she started trying to spring forward in her life. After blowing the $10,000 her ex-husband gave her, she moved down to New York to get an MBA at Columbia. Chuck and I broke up shortly afterward, and she started hanging out with me. Unfortunately, her alcoholic behavior was in full bloom. I was aware she was fucked up and attributed it to booze. I would take her to a party, and she would get so drunk she passed out. I had to drag her out of there.

My Aunt Ruth, who, along with my brother Rick, were the two family members who always had my back, got in touch with me. She warned me about Susan and reminded me how Susan had put me down constantly in her youth. I'd blocked a lot of it out, though there always was tension between us. "Stay away from her," Ruth added.

• • •

"Can you help with the Intervention?" Bert Draesel asked again.

"Yes, of course," I said, gritting my teeth.

This time, I went to the Smithers Center for Alcohol and Drug Rehabilitation to learn more about how an intervention is supposed to work, and how it might lead to success. In Susan's case, there would be only one measure of success: complete abstinence from all alcohol and substances, and full commitment to living in sobriety. The professionals explained to me an intervention works very few times, must be properly rehearsed, and plans must be made in advance. That sure was a lot different than a drunken brother pounding insults into her head!

I got right to work on my part in this: assembling a team of concerned family members. I asked my brother John to fly from Memphis, as well as my first cousin Frank, a psychiatrist who lived in Connecticut. I also asked Bert to join us. We moved through a few practice sessions, going over what each of us would say, basically building a narrative toward the crucible point: *you need help, and we're here to support you in that.* It also required us to address any of her responsibilities that would need attention after she entered rehab. Frank was willing to board her dog at his place in the country, a big help. The whole process was emotionally draining, and I didn't know if she would agree to get sober.

When we met again with the woman in charge of the Intervention, she recommended that I join Alanon, a program for those directly impacted by the user, either as enablers or as recipients of the emotional turmoil and abuse. I thought, *aren't we here for Susan? Why do you think I have a problem?* I ignored her. As I realized later, by simply saying "okay," my life would have been a lot easier. I, too, was living in denial without realizing it.

We held the Intervention and achieved the desired result: Susan agreed to enter rehab at Hazelden. That was the all-important first step. But still, just a first step. Staying sober involves many steps, and it is an incredibly difficult road to navigate for those used to drinking and medicating their troubles, sorrows, successes, and failures away. Only ten percent of people who enter rehab stay sober. But Susan caught a wonderful break—some would call it a blessing—while inside. She met a very good friend who lived in her neighborhood, Pat Dufy. They could attend AA meetings together and later constantly talk about their lives and the 12 steps of AA while walking their dogs. That was important.

Susan was not studious—which might come as a surprise at first glance, considering she received a degree from the University of Pennsylvania and an MBA from Columbia. The truth is, she never studied, even for the MBA. But she changed her tune at Smithers, following all the steps they suggested. She even entered a halfway house-like rehabilitation center after rehab before finally going home. She not only attended AA meetings constantly and faithfully but was such a proponent of AA that we called her "Sister Mary Sobriety."

With Susan apparently in good stead, adhering to her program, and spending quality recovery time with Pat, I felt I could take some deep breaths again and move beyond this latest family crisis. However, when long-time alcoholics and users achieve sobriety, a major part of remaining sober—and of working an honest 12-step program—is to dig into the deeper origins of the disease, the root causes. In the course of doing that work, she learned something else had happened from all of those years of drinking and drugging: her mental and physical health had deteriorated. She found out she was manic depressive, probably since childhood, and the alcohol and drugs were her way of coping with it. A helpful psychiatrist put her on medication so she'd never go back to her previous form of self-medication and to balance her moods. Then, she went to the dentist, only to find out she needed all of her teeth pulled. Damn— one thing after another. She managed to get our brother Peter to pay for the dental bills. She struggled hard, but she moved forward. She really worked on her life.

. . .

When I was convinced Susan's forward progress would last, or at least last awhile, I moved forward, too—2,500 miles forward, to Southern California. I made good on my long-held wishes to get into that sunshine-driven lifestyle and growing art scene, and I moved to direct the Salander/O'Reilly Gallery in Beverly Hills while maintaining a firm presence in New York. Salander/O'Reilly paid for my move; it was great! I'd been working bi-coastally for five years; now, I simply switched where I woke up most mornings.

For her part, Susan made use of that MBA and landed a great job as a business advisor at the Hazelden Treatment Center in New York; it is not unusual for these centers to hire former patients who have the requisite skills. What better way to motivate people in treatment than for them to see their former peers "out there" now leading successful lives—and helping them on a journey both parties knew better than any other? Susan not only worked there but fixed the place up and improved it in several ways. But as she found out, living in sobriety has its very big ups and downs; the world can still be cruel, for one thing. Eventually, Hazelden changed ownership, and she lost her job. They offered her a settlement, which she felt was a pittance compared to her worth—and she fought it. Unfortunately, she hired an incompetent lawyer.

I'd been staying with Susan for four months a year when I wasn't in California. I'd since come to my senses and entered Alanon, realizing my life felt inwardly chaotic. We found we finally had something to talk about—my Alanon program, her AA, and sobriety. I joined a gym in the building, and really tried to get into this new life with my roommate sister. However, when Susan kept losing jobs, her increasingly sweeping moods and complaints became too much for me. All the old triggers hit, and I realized she was smothering me. Plus, she wanted me to pay all the living expenses, since she was no longer working. It was cra-cra in there, and I wanted no part of it.

This time, I had the strength to act in the interests of my own emotional and mental health, rather than focusing on and enabling the other person at my own expense, so I started searching for other places to live in New York.

Finally, Susan got a job speaking about throat cancer for a charity that focused on the relationship between smoking and cancer. It was a *de rigeur* topic: after a century of covering up the effects of nicotine, the tobacco industry was finally being forced to come clean about the relationship between their treasured addictive ingredient and cancer. Susan was personally motivated as well; after I moved out, she contracted throat cancer herself and was treated with radiation. Then, her cancer recurred, and she had to undergo chemo.

Susan was a good speaker. She even had the famed photographer Richard Avedon take a picture of her in a magazine. Richard, who was schmoozing her, said she didn't need makeup. Knowing Susan, I thought, *oh well, this will be a doozy.* And it was. She hated the picture, finding it woefully inferior to the way she viewed herself: as Miss University Homecoming. *That* picture was now twenty years in the past, but not in her mind.

. . .

Downward spirals are like tornadoes. Not only is the central spiraling event a danger—in this case, Susan being fired from Smithers—but it tends to sweep in poor decisions and a whole series of negative events from all the factors surrounding it, making it worse. That is, unless the person involved immediately sees the central danger, deals with it promptly, has a great supporting cast to help her through it, and keeps her feet planted in sober living with those strong 12-step program roots, worked daily.

I knew Susan had just fallen into a downward spiral of which I wanted no part. Together, she and my mother put me down as a kid, demeaned me for going to Temple, told me I would amount to nothing more than a substitute teacher *after* my career started in the art world, pooh-poohed both me and the Hamilton Gallery, and then pulled that strange platonic three-way relationship dynamic with Tom Bergen during and after Tom and I were together. My mother always saw Susan as golden, me as the unworthy daughter, and held no discernible love for me.

I had begun a course of therapy when I was dating Chuck, during which I looked for the first time at the relationship with my family. It's too bad I wasn't into Alanon at that time. In Alanon, I realized how similar my mother and sister were. They could be incredibly mean and put me down constantly. I always said Susan inherited the worst part of my father's and mother's personalities. She was manipulative as hell like my mother, and a drunk and a mess like my father. When she got sober, she developed a sweet, shy side—but it always seemed to come with a price. Now that I saw the pattern, I was determined to keep my distance.

A few years after I moved out of Susan's apartment, my mother moved in. Though her vision was impaired by macular degeneration, she and Susan began a new escape habit: watching TV 24/7. It was sick. Shortly thereafter, Susan received her second throat cancer diagnosis, and had to move my mother into a nursing home because my mother couldn't walk or take care of herself, and she wouldn't leave Susan alone long enough to even take a nap. Plus, she was showing signs of dementia. But to my sister's credit, she visited my mother every day, the dutiful and attentive daughter, giving her a purpose in life.

After my mother died at age 93, Susan lost her purpose. She ran out of money, was being sued for disability, and her rent tripled. She managed to drive me out of her life.

The final straw came one Christmas when I would no longer let her visit me in California. I sent her something very expensive from Divine Design, a program where designers list items for sale at 50% off, then on the last day of the sale, escalate to 90% off. Truly divine, if you're on a budget. I sent her two Divine Design gifts, and she scoffed at them, though they were the only Christmas presents she had received.

After I got off the phone and said out loud, "I'm done." I walked away as a matter of my own mental and emotional health. Tough as it was, I had to. She brought me down, always wanted money, and was a complete burden. I never spoke to her again.

Sadly, Susan saw no way out of her inner and outer hell. This gorgeous, bright sister of mine, who could've had the most successful of lives, and who had beaten cancer twice, finally took her own life. Her mental illness did her in. So did the fact that she was sued by her disability insurance carrier. She had talked about killing herself often, so I was not surprised. I even warned our brother Peter about it, but he was too caught up in the Greenwich, Connecticut scene to care; she had embarrassed him too much.

I tried to save Susan so many times. But in the end, I could not save her.

CHAPTER 13

The Recession and Salander O'Reilly Gallery

While reeling from the efforts to help my sister, I sensed more trouble on the horizon: a recession. We'd just ridden through five wonderful years between 1984 and 1989 when I reinvented myself as an artist's agent, rented 112 Greene Street in New York two to three times a year for exhibitions, traveled to Europe, rented houses in the Hamptons every summer, darted back and forth from California, and pretty much lived the high life. The whole decade had an economic Wild West feel to it, whether you were selling art in New York or buying into the ocean lifestyle in California. Glammed-up, brand-conscious Baby Boomers supercharged the business and marketing worlds, and bolstered by plenty of money in the economy, we let it fly with our fearless "sky is the limit" approach to just about everything.

Much of it felt too good to be true. Beginning with the Wall Street crash in 1987, our bonfire of the vanities, to paraphrase Tom

Wolfe, began to burn out. By the end of the decade, business had really slowed down. And when business starts a downturn, you can bet the art world has already been feeling it for some time.

Suddenly, shows weren't selling out, and I wasn't able to do as many deals. I smelled not only a downturn but also a looming recession. Since I specialized in mid-career artists, the signs of a recession quickly became apparent. Whenever a recession hits, the first sales to drop off are those of mid-career artists. Clients feel they can always purchase the work, since it's not blue chip. If they have to wait until money loosens up again, they'll wait. Great for their budgets, but bad for mine. Both blue-chip art and younger artists still sell during recessions, but I only worked the edges of those two categories.

In the midst of this sea change, which cast a cloud over the go-go-go 1980s economy as thick as the threat of a new war looming in Kuwait and Iraq, I headed back to California in the winter of 1990, focused on persevering through this bump in the road. I rented a space in Santa Monica, which I built out as a gallery, and curated an exhibition for Peter Reginato and Sigrid Burton. Peter enjoyed strong success in California, and had a solid following, so it wasn't a stretch for him to expect sold-out shows. For her part, Sigrid was from Pasadena and could bring along all of her family contacts.

It didn't quite turn out that way. Both shows sold decently, but not extremely well. They were certainly not sell-outs. Given the built-in audience we could reasonably expect, this became another troubling sign for me.

Peter added to the difficulty. He spent money like a drunken sailor and was very demanding. He thought nothing of calling me during another artist's opening to divert my attention to his career. Most artists have robust egos, but pulling me from another artist's opening? He could be beyond the pale. Once, he called me at the Brooklyn Museum, when Peter Gourfain was having a one-person show, to talk about a sale. After all, who was more important than himself?

Well, this time, he called in the middle of Sigrid's opening—and wouldn't get off the phone. In Peter's very self-obsessed eyes, no one was allowed any of my time but Peter. Since his work sold well, he felt he was able to monopolize my time, no matter what. As for my career, my trying to make a living? Which required representing more than one artist? He never gave it a thought. In 40 years of selling art, I never met a more narcissistic artist.

After that fairly demoralizing experience, I came back to New York a bit depressed and found a good temporary remedy: mounting an incredible show for Isaac Witkin. Not only was he one of my favorite people, but he was also a world-class artist. He continued to fabricate huge and gorgeous poured-abstract bronzes. I put together a catalogue and Gerrit Henry wrote the essay. Gerrit was a nationally known art critic, who reviewed for the *New York Times, Village Voice, Art in America Los Angeles Times, Art International, The New Republic,* and *Art News,* among others. It was great to have him aboard. Pleased as could be with the show preparation, our selections, Gerrit's piece, and the catalogue, I excitedly fired off catalogues to all the appropriate people and did all the things that usually worked.

Nothing sold.

Isaac was such a gentleman that he didn't blame me for the lack of success of the show. He also smelled things were getting bad. Even the Chicago Art Fair, which happened that spring, was a bust. Things were about to go south.

Thank God this didn't happen with Peter Reginato.

One weekend, I drove up to visit John Elderfield, a chief curator at the MoMA, and his wife Jill Moser, a painter, in their Upstate New York home. Jill told me that Salander-O'Reilly was opening a gallery in Beverly Hills. After an underselling Reginato show, a non-selling

Witkin show, and a bad Chicago Art Fair, all I could think of was that old Drifters song, "Get a Job." I called Billy O'Reilly when I returned to New York and made a date to see him. He told me they had already hired a director for the California gallery and introduced me to his partner, Larry Salander, who was exactly my age, 41. After talking with me for ten minutes, he decided to release the guy they had just hired and bring me on instead.

In retrospect, the speed and suddenness of all this should have given me a sign that maybe Larry, a bald, wiry, and energetic guy, was impulsive and didn't think things through. But we were entering a recession, and I wasn't in a retrospective or contemplative mood. We negotiated a salary, during which I insisted on an employment contract that my attorneys would draw up. I had a couple of simple reasons for this contract: I was willing to move 3,000 miles to L.A. and wanted job security.

I called my lawyer, who referred me to a specialist in her office. "Please write a letter that doesn't sound like it's being written by a lawyer," I said. The letter guaranteed me a year contract, moving expenses, and health insurance. It was a simple, legally binding agreement.

Larry signed it without consulting an attorney. He knew I intended to see an attorney, but because the letter was so simply written, he assumed I decided to write it myself. Not smart. Then I tried to convince Larry to take on some of the artists I was representing as an agent, but he refused. It became very clear to me that Larry was the real authority in the gallery. Bill was the charming partner, the person I liked, but Larry was the power. I wanted to convince myself that I liked and admired Larry, but in all honesty, we were like oil and water from the day I walked in the door. He was smarmy and creepy, and his ideas, which he thought were innovative, were strange and incomprehensible to me.

Also, as it turned out, it was quite illegal.

With a letter of agreement and a gallery director job in hand, I called all my friends and family to tell them I was moving. I told the artists I represented that I would refer any calls I received to them and didn't want a commission or anything. I wanted to leave on good terms with everyone; I'd represented some of these artists since leaving Hamilton Gallery, and we'd done some great business and shows together. Then it was time to sublet my fabulous New York 5th Avenue apartment to a trustworthy individual. Rebecca came to mind, but I wanted to do major construction that would have resulted in me being kicked out of the lease. I settled on a friend of Terry McInerney's, Dan Walker, a curator of Islamic art at The Met. He and his wife were responsible, and if for some reason things didn't work out in L.A. and I wanted to come back to New York in a year or two, I knew I wouldn't have a problem.

In the Summer of 1990, I moved to L.A. I lived in the gallery apartment in Beverly Hills while I went about the necessary business of looking for a place, buying a car, and getting settled. Bill and Larry had rented the apartment to stay in when they were in town, a two-bedroom on Burton Way in Beverly Hills. I stayed there for about a month and furnished it, then got my own place in Hancock Park.

I was now situated in L.A .and ready to make Salander-O'Reilly great . . . but I quickly started to smell a rat that things were not so good. Paychecks were late, American Express cards were not being paid, and the guys building the gallery in Beverly Hills weren't being paid. Larry had an interesting approach to dealing with the mounting financial issues, which impacted all of us at the receiving end: he simply was convinced that if he yelled and screamed, people would respond. In California, though, that just does not go over; the contractors and others just stopped showing up for work. Because of this, the opening of the gallery was delayed a few times.

Larry's cheap approach carried over to the gallery design itself. It was not designed by an architect, and consequently, looked cheap and shoddy. Things were left unfinished; nice furniture was never purchased, as if it was just slapped together. For instance, the viewing room was shoddy; it should be the most beautiful room in the gallery, drawing you in and keeping you there. Nor was there any furniture. I didn't even have an office, which is a standard staple of the director's work environment. They were scrimping in all the wrong places, and it was obvious.

I thought about how we did things at the Hamilton Gallery. Every corner of our space was painted. If a piece of gallery furniture didn't arrive on schedule, we rented designer furniture so it didn't look like we were unscrupulous misers like Salander-O'Reilly. My office was designed and appointed to the tees. The racks were finished. I saw none of this at Salander-O'Reilly.

To throw another surprise and challenge into my new directorship, Larry teamed me with Ron Gersten, a family friend also coming from New York to be a gallery employee. This definitely was a sign. Ron dressed horribly, and because of his appearance and lack of knowledge, I would no more let him talk to a client in my gallery than cut off my right arm. When he got to L.A., he began smoking dope all day behind the gallery. That's just what we needed—a stoner employee. Not exactly the way galleries were run in New York, especially galleries that I ran or curated for.

I never saw a more incompetent gallery staff than the team with which I was saddled at Salander-O'Reilly. Most of the employees had never worked in an art institution, nor did they have any notable world training besides parroting the wit and wisdom of Larry Salander. In some cases, they were fully uneducated and crude; eloquent communication techniques and riveting conversations were in very short supply. Not to be outdone in displaying unenviable personality traits, Larry was positively abusive to his staff. He certainly found plenty of occasions, as they screwed up constantly. He would berate them with language that would make a sailor blush.

Yet, despite this internal mess, Salander-O'Reilly had managed to take on many of the color field painters from the Andre Emmerich Gallery, one of the best in New York since the 1950s. These artists included Ken Noland, Jules Olitski, and Larry Poons. Larry was trying to create a new market for color field painting, and to do so, he chose to quadruple his prices. Unfortunately for Larry, the auction records did not support his theory. As for Ken Noland, you could buy a striped painting at auction for $40,000—or go to Salander-O'Reilly and get one for $200,000. Larry thought people in California were rich and stupid, as opposed to New Yorkers, and wouldn't be so astute as to check auction records. He even instructed me on how to handle this: when a buyer questioned prices, I was told to say the paintings at auction were damaged, and that was why the value was so low. My question, Larry: How low can *you* possibly go? Further, Larry was in business with Houston dealers Meredith Long and Asher Edelman. They guaranteed money and sales to Olitski and Noland that were unsupportable.

Clients discovered the asking prices for color field paintings at Salander-O'Reilly and wanted to sell there for obvious reasons—like making a lot of money. So, we had a wide stream of paintings flowing into the gallery for resale at Larry's ridiculous prices. Needless to say, they wouldn't sell.

In Larry and Billy, I never had seen two dealers who showed more personal extravagance in their lives and choices yet were dirt cheap with gallery services and staff. They would fly first class to L.A. at the drop of a hat but demand that someone from the gallery pick them up at the airport at all hours to save cab fare. Rather than ground ship the work, as most do with expensive pieces, they wanted to FedEx it. They never wanted to pay for proper conservation when the damage happened, either. But they saved some of their worst enmity for the staff and contractors: they expected people to work overtime constantly for no extra money, didn't want to pay for proper photography, and didn't want to buy computers.

In spite of all this, I really wanted the gallery to succeed—and I wanted my job to last, too. So, I went into solution mode, leaning on my knowledge of cutting corners as a gallery owner for years. I offered to lend the Beverly Hills gallery my computer, typewriters, and library. I turned them into buying office supplies at Staples. I knew how you had to take risks and how to treat the work and the staff. First, you treat the staff nicely, respectfully, and fairly. And you pay them fucking overtime if they earned it. If you are condescending to them, you get sub-par work and discourage initiative.

And we still hadn't opened yet. But October 1, 1990 was fast approaching amidst this mess.

Larry's director in New York, Lori Bookstein, was a lovely person. However, her entire gallery experience amounted to moving up the ladder at Salander-O'Reilly. She didn't visit other galleries and look at art, one of the most basic ways to gain perspective and ideas on presentation. She had a husband and a child on the way and worked long hours. She went along with anything Larry wanted to do. Later, though, she wised up and, on her husband's advice, left before things got ugly.

Another huge problem with Larry was his color blindness when following the law. He asked everyone to do illegal things. For one, he would tell an artist or a client the gallery hadn't been paid when, in fact, the checks were already received, deposited—and spent. I realize this is an old gallery trick, but as far as I know, Larry was the only gallery owner asking his staff to participate in his lies. The others who perpetrated this fraud tended to keep their employees out of it.

No one knew of Larry's scheme better than Leigh Morse. Leigh replaced Lori Bookstein as director in New York after I'd begun in Beverly Hills. Leigh's husband suffered a traumatic brain injury from a car accident, and she needed to support him. She called me before taking the job, and I warned her off, but she really needed the money and took it anyway. Naturally, Larry started owing her money. To settle the debt, she sold a Robert de Niro painting (the father of the great actor, an art patron in his own right), and Larry told her to keep all the money, which would pay her back salary. Leigh naturally assumed Larry had already paid the artist, the normal course of business.

Be careful what you assume. What seemed like a simple solution was in fact a crime. When Larry was later convicted of misleading artists about the status of artworks, the courts found Leigh guilty of complicity. She owed $1.7 million and really suffered for years, and even spent weekends in prison. Keep in mind that she took the job because her husband was permanently disabled.

. . .

It wasn't before long everything that was wrong with the gallery under Larry's and Bill's direct actions and supervision became my fault. The abusive behavior and cutting remarks followed. Isn't that always how it works with abusers? Just before the gallery opened, Larry started yelling at me. Generally, he would start conversations by calling women, "stupid fucking cunts." No one will accuse me of having the cleanest-cut mouth in the world, but even I knew you could not call your staff names like that.

I realized before we officially opened that it would not work out.

On October 1, we opened with an overpriced and unsalable Ken Noland show, for the reasons I laid out earlier. The gallery was in Beverly Hills on Camden Drive, which is not a great street for people to walk on. Not surprisingly, it received unfavorable reviews in the Los Angeles *Times*.

Meanwhile, Larry and Bill were at their wits' end about walk-in traffic and getting people to come into the gallery. I tried to convince them that business in L.A. is done at country clubs, parties, and through social connections—and to send me out to the network. I'd spent the past 13 years as a successful gallery owner and an artist's representative; I knew how to network. I hadn't been in L.A. very long, but I'd already figured that out—hadn't they done any homework at all? Well, no. Why lower their almighty selves to the level of what they saw as stupid rich Californians? They did not understand the L.A. market, and to complicate things, we were at the beginning of a major art-world recession. So, they didn't listen to me—but they *did* listen to Ron Gersten—who I'd nicknamed the "corporate spy"—about how to advertise.

Amidst all this, Larry and Bill hired a receptionist with whom they both wanted to have sex. Not surprisingly, she was completely useless. I called her the resextionist. She'd been a print dealer in L.A., and took the job because of the recession, which I can understand. However, when I found out she was trying to cut private deals behind their backs, we got rid of her. I found and they hired a registrar, so at least I had one ally at the gallery.

The next Salander-O'Reilly Gallery show was Jules Olitski. Again, it was overpriced in any market, let alone a recessed one. The work didn't move. I liked his art, but the asking prices were through the roof. And whenever help seemed to be on the way, they scoffed at it. They were unwilling to work with private consultants and dealers and told them to add to the already inflated prices. When galleries work with consultants, it is an unwritten rule to give the consultant a 20% commission from retail out of your commission. Larry didn't want to do that.

But they did ensure we never had a steady rhythm or flow to the gallery. Every time Larry and/or Bill flew in from New York to lord over the gallery, they would change the hours. One time, they wanted the gallery open six days a week, then until 10 p.m., two nights during the week. Then they would be surprised that the gallery hours, which they had changed again a week earlier, were not listed properly in the local and national guides. Well, national gallery guides need a six-week notice. Insane!

One Tuesday, I came into the gallery, and Larry started screaming at me. I looked at him incredulously. *Okayyy . . . what this time?* Apparently, Ron Gersten and another employee had worked the day before, and there was no toilet paper in the men's room. He went ballistic on me; naturally, it was all my fault. *Well, let's see, Larry. I'm a woman, I'm not going to check the men's room.* I almost laughed. What a ridiculous temper tantrum. He fired me on the spot. My first thought? *Thank God I can leave this hell hole and still be paid for a year.*

As I digested this news, Larry promptly asked me, "What do you plan on doing?"

"Well," I said, holding my fury back at his latest abusive behavior, "the first thing I will do is call my attorney to have the contract enforced."

"You fuck, you fuck, you fuck, you fuck!" he spewed. "If you call your attorney, I'll call mine, and the only ones who will make money are the attorneys."

I shrugged my shoulders. "Fine. I like my attorneys, and I plan on taking out an ad in the *New York Times* in the weekend section saying I am no longer director of Salander-O'Reilly in Beverly Hills because there was no toilet paper in the men's room."

"Do you know what the fuck that will cost?" he asked, his voice tumbling down like a waterfall of pure toxic male maliciousness.

I nodded. "Yes—$1,732 if I get the combination rate, and I will. It will be the best $1,700 I ever spent."

"Okay, okay you can stay," he finally said, storming out the door. I guess he wasn't used to someone calmly holding their ground and stopping him in his tracks.

I then called my attorney. He told me that I had to stay six months for my full year's contract to kick in and receive the pay for the entire year. It had been four months since I first walked in the doors. "Stick it out for another two months and start a diary. Keep an accurate diary of the abusive remarks Larry made and, if possible, get a witness," he added.

Someone had witnessed Larry's morning abuse of me, which I documented. *Game on.* This was war.

They shifted to another tactic, making it clear they were trying to make me quit, which would've nullified the full-year payment on the contract. Nothing was selling at the Salander-O'Reilly prices, and they thought it was because I was a bad director. When the holidays arrived six weeks later, they gave everyone days off except me. I worked through Thanksgiving and Christmas. Larry even kept the gallery open until 6 p.m. on Christmas Eve and kept calling me to see if I was there.

One day over the holidays and during the Olitski show, Michael Jackson came in with a young boy. I was the only one there operating the front desk. Michael told me he wanted to buy really important American art. And he kept asking the 12-year-old boy what he thought of the art. I thought to myself, *what the fuck is this?*

I turned to Michael. "I can help you," I said. We were mounting a Willem de Kooning show to start January—that's pretty important American art, right?—and I promised Michael a private viewing. I got a phone number I could call to let him know when he could come in. This was well before Michael's life came under intense scrutiny, when he was a global icon as the top-selling musician in history. *Any* gallery in L.A., New York, Chicago, or anywhere else would've loved to bring Michael Jackson for a private viewing. It was a nice, positive moment when not much else at Salander-O'Reilly was nice or positive.

Well, we can't have that, right? Just before the de Kooning show opened, I got word from several sources in New York that Larry and Bill were going to fire me—again. They had already hired my replacement, a friend of a friend of Larry's. Of no consequence to them was the little detail that she had never worked in a gallery or been a director before. *Good luck, Larry.* On the morning of my presumed firing, a Sunday, my dear friend Terry McInerney told me not to go to the gallery in jeans. Even though we were installing the de Kooning show, normally a very good occasion to wear jeans, I dressed in my finest clothes. I also brought a friend with a truck so I could walk out of there with my computer, typewriter, and library. For good measure, I brought along a copy of my contract.

When Larry did fire me, confirming the rumors, I asked him to re-sign the contract. Which, incredibly, he did. "And I want to take my things," I added.

"Fine. You can come back for them."

"Well, I have a truck and a friend in the parking lot." We left with my things.

Know what amused me the most? The aftermath. They had to drive to Kinkos to get labels and price lists done for the de Kooning show. They also picked a wrong time to open the show, a benefit: it was the night George HW Bush unleashed Operation Desert Storm on Baghdad. The show was a bust, and I couldn't have been happier.

My life went on in L.A., but Salander-O'Reilly's time in Beverly Hills only lasted two years, during which they went through six directors. I was still on full salary for the entire year of my deal. I figured if I couldn't make a go of it, I could always move back to New York. I had only sublet my apartment, so I could even move back there. Further, as part of my employment contract, Salander-O'Reilly had to pick up the moving expenses.

Larry Salander's life as an art dealer did not improve with time. After closing the Beverly Hills gallery, he continued to show work in New York and Berlin. In Germany, he hired an entire staff that did not speak German. Real smart. I guess they thought if they spoke really loudly, the Germans would understand. What they fully understood, though, was the degree of insult Larry showed them.

In New York, Salander-O'Reilly did get a lot of positive feedback, even being cited by *The Robb Report* as one of the best galleries in the world. Larry had also developed a passion for European art made between the 12th and 18th centuries. Since he was not a trained art historian, he relied purely on instinct rather than experience. Consequently, he wouldn't have known a fake from a real piece. He moved his gallery from 79th Street to a lavish townhouse on Madison Avenue, where he paid $125,000 a month in rent. His lifestyle continued to remain lavish: private planes, country homes, townhouses, and even a birthday party for his new wife at the Frick Museum.

Well, all good and larcenous endeavors eventually come crashing to the ground. In 2007, it must have sounded like an explosion in his brain. First, he filed for bankruptcy. Then, he faced 29 felony counts of grand larceny, for which he was convicted in March 2010. Prosecutors proved that Larry was running a Ponzi scheme and had stolen more than $100 million from clients by selling half-interest in a painting to eight people at a time. Sound familiar? It does if you followed the Bernie Madoff fiasco that was happening at the same time. Larry also stole paintings outright. Earl Davis stored the work of his father, the great American painter, Stuart Davis, at the gallery. He lost 96 paintings. Larry was so unscrupulous in his choice of victims that he even stole from friends and family.

While Larry was in prison, he was served with divorce papers. He later had a heart attack and was released early. He now lives in upstate New York with a woman he'd corresponded with through the prison letter-writing system. He's also painting. However, no one will do business with the Bernie Madoff of the art business.

CHAPTER 14

Blue Chip Art Consulting in Hollywood

One might think enough was enough. After the topsy-turvy course of my life and career over the past eight years, starting with my brother Rick's cancer diagnosis and ending with the Salander-O'Reilly debacle, I'm sure anyone would understand if I simply decided to pack it in and head for destinations unknown. I was flat broke; it would've been understandable, and it was the human nature thing to do. *Cut your losses and start in a new direction.*

However, I lived and breathed the art world. I loved being blown away by a work of art, what it said to me, how it moved me, and how I believed I could put it into the right collector or buyer's hands. And then hear how it enhanced their homes and lives. There's a reason why masterworks stir us centuries after they were made, why they stop us in our tracks in museums and galleries. Great art has an essential power in its composition, beauty, and movement that connects to our psyches and our souls, and it was an equally essential part of mine. I also loved advancing the careers and reputations of the artists who created these works and the conversations and rapport I had with the artists themselves.

Besides, I didn't know how to do anything else. I couldn't; I had no schooling or job skills in anything outside the art world. How was I going to support myself? Doing what? I'd made my living in the art world since I was 21—half my life, at this point—and couldn't imagine taking up any other vocation. Or perhaps even knowing how.

So, while I definitely felt the need to dust myself off after dealing with Larry Salander and Billy O'Reilly, and the way they treated me and everyone else under their employ, I knew I would again land on my feet squarely in the art world. Since I was being paid a salary from Salander-O'Reilly for a full year following my firing, I also knew I had the time to develop a new business. I spent some time going back and forth between California and New York, but I knew immediately I wanted to stay in LA. The combination of LA's emerging art scene and the sparkling year-round weather fed my needs for work and playing tennis and swimming equally well. It felt new and fresh to me, and it was time to make LA. my permanent home.

I started moving forward. One of the people I met in Beverly Hills through the Salander-O'Reilly Gallery was the art consultant Connie Lembarck. I quickly appreciated her big heart, and we got along well. Connie was about thirty years older than me. She had worked and lived in L.A. her entire life and knew the art community very well. She owned a poster gallery for years, and then became a consultant. She even wrote *The Prints of Sam Francis: A Catalogue raisonné 1960-1990,* on the famed printmaker, a collector's item which today goes for $450 and up through third-party sellers.

Connie really wanted to guide me in the right direction, her Jewish mother thing, and suggested I become an agent. Also, she wanted no part of my business. Her intentions were pure and caring.

Soon, Connie introduced me to her old high-school friend, the musician Herb Alpert, who in 1962 shot to fame with Herb Alpert &

the Tijuana Brass and his huge hit, "Lonely Bull." A few years later, you couldn't turn on the radio in the late 1960s without hearing Herb's brilliant jazz trumpet belting out the iconic "Spanish Flea." In fact, millions of Baby Boomers exited their early adult years and adolescents with that riff glued to their brains on eternal instant recall; it's one of the most memorable combinations of notes ever played on a trumpet or any other instrument.

Herb has achieved more than almost any musician, alive or dead, with five No. 1 albums, 14 gold and 15 platinum records, a total of 28 albums on the *Billboard* charts, nine Grammy Awards, and sales of more than 72 million records. If you're under 90, you've heard his music, whether you know it or not. That's known as making an impact. What I especially love is that, as of this writing, Herb is still recording and touring. Music drives him as much as his next breath. What a lot of people don't know is that Herb also co-founded A&M Records with Jerry Moss in 1962 and signed Burt Bacharach, Sergio Mendes, The Carpenters, Carole King, Cat Stevens, Quincy Jones, Janet Jackson, and Liza Minnelli, among others.

He and I had something very much in common: we built others' careers. Of course, he also had his own legendary career to manage.

Herb had a second creative love and outlet—art. However, when I first met him, I quickly realized his paintings were terrible. After some introductory chatting, I suggested that he take drawing lessons.

"How important is it?" he asked.

"Well, how important is the knowledge of the scales if you want to be a musician?"

To his credit, Herb understood right away. He totally got it and started lessons right away.

Midway through my representation, he switched to sculpture. He worked hard, very hard—hard work being no stranger to him— but Herb's sculptures never rose to the level of mastery of his song-writing, trumpet playing, and music production. Like many celebrities, Herb was not trained as an artist, and it showed. Like his music, he produced a lot of work. But these sculptures were not anywhere near the level of his songs.

As mentioned, Herb was prolific. The way he cranked out great albums, I shouldn't have been surprised. He was also an absolute sweetheart, every bit the gentleman he appeared on television and onstage. Unfortunately, though, he lived more in the world of a long-adored musician, so he surrounded himself with people who thought he was van Gogh. Most importantly, Herb's sister, Mimi, convinced him that he was a genius. When you need to exercise the humility necessary to deconstruct what you thought you knew about art and sculpture, take drawing lessons, and build a career in a field, you do not yet master what he did with his trumpet; living in the bubble of global adulation does not help. Worse for me, Mimi didn't like my suggestion for what Herb was doing as an artist.

At the same time, Mimi had a relationship with the elderly Los Angeles dealer Sig Wenger. From her rather biased perspective, Mimi didn't like my sound suggestions to Herb. Suggestions meant to bring out the best in his ability as a sculptor. She also felt Sig was far more knowledgeable than me. When I signed a letter of agreement to work with Herb, she wanted me to pass all decisions through Sig. I refused; I had never heard of the man. So, she took the initiative. From then on, she passed through Sig whenever I wanted to do something. He denigrated every idea I came up with because he saw Herb as his meal ticket and didn't want anyone interfering. Welcome to the insidious side of show business, the senseless buttering up of the *star to remain* on the gravy train. Every major celebrity who doesn't police their "entourage" carefully has someone like Sig in their camp. Unfortunately, Mimi had positioned him to make my job extremely difficult.

I really was only able to accomplish one major thing for Herb, despite the many things I could have done to advance his career as a sculptor. I introduced him to an artist, Kristan Marvell, who was starting a bronze foundry in downtown LA and doing great work for other artists at half the price of other bronze foundries (even foundries at which these artists worked!), so I knew he would be a good fit for Herb.

One day, I got a call. It was Herb. When I connected him to the bronze foundry, it apparently sent his creative mind and ability to produce and finish into hyperdrive. "Can you come over to my home in Malibu and look at the 60 sculptures I made over the weekend?" he asked.

Sixty sculptures? On a weekend? Are you shitting me? Did he write songs like that, too?

When I arrived, dumbfounded, he told me he wanted to fabricate all 60 of those pieces. "No one does 60 good works over a weekend," I said.

Herb and I went through all of his works, my eye sharply attuned to what could truly make a mark. Also, I was thinking hard about what it would look like if a man with Herb Alpert's stature in culture came out with shitty work. After much back and forth, I convinced him to fabricate only five of them.

Once we got Herb off and running as a sculptor, things started getting too complicated, with everyone adding their two cents to everything I was doing for Herb. At one meeting, Sig said I only acted as a consultant to clients. "Have you ever heard of the Hamilton Gallery?" I asked. "Or the book '*The Art Dealers*'?"

As it turned out, no on both counts. He'd only asked a single New York consultant. He never checked up on me, preferring to look at me as an unseasoned little thing. He treated me in that demeaning way, too.

After that meeting, I decided it was time to leave. Sig was close to 80 years old and never even went to NYC. He was a fool. For my part, I was sad to be parting ways with such a genuinely good and sweet man as Herb but relieved I didn't have to deal with his sister, Sig Wegner, or anyone else in that entourage anymore.

. . .

My enthusiasm for jumping back into the art world grew, as did LA's art scene. I started going to studios and attending all of the L.A. gallery exhibitions, fairs, and other events. I went to the Brewery Projects, and several studios impressed me, especially John O'Brien. Then one day, I got a call from Ellie Blankfort, an art adviser, and we had lunch. She was sympathetic to what had happened to me at Salander-O'Reilly. She was also married to Peter Clothier, an internationally known writer on art, politics, teaching, the creative process, religion, and culture, and the author of *Slow Looking: The World of Looking at Art,* among other books. It was fun having dinner and talking about art with them. Most of all, it was fun having someone interesting to talk to.

By this point, I was pretty isolated and needed good conversation and company. When I was working at Salander-O'Reilly, all I did was work, so I hadn't developed a strong group of friends for support. It was a far different experience than at Hamilton Gallery, where I was quite often out and about; over the past couple of years, there was all work and no socializing, too. I did have James Ulmer, a friend from New York, working at the *Hollywood Reporter,* but he was flaky and unreliable. He would forget about dinners or devise preposterous excuses about why he didn't show. Then there was Larry Miller, a friend of my brother Peter's from college. He was starting to make a splash as a comedian and had some small roles in movies like *Pretty Woman.* He was fun to be with when we got together, but again he was unreliable. Calls would go unreturned for weeks.

It seemed like a great idea when Ellie suggested we partner up as art advisers. We were already going to all the openings together, especially the L.A. County Museum and gallery openings. She told me she was very good at selling and also had existing clients. Ellie knew everyone, that's for sure, but I could quickly tell she was not a natural salesperson. She was the daughter of the late Michael Blankfort, the screenwriter and novelist whose works included classic movies *The Caine Mutiny*, *The Untamed*, and *The Plainsman*. He also fronted for blacklisted screenwriter Albert Maltz on the official credit for *Broken Arrow*, which the Writer's Guild of America returned to Maltz in 1991.

On one level, Ellie acted like a collector and treated artists and dealers accordingly. On another occasion, however, she felt she could critique work and advise artists on how to make work. This was not always appreciated. I also recalled how uncomfortable I was whenever Michael David came to me and asked me for ideas on what he should paint. That's the artist's job. Also, Ellie was no business person. She didn't know how to cultivate clients or close a sale.

Nonetheless, I liked the positives of what our potential partnership had to offer. We got to work and wrote a letter advertising our services. I then went to Larry Miller and asked him to send the letter to some of his Hollywood friends. For some reason, Larry directed me to start the letter with, "Dear friend of Larry's and potential sucker:"

For some reason, I followed suit.

In a direct response, I received a call from comedian Paul Reiser, whose new TV series *Mad About You* was about to begin (it would become a major career-making hit for him and co-star Helen Hunt). I called Ellie the day Paul made an appointment to meet us with the great news—*we already had a potential client!*

"I have my heart set on going to a dog show in Laguna today," she said. "Can we reschedule?"

I was incredulous. Our first possible client was getting backseat billing to a *dog show*. "No, we cannot reschedule, but if you want to go to the dog show, fine," I said, my tone of voice the texture of steel. "I will handle the Reiser business without you."

She came to her senses and made the appointment. We left with a new client in hand.

Soon, we started working with the Reisers in their newly purchased home on Astral Drive. This classic old Hollywood Hills home included a beautiful winding staircase, and Paul and his wife wanted to commission an artist for a piece that would run up the stairwell. We settled on Simon Toporafsky, an artist that Ellie knew. He listened patiently to the Reiser's requests and worked very hard on a multi-faceted piece that combined paintings and sculpture.

Ellie and I went to the studio to see the piece. She liked some aspects of it but not others, but that's because she was unable to look at the piece as a whole. That's a problem of having an overly critical eye, a problem many art critics have—and music critics, for that matter. Plus, as mentioned earlier, our role was to consult and see the project through, not pick at the artist. Ellie decided she wanted to send extra paintings to the Reisers from the studio she liked, which had nothing to do with the commission we'd been entrusted to shepherd to completion with Simon.

After the studio visit, Simon called and complained about Ellie, and with good reason.

I quickly canceled that idea. Simon wanted to finish the work, so he promised the Reisers that if they ever moved, he would be happy to reinstall the piece at their new place at no cost. That is no small request; installing a piece that works to the contours of a stairwell in relation to the room is an artistic process in and of itself. However, he committed, and I applauded him for it.

During this time, I invited Simon for dinner and we had a remarkably good evening. He was originally from Philadelphia, so we shared hometown roots. Sadly, he too was estranged from his family, but he also loved to cook and was charming and funny. It was the beginning of a good friendship between two people in the art world with several common interests—or so I thought.

Years later, the Reiser's moved—but Simon apparently was stricken with amnesia. Or second thoughts. Or the idea of making a quick buck. He did not keep his promise. Now he wanted a fee, undoubtedly motivated by how much Paul Reiser's star had risen in the Hollywood sky since we worked with him. *Figures.* I installed the piece myself.

Simon wasn't the only one with whom I had a parting of the ways. I seemed to be working the contacts almost exclusively. And I was finding good opportunities. Through my social connections, I knew a decorator who turned us onto a client who wanted her whole house done in art. We found an artist who painted whales, and she commissioned a painting.

After about 18 months of working with Ellie, though, it became clear that her so-called carryover client list was not much of a list at all. My clients, or those I acquired on my own, made up all of the business we were doing. There simply was not enough business for us to continue to work together.

We ended our relationship amicably. Today, she is head of the Davyd Whaley Foundation, established in 2016, which offers grants and scholarships to artists to assist in their endeavors. It was created in honor of Davyd Whaley, a resident at the Santa Fe Art Colony in downtown LA, who had a wonderful saying: "Painting Manifests as Alternate Universe." An engineer before he became a painter, Davyd enjoyed a successful career while also teaching art to terminally ill and war-scarred children. Sadly, he met an untimely death in 2014 at the age of 47. A wonderful book of his work was put out in 2016.

The Davyd Whaley Foundation directorship is a perfect job for Ellie. She's great at it. Meanwhile, Connie had also suggested I could be good as an artists' agent—a road I'd traveled in its very first days.

CHAPTER 15

The Doug Chrismas Story

> "**N**otorious Los Angeles art dealer Douglas Chrismas has been arrested on federal charges that he embezzled funds amid bankruptcy proceedings related to his longtime gallery, Ace.
>
> "According to a Justice Department press release, Chrismas allegedly embezzled over $264,000 around March and April 2016, "including a $50,000 check that Chrismas signed, was drawn against the estate and was paid to a separate corporation that Chrismas owned and controlled."
>
> —ArtNews, July 22, 2021

. . .

When I first heard about Doug Chrismas from Ace Gallery in New York, I rolled my eyes, considered his name, and thought, *well, that's what they can get away with in California.* Turns out that was a prescient thought.

As with any other business or industry, there are dirty players and fraudsters in the art world. Like other unscrupulous managers in the nascent years of rock and roll, sports management, and other endeavors, they circle the naïve, gullible *sources of their income*—musicians, athletes, artists. They prey on the artist's desire to be shown and to sell paintings, the musician's desire to be heard and to sell records, or the athlete's willingness to receive a big contract. Through any number of backroom deals, fueled by their absolute lack of ethics or morality, these people screw their clients one way and then the next, enriching themselves off the backs of clients who are left wondering what happened to their earnings. Or, worse, empty-handed when their careers are over. I think that's far-fetched. You might want to check in with Tai Babilonia, the beautiful American figure skating great who, with Randy Gardner, became a household name and half of the figure skating world's finest pairs team in the late 1970s and early 1980s. Tai later invested a good part of her life savings with Bernie Madoff—and promptly found herself starting over in her early 50s.

These sharks don't care about anyone's enrichment but their own and are very good at what they do.

I've had my run-ins with these people, too, as I shared earlier. Sometimes, they hid earnings from the IRS by counting everything they ever did as expenses. Others, like Larry Salander, paid themselves and every other obligation under their sun before bothering to compensate the individuals whose work brought in the money in the first place—the artists.

But I have to say, no one did it quite like Doug Chrismas—who, as of this writing, awaits his delayed trial on all of the charges that led up to his arrest by the FBI and the end of a decades-long string of frauds. He's been sued by artists, dealers, collectors, private investors, service industries, landlords, and former friends—pretty much every corner of his world. He's also been sued under three different surnames and nine different business names—and we're talking about the lawsuits in LA alone. Like I said, this guy takes the cake, at least in my half-century of experience in the art world.

I got to know about Doug and Ace Gallery in the 1990s when I was establishing myself in the L.A. scene, and the more I heard, the more I wondered to myself, *How the hell is this guy getting away with it?* I knew he had a mercurial personality and could project himself as three different people at once—abusive to his staff, charming with clients, and ruthless with lawsuits. That takes the type of dark talent reserved for true sociopaths who care not at all about anything but their own best interests and pockets.

. . .

Doug started off impressively enough. Born to a middle-class Vancouver family with no ties to the art world, he showed his slight disdain for his upbringing to non-artistic parents in 2003 when he told Kristine McKenna in her revealing Los Angeles *Weekly* story, "My father was an interesting man who designed airplanes, but I haven't seen him for years and don't know if he's still alive. I have a brother who got a doctorate in geology, then became a photographer."

As Doug told the story, he accidentally walked into an art gallery, sensed something about the environment, and then opened Ace Gallery in 1961 when he was just 17. It sounds awfully young, but the story is corroborated by Canadian architect and art consultant Ian Davidson, who remembered him running a framing shop and also building furniture. In fact, Davidson and his partner sold him what became Ace, the first contemporary gallery in Vancouver. A friend, former dancer Teresa Bjornson, introduced Doug to Robert Rauschenberg and other fine early '60s artists, opening the door for him in a big way. However, according to Davidson, Doug denied Teresa had anything to do with his good fortune, claiming he met Rauschenberg alone when the artist came to Seattle. In the interest of sharing the truth, I'll stick with Davidson's account.

In 1966, Doug and his then-girlfriend, Jane Erickson, moved to LA after, as Doug put it to *LA Weekly*, "Warhol told me LA was the future, so I decided to come to LA on Andy's advice." He closed his Vancouver LA and opened the LA version of Ace in a warehouse space below the Factory, a West Hollywood nightclub owned by entertainer Sammy Davis Jr. Soon thereafter, he presented his first avant-garde show at Ace, a Sol Lewitt drawing show, and also showed plastic sculpture by Peter Alexander, DeWain Valentine and John McCracken, among others.

A few years later, Chrismas closed that space and moved into minimalism, earthworks, and light-and-space installations, all requiring big spaces to fill (as I learned from working with Isaac Witkin and others) and were big-time in Southern California. It fits in perfectly with his love of architecture as well. He began creating galleries to accommodate it, beginning with one in Westwood. He committed to minimalism, earthworks, and the Light & Space movement, a solid-object reaction to abstract expressionism, like no one else in California. He built absolutely beautiful galleries and encouraged his artists to show enormous works, then exhibited and promoted the works. Robert Irwin, Larry Bell, James Turrell, Peter Alexander, Craig Kaufman, Dewain Valentine, and Fred Eversely were primary artists (Peter is now considered blue-chip).

Doug Chrismas was off and running. However, he routinely and frequently engaged in terrible business practices. People just weren't catching on yet.

He kicked off the 1970s by setting up in Venice, the beach community of LA, where art and music were all the rage. From The Doors to a host of artists, the former home of Charles Chaplin and a long-time bohemian enclave became one of the hottest underground scenes in the country. Chrismas set up two more galleries, and they were regularly filled with quite the mix of people, from New Yorkers and Europeans to artists and art students, actors and models, wealthy collectors, and anyone else who wanted to be tied in. In 1972, he mounted one of the best installations of the time, Robert Irwin's *Room Angle Light Volume*. He also had quite the New York connection, bringing in museum-quality shows by

Andy Warhol and Robert Rauschenberg. You can't get much better than that.

But there was this other side. There's a story that Christine McKenna related in *LA Weekly* about Chrismas inviting artists up to Vancouver for a major show, picking them up at the airport, then forcing them to put their bags in the front seat instead of his trunk. Why? It seems he had something in the trunk. When the artists kiddingly joked to him about what that "something" might be, since stuffing a bunch of luggage in a car full of grown adults created a bit of a squeeze, Chrismas grew very defensive and plaintive about not opening his trunk. Those still around still don't know what was in there.

By the mid-1970s, people had started to catch on to his shady business practices. Artists Doug Wheeler and Bruce Nauman defected Ace Gallery, even though Chrismas' second Venice gallery was also going strong, and he'd just opened a third in the old Ferus Gallery space on La Cienega Blvd. He represented many leading artists, and by all accounts, could've been one of the top gallerists in the world—*if he'd paid them and taken care of them.* Since this businessman, who wouldn't flinch when the stakes got high, seemed to be allergic to paying his artists, they began leaving. Strange to me that a guy who took chances no others took—and created a number of now memorable careers in the process—would have a problem paying those whose works made his cavalier and innovative approach so impactful.

He brushed it off, marching right ahead with his "Big is Beautiful" approach, both in the scope of his shows and the artists involved, including Robert Motherwell, Frank Stella, and Michael Heizer.

Then, in 1977, the California Law Center sued him in a dispute over a Warhol drawing that had been stolen from Ace/Venice. Warhol was also having trouble getting paid from Chrismas, as he noted in his 1989 autobiography. A year later, Motherwell sued him after nine pieces he'd consigned to Christmas, valued at $493,000, suddenly vanished. On and on it went, right through the 1980s.

Meantime, Chrismas' love for big spaces, big showings, big attention, and all else never stopped. In 1990, he opened Ace/New York in the former Longshoreman's hiring hall, a 20,000-square-foot building. (For perspective, keep in mind that my Hamilton Gallery, a prominent space on West 57th, was 5,000 square feet). A decade later, Chrismas took out a 10-year lease on a former bank building in Beverly Hills and, in May 2001, opened his second Ace Gallery in LA proper—adding 17,000 square feet to his mounting collection of gallery space from coast to coast. Not big enough, apparently, because he later expanded the gallery and added condos above it. He even had spaces in Mexico City and Berlin. The total of all his spaces was added up in the early 2000s—how does the equivalent of a football field and an indoor soccer pitch sound? And guess who was paying for it? In many cases, the artists—with their own unreimbursed works.

. . .

In 2003, Kristine McKenna's Los Angeles *Weekly* article exposed the dark underbelly of Doug Chrismas's flashy art-dealing career. By 2003, he had been the defendant in 55 lawsuits and had done business under three pseudonyms and nine companies. Besides stiffing artists, he was sued for everything from producing and selling unauthorized fabrications of sculptures, poaching artists from other dealers, and occasionally selling artworks he failed to deliver to the buyer. Not to mention Warhol drawings or Motherwell paintings that "were stolen" . . . makes you wonder. He had an accounting system that no one could understand. Kristine's article exhaustively outlined his difficulties, completely with interviews with many who sued him (some either did not wish to be interviewed or took a high-ground approach and talked of his overall benefit to the scene).

But perhaps his great gift? Being elusive and evasive. He loved the light shining on him and his galleries, but do an interview? When the reporter wanted to delve into *how* he built this small empire of galleries. Not a chance. He even told his staff not to talk. In my eyes, he is the epitome of an art fraudster.

The avalanche was just starting to roll down the mountain of a mess he'd created with his own nefarious business practices.

Chrismas declared bankruptcy so often that the courts intervened and wouldn't let him declare bankruptcy again. Staff would go weeks and be told not to cash their paychecks. My friend, Burnett Miller, worked for him as a Director at ACE Gallery and told me how he ran up huge bills on his AMEX card on behalf of Ace Gallery, all in the course of doing business. However, Burnett couldn't get paid his expenses—or his earnings. He later sued and won.

In 2006, Chrismas went bankrupt, and a forensic accountant was put in charge of the gallery. All parties agreed Doug would still be involved in sales since keeping him engaged in generating revenue would help pay off debtors. That didn't last long, though, because the accountant, Sam Leslie, discovered Doug had cheated that bankruptcy court; all told, over $260,000 that was owed the bankruptcy court was put into one of his many shadow corporations.

Seven years later, Ace Gallery and its 40-year history began its final demise, and so did Chrismas. In 2013, Ace filed for Chapter 11 bankruptcy in L.A. It maintained operations as a bankruptcy estate, with Chrismas acting as the gallery's president, trustee, and custodian, giving him access to the gallery's property. I'll never know how he swung that arrangement, but that's what deceptive, convincing fraudsters do. He remained in control for another three years, when the bankruptcy court finally wised up, and an independent trustee was appointed to run the bankruptcy estate.

With that, Doug's long ride was finally over—except we're talking about Doug Chrismas here. A $50,000 check, signed by Chrismas, was drawn against the estate and paid to a separate corporation that Chrismas owned and controlled. Then, he also allegedly embezzled $100,000 owed to Ace Gallery by a third party for an art buy, again directing the funds to his separate corporation. Another $114,595 owed to the gallery by a third party went instead to a creditor on another matter.

That's over $264,000—the exact amount of the Justice Department's complaint against him in the July 2021 filing.

It wasn't for lack of trying. In 2016, creditors filed numerous times against Chrismas for "avoidance, recovery, and preservation of fraudulent transfers," according to court filings. A forensic accountant then took it several steps further, telling the bankruptcy court that "millions of dollars [were] diverted to mysterious accounts and dozens of works of art that have been moved to private storage," according to filings.

So, not only did Chrismas commit fraud, embezzle, funnel money to outside corporations under his name and other obviously criminal practices, but he did it *while under the thumb of a bankruptcy court*. You can't get much more brazen than that. Like I said, I'd never seen anything like it—and from Andrew Crispo to Larry Salander and Mary Boone's losing dance with the IRS, I've seen plenty.

Finally, in July 2021, the net dropped on Doug Chrismas' head when he surrendered to FBI agents in Los Angeles. He was released on a $50,000 bond after pleading not guilty. His trial was supposed to take place in September 2021, but COVID-19 restrictions and typical pre-trial delays have kept moving it back. As of this writing, he is still awaiting trial, but if convicted, he is looking at a maximum of 15 years in federal prison.

But Sam Leslie didn't stop at a Federal trial. He sued him for $14.2 million in May 2022 for the profits from artworks and sales and for hiding inventory, 60 pieces, not involved with the regular bankruptcy in California court. It was a summary judgment. Summary judgments are generally held when the evidence is so overwhelming that a judge alone makes the decision. Sam Leslie won.

For anyone, that is daunting—let alone a 77-year-old man. But I think of the artists, collectors, and others who have been swindled and victimized by him and the terrible black eye he created on the L.A. art scene—let alone what could have been a memorable legacy.

He deserves everything coming his way.

CHAPTER 16

Artist's Agent

I faced a new dilemma, another challenge. I wanted to continue living in L.A., I loved my new lifestyle, but I needed to make it work financially—not easy then, not easy now.

This time, though, I knew which steps I wanted to take. I wanted to continue with some art consulting, as well as the agenting. I had a knack for both. Opening another gallery was out of the question as well; the last thing I wanted was the pressure of making sales to cover high overhead. Then the art adviser Connie Lembarck and I got together for lunch, and she made a suggestion: "Why don't you become an artist's agent, like Dudley del Balso?" Among others, Dudley championed L.A.-based artist Robert Therrien, whose large sculptures reimagined and reinvented objects from everyday life, turning ordinary items like tables and chairs into monumental sculptures you couldn't help but be drawn into.

Later, I called her and discussed the parameters of being an agent with her. I knew something about agenting already, after spending five years as one of the first full-time agents in New York after closing the Hamilton Gallery. I'd enjoyed good success, while continuing to curate shows here and there. Now though, a decade later, everything was flipped: I would be doing it from the other side of the country, in an entirely different art world. I represented artists who needed an agent, mostly to kick-start their careers. I worked primarily with California artists but was also open to representing New York-based artists. We shopped their works around half the time in New York, and the other half in New York.

From my time in LA, I knew well that California artists wanted a New York gallery to show their work and additional connections outside of L.A. I had something to sell. Connie gave me two good names with whom to get started: Peter Alexander in L.A. and Robert Zakanitch in New York.

Peter was a well-known L.A. artist (now considered a blue-chipper) who had exhibited worldwide in galleries and museums since the 1960s, beginning with his resin sculptures; he was also a major proponent of California's Light & Space movement. In 1971, he was even featured in the PBS "Artists in America" series, and in 1980, received a Fellowship from the National Endowment of the Arts. He sold commissioned public works to the Venice Art Walk, the Walt Disney Concert Hall, and the 777 Building in Los Angeles. He was part of the "Eight West Coast Artists" installation in Barcelona. In 1984, his "Amphitheatre of Light: A Prelude to the XXIII Olympiad" was exhibited in the Hollywood Bowl (right down the street from where I live today). Strangely, he had yet to enjoy any strong exposure in New York. He was the younger brother of the New York dealer, Brooke Alexander, who owned a gallery in the same building on 57th Street where my Hamilton Gallery operated. He even visited my gallery when I was in business. Peter was tall, good-looking and well-bred. He attended the University of Pennsylvania and studied architecture before becoming an artist. He was also delightful, smart, and funny.

When I contacted Peter, he had recently made a series of paintings, the "Las Vegas" series, which involved spray-painted images on top of landscapes. Some described the works as "aerial lithographs." Not surprisingly, given his roots, light was the most important aspect of his work. He was a visionary. You could actually *see* the buildings and images, but the buildings were obscured so it was hard work on the eyes. Still, I felt I could get him a show in New York, so we agreed to work together.

Robert Zakanitch was a much different artist than Peter, but in my opinion, just as prestigious and prominent. For my money, he was the best painter in the Pattern and Decoration Movement of the late '70s. In 1976, he and Miriam Schapiro created an organization in New York around Pattern and Decoration artists after meeting a year prior at the University of California-San Diego in La Jolla, where he was a guest instructor. History proves my point about the quality and staying power of his work; today, at age 87, he can walk into the Philadelphia Museum of Art, Museum of Modern Art and the Whitney, among others, and see his works held in collections. During his career, he has moved from Abstract Expressionism to Minimalism, and as *AskArt* put it, "has done contrasting work of lush, exotic botanicals of seemingly boundless imagery." One of his comments on his work? "I don't want any dehumanization in my work. I am more interested in planting the seeds of healing and civility?"

How can you not love an artist with that point of view? I had always been a big admirer of his work.

I visited Robert's studio and was really impressed and very enthusiastic about working with him. He had finished five enormous paintings, each measuring 10 x 30 feet. He called them "The Big Bungalow Suite." He not only needed a gallery exhibition, but also wanted to put together a museum show featuring of these works. Since they were not mounted on stretchers, they would be fairly easy to transport. It was a great idea.

Robert's work moved me. Deeply. Very few times in my life have I dreamed about an artist's work after making a studio visit. My dreams usually involve everything but paintings or sculptures, probably a good thing; imagine the confusing muddle of images when hundreds of artists' works are trying to sort themselves out in my subconscious! But with Robert, it was different. It happened to me the night after I saw "The Big Bungalow Suite" paintings for the first time. I was floored.

Bob also had a stable personal and family life, which was not always the case among artists, as my experiences and stories have certainly made clear. He was married to the feminist artist Patsy Norvell, who had been active in the women's art movement since 1969, and they were the proud parents of a daughter, Amelia. They were both bright, and I looked forward to working with him and getting to know his family.

. . .

Not everything can go perfectly, can it? Sure enough, my family life came back to haunt me once again.

My oldest brother Bill, who had flipped out at Dad's funeral, began spending a lot of time in L.A. At least once a month, he would come and stay in my apartment. At the time Bill was technically sober, but to be more accurate, was a "dry drunk." He gave up alcohol because he is an alcoholic and it was slowly killing him, but he did nothing to figure out the underlying reasons why he drank. He never went to AA, for example. Rather than viewing his decision to quit as a life-saver, a game-changer, a new lease on a happier, healthier and simply better life, the point that recovering alcoholics who work their program attain, he was pissed off that he had to give it up. And so, the underlying causes reared their venomous heads. My brother, who died in the spring 2023, also suffered from narcissistic personality disorder and was bi-polar. He was tough to be around, triggering all the past feelings and difficulties I'd worked so very hard to disassociate from my life, and I didn't know how to tell him he was not welcome in my life. When Susan died in 1998, he even told me he was going to break into her apartment, cut the paintings

I'd gotten for her out of the frames, and steal them. "Finders, keepers," he said. He thought it was funny.

I never spoke to him again.

Unfortunately, Peter Alexander was also a dry drunk. During this same time, Peter was in a crisis, had broken up with his girlfriend, had stopped drinking and was depressed. On all levels, I was having my buttons pushed by "dry drunks."

I didn't handle it well. I went into a deep depression, during which I concluded that most of the important people in my life were either alcoholics, children of alcoholics, or married to alcoholics. I was surrounded by them physically and emotionally, and they were beginning to tear me apart with behavior I didn't know how to deal with. Often, I enabled it, even though I didn't fully understand that concept yet or how to move beyond it.

But I would. Mary Weatherford, a wonderful artist and friend from New York, suggested that I go to an Al-Anon meeting. Little did I know that my decision to attend would permanently change my life and bring me the peace and serenity I longed for. I instantly felt at home at my first meeting. I belonged in the room, their story was my story in many ways, and I felt myself among people who understood from direct experience—and hard work—what I felt inside. Everyone there was severely affected by the disease of alcoholism. Either they grew up in an alcoholic family, married an alcoholic, worked with alcoholics who affected their performance, or had close friends they'd tried to help. These were characteristics I could relate to.

What I related to the most was the root of all the problems: feeling unwanted, unloved, and alone. Just like I felt growing up in my family home and many times thereafter in my career. Growing up in an alcoholic family meant that all the attention went to the alcoholic. If he or she was in a bad mood, the collective mood of the family went south along with them. Life was always very dramatic, and everyone played the "blame" game whenever anything went wrong. Or, they tried to do everything possible to "make everything okay," to settle down the alcoholic's rage . . . to enable. But If you made a mistake, you *were* the mistake.

In my family, like most, alcoholism was the symptom of a deeper problem. In our home, things were complicated by mental illness. My father and siblings were self-medicating with alcohol to get them through debilitating depressions. It is not uncommon for people with severe depression to drink or use drugs to feel better. Then the drinking becomes a habit. My father's famous expression was always, "It must be noon somewhere." So much for 5 p.m.! He considered noon an acceptable hour to have his first drink.

However, I'd found my place of support and the people to support me, accept me for who I am and what I'd been through, and show me ways of addressing and moving past the impact the alcoholic makes in our lives. I'd found Al-Anon, and my healing happened.

. . .

It was a good thing, as I was quickly learning how different agenting was in the 1990s than the 1980s. When I was a pioneer agent in New York, so to speak, I was paid commissions on works sold, similar to a literary agent today. Now, in structuring my new approach to agenting, I asked artists to pay me a monthly fee to manage their careers. I didn't understand that if artists were paying you retainers, they felt like they owned you to some degree. They wanted to know what you were doing for them on a daily basis, and expected you to revitalize or create huge strides and open doors in their careers in six months. It became much too tall an order, emotionally and otherwise. I found that these retainer-based relationships lasted a year, and after that, if I continued to work with them, I reverted to being paid in work by commission. Nevertheless, I managed to work with quite a few interesting artists, but when I started out, it was just Peter Alexander and Bob Zakanitch.

It didn't take long with Peter. In the Fall of 1994, I immediately landed him a show in New York with the Barbara Mathes Gallery. I also worked with him for the final show at the James Corcoran Gallery, which featured his work. But not without tragedy along the way: right before his show opened, his dream house burned down. What a traumatic experience for anyone. He was a wreck. He had gotten back together with his girlfriend; emotionally, she bore most of the brunt.

I continued to support him in his work. At James Corcoran, he showed the Las Vegas Series. Later, I helped organize his large "Century" show at the Laguna Art Museum (where some of his works still hang today), but it was clear our relationship had reached its logical conclusion. Peter joined the Franklin Parrasch Gallery in New York, and they opened a gallery in L.A. It was after he landed in the Parrasch Gallery that his career truly soared to blue-chip status.

Sadly, Peter recently passed in the summer of 2020. Fortunately, his estate planning is absolutely in the right place for his brilliant work to live on. Franklin Parrasch is devoted to the work and will promote him for many years to come.

I also was busy with Bob Zakantich. In the Spring of 1994, we showed the "The Big Bungalow Suite" with Jason McCoy Gallery. Jason's space on 57th Street was not large enough to show the paintings, so he rented a space in SoHo. I worked very hard on publicity for the show, recalling all of my efforts as a curator and my years with the Hamilton Gallery—as well as my still-strong press connections—and his painting ended up on the cover of *Art in America,* on an issue about painting. You can't receive much more prestigious coverage than that. Unfortunately, though, Jason was not very interested in working with me on promoting Bob's work—why wouldn't he be? With the way Bob's work drew collectors, buyers, and the press in? Sometimes, I just had to shake my head at people like Jason and wonder. Well, many times.

Not surprisingly, our relationship became adversarial. He thought I had nothing to contribute. How about *tying the cover of an issue of* Art in America *to his exhibit?* I also had very ambitious plans for this brilliant suite of paintings, whereas Jason was much more provincial, never sharing the vision. Specifically, I wanted to travel to the exhibition of the large canvases to museums all over the country. I handed Jason 200 letters I had written, asking him to send catalogues from the show to the museums with personal letters from me offering the show.

Jason threw them out. He decided they were badly written.

When I found out, I resent the letters myself. The show did indeed travel to more than five museums, but for every museum that said yes, twenty others said no. It was a lot of work, which Jason was unwilling to do. He also was unable to sell any of Bob's work. Apparently, he just figured he would exhibit the work, and it would sell itself.

. . .

While I was in New York, my friend, Christopher Ford, stayed in my Hancock Park apartment in L.A. One weekend, I was robbed, and I knew it was time to get out of the neighborhood. Christopher had an old boyfriend, Cliff Benjamin, who rented a huge house in the Los Feliz neighborhood of north L.A. He was leaving for Phoenix and turned us onto the landlord. The timing couldn't have been better. We were able to rent that huge house—five bedrooms—for a very reasonable price.

That same weekend, my sister's 90-pound chocolate lab died. I had never taken care of dogs or had them as pets as a kid since my mother had asthma. However, this lab was really sweet; she changed something in me. I fell in love with her, and then and there,

I became a full-fledged "dog person." My sister was devastated, and someone at her church offered a very young yellow lab in California that they wanted to sell. My sister wasn't interested, but I was. I thought she would be a good companion and protection in case Christopher was not at home.

When I returned to California, I drove to Orange County and picked up Chardonnay, who was just one year old. It was love at first sight. We then came up with the bright idea to breed her and ended up with seven yellow labs. We put them all in the basement, where they slept, and then they would spend afternoons in the backyard.

With the basement occupied by seven labs, I promptly turned the garage into a gallery space. It's not a hard conversion. Cliff, the previous occupant, was an artist and had worked in the space. I hung paintings by the artists I was representing. The puppies and I then came to a basic understanding, which they obeyed: they were never to enter the gallery. One afternoon, a client came by to see a painting by Nabil Nahas, one of my artists. All the puppies lined up in front of the garage and wagged their tails furiously, like a scene out of *101 Dalmatians* or something. The client turned to me, her eyes wide, and asked, "How can I look at these paintings with these adorable puppies in the way?"

"Buy the painting and I will throw in a puppy," I said.

Talk about a deal closer! She bought the painting and brought one of the puppies to its new home.

. . .

When Connie Lembarck and I first talked about my becoming an agent again, she recommended a third artist, Fletcher Benton. Fletcher was good-looking and quite lovely. Also, his wife Bobbie and I had a lot in common, so we hit it off. He also made steel constructivist sculptures and enjoyed a very successful career in San Francisco. He owned a fabulous studio in downtown San Francisco, a large home in Japantown, and a home in Napa, the center of California's most prestigious wine-growing region. He wanted to be exhibited in a New York gallery and also some help landing and creating museum shows. His wife, Bobbie, and I had a lot in common, including our love of reading and watching movies. However, no one wanted to show constructivist steel sculpture in New York, though, and I was unable to get him a dealer there.

Eventually, the business relationship fell apart, but the friendship remained. Fletcher also sponsored an annual artist's tennis tournament at his home in Napa, which I attended for years. These were hilarious events, with every well-known artist in San Francisco participating and bringing their favorite food. Bobbie and I remained friends until Fletcher died in 2019.

I continued diligently working on my Al-Anon program, which led to major fringe benefits. I had a friend in the program who lost a lot of weight and suggested I look at a 12-step program about compulsive overeating. I joined what I call "the Nazi Party of Overeaters Anonymous," called HOW. They told you what to eat—and when. No deviations, no exceptions. The basis of keeping the weight off was to abstain completely from sugar, white flour, and alcohol—for the rest of your life. As in, "never eat sugar, food with white flour, or touch a drink again."

There is not a program in the world that works when the word *never* is involved. It is too tough of an ask, and besides, I don't know about you, but you know how I tend to react when someone tells me, "Never?" Moderation, of course, and occasionally a yes, but *never* does not work. However, I really stuck to the program diligently, lost 50 pounds with HOW suddenly became interested in dating again.

CHAPTER 17

The End of Romance

I felt great again. After working on myself through Al-Anon, getting a better handle on how to deal with the alcoholics moving in and out of my life, and also losing 50 pounds, I was light on my feet again—and ready to find someone.

In that buoyant spirit, I flew to New York in the Fall of 1997 for my annual six-week stint to stir up business and promote artists. While I was there, my friend Dick Pollich, who owned the prominent bronze foundry Tallix, introduced me to a man whose brother-in-law was an artist. I took a train to Garrison, New York, about 60 miles north of the city, to meet Dick and his friend, Paul Mayen, the man who hoped I would represent his brother-in-law. Paul was an elderly European, and I quickly found him very charming; I also sensed that he was gay. His house was unbelievably gorgeous, complete with a glorious garden, tennis courts, an indoor pool, an art collection—and live-in servants. I was pretty impressed with everything from his home to his ability to make pleasant conversation.

My impressiveness didn't last long. Imagine my surprise when he started hitting on me like a ton of bricks shortly after my arrival. *Aren't you gay?* I thought. I was confused. *Is my gaydar screwed up or something?* I'm normally quite good at reading people, and thought

I pegged Paul's orientation from the beginning—after all, new romance was on my mind—but I apparently misread him entirely. I began to wonder about my people-reading skills.

Over lunch, Paul invited me to visit him in Hydra, Greece, that summer. Not your average "let's go for a drive in the countryside" or "how about spending a day together in the Hamptons" invitation. No, he was going for the ostentatious entrée, right over the top. I was a bit overwhelmed. We decided to get together in two weeks, during which my head spun over his obvious attraction to me and his desire to spirit me off to Greece for a summer of what I assumed would be romance if he had his way.

Two weeks later, we had lunch in New York. Afterward, we passed by the Armani store and walked inside. "How do you think you would look in a black suit?" he asked me. It was a rather unusual question for a man to ask a woman, but I found it considerate.

"Well, as a blond, it would be a very flattering look," I replied. Shortly afterward, we left the store.

That weekend, he invited me to his house in Garrison for the weekend. I have to admit, I was a bit hesitant to make the trip, because I was not really attracted to him. He was quite a bit older, I felt like I was misreading him, and I was confused as to where this might be leading. I took the plunge and went anyway. Sure enough, Paul was all over me the entire weekend.

On that Saturday night, we went to dinner and had a wonderful time. It was lots of fun. Later, when it was time to go to bed, he kissed me and said good night. He didn't try anything further physically, which was both appropriate and very much welcomed by me. However, when I walked into the room where I was staying, I noticed a black Armani suit. My new black Armani suit. Our quick dive into the store led to a very nice gift.

The next morning, Paul felt it necessary to explain to me he had prostate cancer and was taking medication that rendered him impotent. Did he feel guilty he hadn't tried to go further with me the previous night? Or was he truly the perfect gentleman, letting me know his medically necessary limitations? I couldn't tell. "How do you feel about an old-fashioned romance?" he finally asked.

"Just great," I said. And I meant it: I figured I would be in love with him by the time the Greece trip happened the following summer—or skip it entirely. For me, "old-fashioned romance" meant *no sex until Greece.*

Then I asked him about being single his whole life. He told me about one woman after another he had lived with, giving the impression of being a ladies' man.

Finally, I needed confirmation on the big question in my mind: "Are you gay?" I asked.

"No, no, no," he said, vehemently denying it. Like I said, my "gaydar" wasn't working as well as I thought.

Shortly afterwards, my six weeks in the city were up, so I flew back to L.A. for a few weeks. I desperately missed the dogs and being in my own home. Paul and I continued to talk on the phone, and I still planned on visiting him in Greece; we'd decided that I would come over for ten days. Every time we talked, he proved to be ever so romantic on the phone, so I chose to ignore all the "gaydar" signals that I had received. Clearly, I thought I was wrong. It really is possible to fall in love with someone over the phone, and I felt that happening to me. I also was projecting ahead quickly. I began thinking of the glamorous life that awaited me and that we would lead together. He also wanted children.

· · ·

In August 1998, I was a woman in love as I boarded the plane for my big trip to Greece. I arrived in Athens and stayed in a great hotel, then took the hydrofoil from the Argolis peninsula of the Peloponnese across the beautiful Aegean Sea to Hydra the next day. What an intimate, romantic island; it was only 13 miles long, both ancient and modern and anchored by a sweet central town. Paul greeted me at the dock in a one-piece outfit that was so flamboyantly gay that I nearly died on the spot, which would've been an inconvenient, premature ending to the trip.

I had chosen to believe his denial of being gay. I ignored my gut. Not a smart thing to do. I was kicking myself inside while standing thousands of miles from home.

Nonetheless, we had dinner, and he presented me with a marvelous necklace. This was the night we were supposed to make love, according to all the signals on our phone calls—who doesn't make love on a romantic Greek holiday? Instead, he kissed me on the cheek goodnight and left it at that. I knew he had prostate cancer, he was impotent, and the other things he said—was he making it up?—but it was still plenty unnerving. I didn't quite know what to do, but I'd learned well from my years in Al-Anon that when you don't know what to do, the best thing is to do nothing.

Shortly thereafter, the Priesters arrived from New York City with their 13-year-old daughter. Bill was a well-known cardiologist in New York, while his wife, Lale Armstrong, was the architect who had designed Paul's Garrison house. She was also the daughter of Paul's lawyer and a very good friend. Paul had been friends with the Priesters for 30 years. For my part, I didn't know Lale, but I immediately trusted her. After a lovely dinner, I decided to talk to her the next day about my uncomfortable situation.

The next day was foggy, so we decided not to go out on Paul's boat, from which we would go swimming and follow it up with an elaborate lunch. I took the opportunity to sit down with Lale. "Is Paul in the closet with everyone, or just me?" I asked. By now, I was listening intently to my gut and my heart. I had no doubt anymore.

She sighed heavily, having known Paul all her life. "No, just with you."

I explained the elaborate game he had played with me for the better part of ten months since we'd first met in Garrison during my fall trip to the city. I added how he even made up stories about women with whom he'd purportedly had long-term relationships. He told me about his best friend, Edgar Kaufmann, and how they were the best of pals, while failing to mention they had been lovers for 30 years.

"Paul asked me not to tell you he is gay," Lale added. Apparently, Paul was blaming the whole thing on my being so hopelessly in love with him, as if I wasn't encouraged in this matter. Plus, I don't recall being the person who was all over the other during our weekends in Garrison; it seems to me he was the one making the moves.

"Go to lunch with him, yank him out of the closet, and make him buy you a ticket back to New York," she concluded. While she had never seen this side of Paul, she was convinced that what he had done with me was very cruel.

I did just that, but gently. "Look, Paul," I began, "my best friend and roommate are gay, and I am friends with tons of gay men, so what is this game you're playing with me all about?"

"I was born a Catholic," he replied, his voice soft and eyes downcast. "I thought I would go to hell if I died a gay man. I saw the possibility of marrying you as my redemption."

Oh, great. Just great. That was a new one.

He was deeply remorseful and happy to buy me a ticket home. Meanwhile, I felt completely foolish and betrayed. The whole experience really devastated me.

Ironically, when I told my friends at home what had happened, my gay male friends were the most outraged. It was 1998, and no one was ashamed of being gay, yet here was a man pretending to be straight and playing with my feelings. Over our years of talking on the phone and talking very intimately and romantically, I might add, I slowly fell in love with him. I trusted him—only to find out in Greece he was a liar who fully manipulated my feelings. He knew how badly I wanted to be in a romantic relationship, which made his actions twice as bad.

This, however, was not the end of the tale. I was still working for Paul as an artist's agent to his brother-in-law. I needed the money, so we needed to retain some sort of contact. Further, Lale and others encouraged me to remain his friend despite the deep betrayal of my feelings and hopes. Why, I cannot imagine. I did a lot of soul-searching and work on this, taking responsibility for my own blindness as I tried to accept reality.

However, Paul was betraying me in another way the whole time. The entire time he was romancing me, he was also courting a gay man who also lived in Los Angeles. I had no idea until later. Paul ended up living with this man and buying a house for them in Los Angeles, only a few miles from me. Once again, he put his friend Lale into the untenable position of having to inform me of his new lover.

This time, I didn't fuck around. I confronted Paul promptly. "We are just friends," he contended. "I want it to be more, but Jed does not." Well, as those words left his mouth, he and Jed Cohen were lovers.

I realized I was dealing with a pathological liar. There was only one thing left for me to do: cut all ties with him. I had no choice; this was about self-preservation, self-respect, and maintaining my sense of dignity. And getting the man out of my fucking life once and for all.

"I will continue to work with your brother-in-law, but will only do it through your nephew and girlfriend, Aldo Radocy and Carol Perrione, and have nothing further to do with you," I said. It was the only way to get him out of my head.

When I arranged a show for Paul's brother-in-law in Los Angeles, I met Jed Cohen and found him completely charming. Interestingly, from that point on, while Paul was still alive, he wanted to keep Jed and me apart because he didn't want us to compare stories.

By the time I was done with Paul, all those questions of whether I had any chance to pick the right guy came roaring back into my head.

. . .

At the same time, I began working with Dennis Ashbaugh, an artist who was painting DNA portraits. He was living with Alexandra Penney, a fabulous woman and author of many books (*How to Make Love to a Man, The Sexiest Sex of All, How to Keep Your Man Monogamous,* etc.), and her essays, articles and short stories were published only in the best magazines. She was very well-connected. I often wished that Dennis' work was as appealing as he was as a person. He seemed more interested in socializing with the rich and famous than buckling down in the studio and making himself great.

One evening, we were having drinks at their apartment, and Alexandra's friend, the writer Nicholas von Hoffman, called. He had just lost the lease on his New York apartment and was freaking out. He lived in Tenants Harbor, Maine, most of the year, but like me, wanted to spend three to four months in New York.

Alexandra told him about my short-term rental on Madison and 65th Street. Nicholas wanted to see the apartment and take me to dinner. She and Nick were good friends. "He is one of the smartest, funniest men I have ever met," she added.

We met for dinner the following week, and I had laryngitis. I could only whisper. He talked all night and kept me on the edge of my seat. Smart and funny? I have always loved that combination—and on that count, Alexandra was absolutely correct. Nick was plenty of both.

He was also well-known for writing *Citizen Cohn,* the definitive biography of Roy Cohn, the ruthless New York lawyer and close friend of one Fred Trump. He would rise to further infamy postmortem when his major influence on the worldview, ways of doing business, and dealing with people of Fred's son, Donald, became universally known. Nicholas had written many other political books, wrote columns for *The Washington Post* and *Boston Globe*, and appeared on *60 Minutes* in the segment "Point, Counterpoint," with Shana Alexander. I recalled that, but as I sat across from him, I remembered vividly the parody from *Saturday Night Live* with Dan Ackroyd and Jane Curtin. Ackroyd, who was riffing on Nick, started every argument with, "Jane, you ignorant slut."

I found Nick strange, but at the same time, very intriguing. We went out a few times in New York and he made it clear he was interested in a romantic relationship. He planned to come to Los Angeles to do an article about computer technology at the Getty Museum. He called the Getty and was not being treated well, so he contacted me to see what I could do. I stepped in and called a fellow ArtTable member working in the Getty's PR department; I was the Southern California chapter president, so I had a little pull. "This is a really important journalist," I said, "so I think you should treat him like a VIP."

They literally rolled out the red carpet for him.

We went to dinner every night Nick was in Los Angeles. For the final night, I planned a large dinner party with a number of my most eccentric friends. The ever-amusing artist Simon Toporofsky and dealers Marc Selwyn and Burnett Miller were there. Everyone brought wine, flowers, or a dish. Except for Nick. The next day, when he called to thank me for the evening, I pointed out that he was ill-mannered for not at least bringing flowers.

Nick felt badly—so he sent me a casserole dish. Now please, mind you, to whom do you typically send a casserole dish? A maiden aunt, perhaps, but not a girlfriend. And *not* in the early stages of a budding romance. As I said, Nick was bright and interesting but strange and awkward in some very important ways.

Shortly after that, my sister-in-law, Dola told me that she and her husband Tom were celebrating their 10th wedding anniversary and would like to buy some art. They were interested in Andrew Wyeth and Hudson River Valley paintings. I was well-qualified to help them with both subjects. I called my old acquaintance Nicholas Wyeth, Andrew's son, who I knew from the watercolor show on which I'd worked at the Crispo nearly 30 years before. I learned that Nicholas lived in Cushing, Maine, close to Nick's home in Tenants Harbor.

I made plans to visit Nicholas Wyeth and thought, why not? I could see Nick at the same time. I flew into Tenants Harbor and called Nick the next morning. His best friend answered and said Nick was out of town in Washington and wouldn't be back for a few days.

Well, that response surprised me. Just the day before, Nick and I had spoken on the phone—and made a dinner date.

I went to see Nicholas Wyeth, who showed me several beautiful and important Andrew Wyeth watercolors for sale. I took the transparency and returned to my hotel. I had brought a present for my friend Nick's dog and knew the name of the street on which he lived, so I drove by. I spotted a teenager walking down the street. "Could you show me which house is Nick von Hoffman's?" I asked. He pointed it out.

When I went up to the house, I found the door open. I walked through the front door to surprise my new boyfriend, took a quick look, and decided he wasn't home, then dropped the present on a nearby table. While on my way out, I heard a dog barking. No sooner had I said hello to the dog than I looked up—and right into Nick's face above me.

"Listen, I'm not stalking you; I merely had a present for your dog," I said, stunned to see him.

"I just returned from Washington, and you can't come in because I'm stark naked," he said.

Nick was having vision problems from macular degeneration, but there was nothing wrong with my vision. I saw a fully dressed man in front of me.

"I can see you, Nick, and you're fully dressed."

"Get off my property!" he screamed.

I was floored. Here was someone I had entertained lavishly In Los Angeles for five days and spoken to at length three or four times a week. I was confused but did as I was told and walked away. On my way out, I thought, *No, this isn't right.*

So I went back for more. "If you didn't want to see me," I hollered, "why didn't you tell me in one of your last fifty phone calls to me?"

"Well, I am telling you now. Get off my property."

Yikes, I thought, *he's nuts.* I ran away.

The next day, I left for Cape Cod to visit Dola and Tom for the weekend. I had found some Hudson River Valley paintings in San Francisco and brought photos to show them—and I also had the Wyeth watercolors, which I'd sought out on their behalf. Their house was in Marian, a home in quaint and beautiful Plymouth County decorated and appointed with great taste. Dola and Tom bought two works by the marine painter William de Haas, and I told them about my visit with Nick. They sympathized, and we even made jokes.

But one thing for sure that came out of my fling with Nick: I vowed to retire from dating. I was bad at it, and I made bad choices. And I was pushing 50. Why bother anymore?

When I got home from Maine, I called Simon Toporofsky. I did as much for him as anyone could. I landed him a show in Los Angeles and another in Phoenix. I even drove to Phoenix with a broken foot for his opening. At a time when I was still smarting both from my experiences with Paul Mayen and Nick von Hoffman, Simon decided it was the right time to sever ties with me.

He did it in the cruelest possible way, too: by calling me one morning at 7 a.m. and reciting all of my character defects, a tirade that lasted about 45 minutes. Finally, I got off the phone, deeply hurt. I needed to put some distance between us and think things through.

After about two weeks, I called him back. "You are not my psychiatrist, boyfriend, or sponsor," I said. "You have no business being so cruel to me."

We never spoke again. I thought this was my friend. However, I learned that this was Simon's ongoing pattern. Whenever he gets close to someone, he exploits them. When he feels he's gotten as much out of them as possible, he severs the relationship in the most hurtful way imaginable. I never like to lose friends, but losing Simon was particularly painful. We talked every day, sometimes four or five times a day for years.

Suddenly, there was nothing.

CHAPTER 18

Re-sale: Playing the Game in Whitley Heights

I returned to LA from the East Coast in the summer of 1998, ready for some sort of life change to switch gears from the emotionally difficult way my year had gone. Apparently, the landlord of the house I was renting read my mind, saw it in the tea leaves or something, because the house went up for sale.

I looked at my finances and how much I loved LA and wanted to anchor there for the rest of my life. I thought of my life situation—being 50 and still renting—and decided to take the plunge, use all of my savings, plus what I had made at a recent sale, and try to buy a house. The sale itself was interesting: during the weekend of my ordeal with Nicholas von Hoffman, I went to Cape Cod with my sister-in-law and her husband. I sold two Wyeth watercolors and some 19th-century Marine paintings by Willem de Haas.

Even with this good sale, I quickly learned the amount I could afford to spend in the pricey Southern California market would only get me a "major fixer-upper." As a single woman who isn't as skilled with hammer and nails as she is with, say, negotiating a deal for a painting, that was not my ideal vision of buying a home.

I decided to take another six months and see if I could earn and save some more money. I also wanted to live in an area with some history, architectural style, and atmosphere to it. I certainly wasn't thinking Bel-Air, Beverly Hills, Pacific Palisades, Brentwood, or other Tony communities within Los Angeles, but I kept my eyes and ears peeled for a modest home in a stylish neighborhood. I rented an apartment, and then my plan worked. Among other things, I sold a huge quantity of art to the same private buyer. The timing could not have been more perfect.

Six months later, I found my home—in Whitley Heights, at the north end of the Hollywood Hills across the street and up the hill from the world-famous Hollywood Bowl.

Whitley Heights had everything I could imagine: homes large and small with great architecture, tight hilly streets mixed with beautiful trees, style from one end to the other, and a century-old history beyond any other in L.A. The neighborhood is built along a steep hillside with panoramic views reminiscent of Tuscany. It even had secret tunnels and underground passages where residents could pass surreptitiously from one home to the next to do God knows what. There is also a long-held rumor that an underground passage from Whitley Heights to the Grauman Chinese Theater on Sunset Boulevard existed for years, presumably so stars and their entourages could avoid their legions of fans, slow transportation and other intrusions of privacy. Traveling in the hills in the 1920s was not so easy. Whitley Heights was no less than the enclave of Hollywood's first film stars, as it was designed by the "Grandfather of Hollywood," Hobart Whitley. It is where the first Golden Age of Hollywood held center court, beginning with the final decade of silent film stars, and continuing right through the advent of talking pictures and the height of the studio era. Stars from Rudolph Valentino, Barbara LaMarr, Ramon Novarro, Maurice Chevalier, and Bette Davis lived there, along with William Wellman, the first man to win an Oscar for Best Director.

The delightful Spanish-style house I bought, built in 1924, once belonged to silent film legend Ramon Novarro. You can't get much more history and legacy in your new home than that! Rudolph Valentino lived directly across the street and talked many of his movie star friends into buying places there. Bette Davis lived on one side, and William Wellman on the other. Ramon was a star in *Ben Hur* and many other classic silents. Later in life, he lived in a Frank Lloyd Wright house in Los Feliz, where I had previously rented before this journey to buy a home began. Sadly, Ramon was brutally murdered by two young brothers looking for cash.

Right below my house, directly across the street from the Hollywood Bowl and tucked in the overflow parking lot, is one of the busiest studios of the 1910s and 1920s, the Lasky-DeMille Studio Barn. Now the charming Hollywood Heritage Museum, the former horse feed barn was first leased by producers J.J. Burns and Harry Revier to shoot Keystone Cops movies. They met the now-iconic Jesse Lasky, Cecil B. DeMille, and William Goldwyn, who had relocated the Jesse Lasky Feature Play Company from New York in 1914 after dealing with great inventor but ruthless East Coast studio owner Thomas Alva Edison. DeMille shot *The Squaw Man* at the studio, the first feature film in Hollywood. DeMille and Goldwyn parted ways, and Adolph Zukor joined up with DeMille, who was in his prolific heyday. Eventually, the Jesse Lasky Feature Play morphed into Paramount Pictures. (For his part, Goldwyn joined forces with fellow New York expat Louis B. Mayer and started MGM). Parts of *Ben Hur* were shot at the studio barn, along with many other films, some epics, others lost to time.

What a thrill to now be living amidst so much architecture and history. And, when in the mood for music, I could walk a few minutes to the Hollywood Bowl—or pull up a chair in my nice quaint backyard and listen from a distance! My backyard garden was designed by Robert Dash and selected for the National Garden Conservancy tour. It was his idea to put river-washed stones in the garden. Nothing fires up one's creative juices and vision than living in such a place; I did not have to make much effort to imagine what home life as a Hollywood star would be like. I was in one of them. My two dogs, a pair of yellow Labs, loved the neighborhood.

Also, I'd been holding dinner parties since the mid-1970s, but now, I had the added space of a beautiful home and yard. I constantly hosted dinners in the new house in Whitley Heights. One time, I threw a party for which I asked people to dress up as 1920s Silent Era Golden Age movie stars. Patti Heid, an artist with whom I worked and the ex-wife of comedian and actor Cheech Marin, won the night despite dressing a decade late; she came as the Wicked Witch of the West from the 1939 classic *The Wizard of Oz*. Two guys went as the Gish sisters. One couple even came as my home's original owner, Ramon Navarro. These dinners were by invitation only, and everyone wanted to be invited.

However, not everything was paradise. The problem with owning a house built in the '20s was both the enormous expense and constant necessity of maintenance. Eventually everything has to be replaced. But oh, did my new house ooze with charm! You can't blame me if I clicked my little ruby red slippers (or boots) together, closed my eyes, and said, "There's no place like home." Only this wasn't a tornado-driven dream in the land of Oz.

· · ·

I continued my bi-coastal career, spending three to four months in New York and the rest in L.A. as the 21st century progressed. I was still representing artists as an agent, but as mentioned earlier, the relationships almost always proved short-lived. Around this time, in the Fall of 2000, I made a connection with Lee Sonnier, who worked for a gallery in Beverly Hills, a highly commercial space. Lee was a very nice guy but knew very little about art. He was good at finding things, an accomplished "runner," to use industry terminology, but he knew very few people in the legitimate art world. He didn't want to make the extra effort to travel to fairs and, most importantly and sadly, didn't care if things were authenticated or not. I was wary of him.

Lee did, however, have a client I found legitimate, a man named Jim Upchurch, an equally nice businessman who collected only California Impressionism. Through his former employer, frame shop owner Chuck Mitchell, Lee met another client named Greg Econn. Chuck belonged to the Jonathan Club, an exclusive downtown club populated by wealthy businessmen with all the right networks and connections that make L.A. run economically. There, he would meet potential clients.

While Lee and Jim were friendly, engaging men with whom I enjoyed conversations, Chuck was a serious misogynist; I immediately hated him. Plus, he knew framing—but nothing about art. The first time he met me, he asked me for a resume. Mind you, I'd been asked for a resume before—by the Whitney, when I was first hired out of college. My work took care of any prerequisites in the three decades since. So I was like, *really? What the fuck?* I should have asked Chuck for his. Instead, I referred him to the *Art Dealers*, the book by Laura De Coppet and Alan Jones, which featured me in a 20-page chapter as one of New York's primary art scene movers and shakers when I owned Hamilton Gallery. Chuck was also bipolar, not an uncommon thing in the art world as I'd long before learned, and did not take his medication regularly. He was a nightmare to deal with, completely unprofessional and greedy.

However, Chuck did find something for me—an early George Inness painting. Inness is my favorite 19th-century American landscape painter whose work I'd curated at one of the Crispo Gallery shows I put together. I had the piece authenticated by Michael Quick, the art historian who was writing the *Catalogue raisonné,* or the complete catalogue of the artist's known work. I also had it professionally photographed.

Unfortunately, Chuck interfered with the sale every step of the way. I finally sold it, in spite of his sabotaging efforts.

Here's what happened: the owners of the Inness also owned an early Norman Rockwell, probably the most universally known artist by the average American and similarly treasured by collectors, not only of art, but of Americana and nostalgia. His popularity may never recede, so this was a hot-ticket item. The specific piece was "The Auctioneer," which has a great back story. One time, Norman visited California and developed a bad toothache. He exchanged the painting for the dental work, since he couldn't afford the services at the time.

Once again, before making the deal, I had the painting authenticated and photographed—which is when Chuck fucked with my efforts. For the appraisal process, he took the painting to a notoriously bad appraiser, not a member of the Appraisers Society of America, and put too high a price on it. I promptly bypassed Chuck, talked directly to the client (who also owned the Inness), and sold the painting after nearly a year.

Here's the thing with authenticating and appraising art: if you don't have credentials, the experience, or the wherewithal, you're going to fuck something up. Doing so in this business takes its toll on money and reputation and can burn both ends of the deal. Sure enough, Chuck's appraiser got the title, year and provenance wrong—and still wouldn't change his final number.

Then and there, I began to study the art of resale, with the full intention of adding it to my portfolio of experience and, of course, taking care of my beautiful new/old Whitley Heights home. I quickly found out that procedures and protocols were different from dealing in the primary market. I learned five rules each person buying a very expensive work of art should follow before purchase:

1. It is vital to have a certificate of authentication. *Vital.* Virtually every artist is connected with an expert or a panel of experts who will authenticate the works of art. There are some exceptions. For Jackson Pollock, Andy Warhol, Keith Haring, and Jean Michel Basquait, and a few others, the *Catalogue raisonné* is complete, and they will not authenticate any more paintings. If that is the case, it is important to have some sort of documentation that ties the work to the artist's studio, preferably a photo of the painting in the artist's studio, a bill of sale or canceled check. And, has the work been included in an official exhibition? That counts toward authentication, too.

2. Possess a rock-solid provenance and the buying history of the painting. This document traces the work from one owner to the next. For those works that have passed through several sets of hands, be sure every owner is listed. The provenance also includes any museum or gallery exhibitions that included the painting. In the $80 million Knoedler Gallery scandal (which I get to in the next chapter), one of the most notorious in recent art history, the big red flag flew right up the pole when the provenances of 60 Abstract Expressionist paintings were called into question.

3. It is important to have a report detailing the painting's professional condition, preferably provided by IFAR, the International Foundation for Art Research, to validate it as authentic. A conservator can tell if the painting has been

repainted or filled in. Another feature that got Knoedler into trouble with the aforementioned 60 paintings concerned the color pigments used; they had not yet been invented in the 1950s, when the paintings were supposedly created. During the investigation, a scientist determined the works were more recently painted. They have methods that determine the age of paint and sculptures. Likewise, they can tell if a work was damaged at any point in its history.

IFAR is an institution that maintains a global database of stolen art. In particular, they offer impartial information on authenticity, ownership, theft, and other artistic, legal, and ethical issues concerning art objects. They offer provenance and web-based research sources and keep the *Catalogue raisonné* database (records of all the works of noted artists). In short, they are the authoritative source formed to maintain integrity in the arts. What they say means something. They were the ones who busted the Knoedler Gallery, and the organization to which Alec Baldwin went with the Mary Boone painting that put her in very hot water as well.

4. Artnet comps. The Artnet came out with the public explosion of the Internet in the 1990s. Since then, it has become the bible of recent art collecting, dealing, and reselling. It lists all paintings auctioned anywhere in the world since 1990. When a painting is for sale, and I'm asked to be involved, I must check it through Artnet. So should you. If I find that the painting was at an auction (or more than one auction), what price did it sell for? Also, if a similar painting (same subject matter, same year, same size) went up at auction, what was the price at which bidding opened? And what did it actually sell for? By finding out this crucial

information, you walk away with a range of real prices, true assessments of resale value versus fantasy prices.

Once, I was offered a painting that had sold two years earlier at auction for $250,000. What is the price the New York art dealer quoted me? $1,250,000. Well, art is a valuable investment, but nothing appreciates $1 million and five times provable purchase value in two years. When I pointed that out to the dealer, she said, "Well, we think it's a masterpiece."

"You sure do," I replied. "You want to make $1 million in profit in two years' time."

They settled for half of the asking price. Had I not checked Artnet, my client would have paid much more.

5. Buy work from a reputable dealer. There are crooked, sleazy dealers sprinkled throughout the art world. The most important thing I have learned is not to put my blind trust in everything a dealer says. For instance, if a dealer tells me the experts say this painting is correct, I ask for those statements in writing.

. . .

Once I got these basics down, and found and developed my market, I moved into reselling with all my heart, knowledge, and expertise. Things really went swimmingly, in all facets of my life. I was doing lots of resale business, living in my dream house with two mellow older dogs, and enjoying life. I spent summers indulging in one concert after another, always taking a nice vacation somewhere in the country or world for a week or two. After a lifetime of family and other drama surrounding the holidays, those days were behind me. I no longer had any expectations from family members.

I usually spent Thanksgiving with friends, and Christmas at Mary MacNaughton's home.

Mary was the director of the Scripps College Museum in Claremont, whom I had met through ArtTable; I was now the Southern California chair, a decade after rejoining when I first moved to L.A. and turned to the organization and its members to help me network and meet people. I would go out to her place on Christmas Eve, then spend Christmas morning opening presents with them. No drama, just nice feelings. Best of all, Mary and I became great friends—just in time for another ArtTable drama.

CHAPTER 19

Knoedler Gallery Art Scam: The Biggest in My 50 Years in the Business

Art dealers work hard. We work very hard, and the more valuable the work we sell, the lower our commissions. We must know the paintings we seek and sell, their histories, and what makes them command the prices the market bears. We must know what our clients are looking for and how to obtain the work for them. All of this is predicated on a chain of trust—the client's trust in me, my trust in the person from whom I'm acquiring the work, and the trust of both parties in the provenance and authenticity of the painting or sculpture.

When that trust is shattered, it can take years to rebuild if you're lucky. More often than not, wholehearted trust is lost forever, and reputations are shattered.

This is why I, along with the entire art world, was brought to its knees by the Knoedler Gallery Art Scandal in the early 2010s. The scandal was so pervasive, and so bad, and so well publicized that it caused buyers to distrust dealers universally. It didn't matter how impeccable that dealer's reputation was—and I'd built my entire career on the fact you could trust me, no matter what, because I was a straight shooter and would play fair with you.

It didn't matter. I, like everyone else, had my trustworthiness called into question. Nothing could be more unfair, especially since I was 3,000 miles away from the mess and had no idea what was happening until the news broke. It didn't matter. Buyers and collectors looked at me with sideways glances for a while, just like they did every other dealer in the business.

How can a scandal that goes down on the East Coast impact an honest broker on the West Coast? When it comes to forged paintings, it forces everyone to look at the works hanging on their walls or in their galleries and museums, and ask themselves, *is this fake, too? And who did I obtain it from?*

Today, the Knoedler Gallery Art Scam remains the largest forgery scandal in modern art history. It's the subject of a riveting Netflix documentary, *Made You Look: A True Story About Fake Art*. The actor Alec Baldwin, who exposed Mary Boone's unsavory dealings from his own experience with her, joined *Vanity Fair* to put out an incredible six-hour podcast on Apple Podcasts, further detailing the Knoedler scam, *Art Fraud*.

Here's my account of what happened, why it turned the art world upside down—and why it made my life and that of other dealers really fucking difficult.

. . .

In the Fall of 2011, I got a call from another dealer. The dealer told me that Knoedler Gallery had closed amidst rumors that they had sold a number of fakes. *This can't be true*, I immediately thought. *Who comes up with this shit?* The oldest gallery in the United States, Knoedler, was founded in 1848 and occupied two townhouses at 19-21 East 70th Street in Manhattan. Over the years, they have shown all the greats, including Rothko, de Kooning, Motherwell, and Pollocks, in beautiful exhibitions. It just couldn't be.

So, I investigated.

Knoedler has always had legendary clients, but most importantly, in 1977, they employed Ann Freedman, who was a cold, cut-throat, very business-oriented sales queen. And also very good. I knew Ann in the 1970s, when she went to work for the Andre Emmerich Gallery right out of college. They hired her as a receptionist, and then she climbed the ladder because of her sales ability. However, she was loathed by the staff. She didn't have a friend on it. So, it was no surprise to anyone in the industry when she went to Knoedler.

After struggling financially in the late 1960s, Knoedler Gallery was purchased by Occidental Petroleum chief Armand Hammer in 1971 for $2.5 million. He hired his grandson, Michael, who knew nothing about art. Not exactly the preferred *bonafide* for a gallery director, but Armand was smart enough to hire Lawrence Rubin and John Richardson. Larry Rubin was the brother to Bill Rubin, the chief curator at the Museum of Modern Art, and a respected dealer. John Richardson was an art historian who wrote a definitive four-volume set on the life and work of Picasso. Knoedler needed new blood to get off the mat as a third-rate gallery. Now they had it.

Michael then brought in the final piece to make the gallery prosperous again—Ann Freedman. She started to sell immediately. Larry had great relationships with artists and kept the prestigious Diebenkorn estate, along with renowned artists Robert Rauschenberg and

Frank Stella, in the gallery. When Larry was forcibly retired in 1994, Michael gave Ann the first crack at directing the gallery. Rather than arrange for Larry to work from his estate in Italy with artist and art historian Donald Saff, which Larry had requested, Michael decided to promote Ann. However, her reputation at Emmerich was also her reputation at Knoedler: She built no relationships with artists, and many clients hated her. She also did not get along particularly well with other dealers.

When that happened, the gallery quickly lost the works of the Diebenkorn, Rauschenberg, and Stella estates. Michael's decision sealed Knoedler's fate.

Right after that, the seeds of a great scandal began to be planted.

Jaime Adrotti, a long-time Knoedler employee, met Glafiria Rosales at an opening in SoHo, and they became friends. Glafiria mentioned to Jaime that she had in possession any number of Abstract Expressionist works for sale. Jaime introduced Glafiria to Ann—and the wheels started turning.

It began with a single painting, a Diebenkorn that Glafiria gave Ann. Ironic since Diebenkorns had hung in the Knoedler until Ann took over. Glafiria said they were owned by a Mr. X., Jr. (not the real name), who had inherited them from his Filipino parents. Initially, Glafiria said the parents were guided by Alfonso Ossorio, a wealthy artist who lived in the Hamptons (who has since died). Had she said that to me, I would've researched the hell out of the provenance, who truly owned the pictures, and made sure Diebenkorn actually painted them.

That's not what Ann did. Instead, she took Glafiria's word for it, and sold the painting.

Then Glafiria came to Ann and informed her Ossorio had offered up some Jackson Pollocks, with whom Ossorio was close. She said they were bought directly from the artist's studio for cash, and then sent to the Philippines. No taxes had been paid. Now I don't know about you, but enough red flags to outfit a flag team are shooting up in front of my eyes just writing this.

Ann saw something else in her eyes—dollars. Big dollars. The dollars needed to get Knoedler out of its current financial predicament. She did no further research and grabbed the paintings. She did ask Glafiria to introduce her to the collector, Mr. X, Jr., and Glafiria promised she would do so, but it never happened. In the meantime, Ann thought she was pulling a scam on Glafiria because she paid very little for the paintings compared to their known market value. Ann then marked them up to that full retail value, making 600 to 800% profit per painting.

The truth is, they were scamming each other. Ann just didn't know it yet.

During this time, a private couple, Jack and Fran Levy, also bought a lot of paintings from Ann through Knoedler. At one point, they were shown a 1949 Jackson Pollock, a small silver drip painting, which Glafiria offered for $4.1 million. Doing his due diligence, Jack Levy insisted Knoedler contact IFAR.

At Jack Levy's insistence and noting the lack of provenance, IFAR scholars got to work. First, they conducted a detailed lab examination of the painting. They looked into Ossorio and asked his former lover if Ossorio ever helped a couple from the Philippines to procure art—and then named the paintings. "No," the lover said definitively. There went the Ossorio connection.

IFAR came back and told Jack Levy that the Pollock wasn't right and they couldn't get behind the authentication. Levy returned the painting to Knoedler, and they refunded him the money.

Blinded and enraged by the loss of a $4 million sale, Ann was convinced IFAR was wrong. She called David Mirvish, a famous Toronto dealer, with an offer to buy a one-third interest in the work. Ann assured him she would personally buy one-third interest, putting her own skin in the game, and the gallery would buy the other third.

Now, any worthwhile dealer would look at the IFAR conclusions seriously and wonder if not only Pollock, but all the work coming from Glafiria, was fake. Ann did ask Glafiria again about Ossorio, and the collector. This time, Glafiria changed her story. She said the actual private dealer was not Ossorio at all, but David Herbert, who had died in 1995. Ironically, the estate executor was none other than Jaime Adrotti, the Knoedler employee. Small world, huh? David had worked in many galleries in the 1950s and was involved in helping artists get paid by making cash sales directly from the studio.

That was enough to convince Ann. She continued to work with Glafiria. However, Ann was not totally naïve. Her own suspicions were growing. She expressed concern about the situation with Michael Hammer, who replied, "Don't kill the goose that's laying the golden egg."

What a golden egg it was. At this point, Knoedler was making millions, a cash flow they hadn't seen in decades—if ever in their 150-year history.

Then, a large drip Jackson Pollock came from Glafiria and they priced it at $17 million. Pierre Le Grange, the buyer, wanted guarantees. Ann said they would return the painting if any real expert concluded it was a fake. That was not enough to satisfy Le Grange. Ann met with the Pollock Foundation, after which she told Le Grange they would update the Catalogue raisonné, include the painting, and reproduce the catalogue in color. Le Grange nodded his head to that, and he bought the painting.

Only one problem: you don't update the *catalogue raisonné* unless there's a lost treasure or archaeological find. These catalogues are the verifiable body of work an artist produces in their life. Once published, no paintings are added. It makes your head spin, doesn't it?

This was just getting started. Next up was a collection of Robert Motherwell's *Elegies to the Spanish Republic,* a set of 108 paintings he produced between 1948 and 1967. He painted them as a lamentation, or funeral song of sorts, to the Spanish Civil War, which had taken place in the 1930s. The metaphoric works contrasted life and death, and the relationship between the two. They are profound and powerful, right from the great artist's soul.

Well, in 2009, one Jack Flam kept seeing paintings from this collection pop up, in multitudes. *How could that be?* he wondered. All 108 works were prized treasures. Jack happened to run the Daedalus Foundation, otherwise known as the Motherwell Estate. He asked to authenticate a few of the paintings he saw, which he deemed authentic. Then he demanded to review all seven. The Daedalus Foundation hired Jamie Martin to do a thorough lab analysis of the paintings. Martin found a pigment that had not yet been invented in Motherwell's day. Clearly, the work under examination had been painted later—and not by Motherwell. All seven were declared inauthentic, and the lawsuits started flying.

In the Fall of 2009, it came to a head that Michael Hammer got wind of the fake Motherwells, and that Knoedler had sold the majority of the fake paintings, so he fired Ann.

Then the second big domino fell, in the form of Pierre Le Grange's marriage. He was in the middle of a divorce and trying to unload the Pollock he'd bought from Knoedler. Neither Sotheby's or Christie's would take the painting. The word was getting out. Then Le Grange remembered Ann's promise to take back the work if he knew it was a fake, and he went to Knoedler. But she was fired, and the gallery wouldn't refund him. He screamed Holy Hell.

A year later, Ann surfaced from rather deep hiding and met Le Grange for a drink at New York's Carlyle Hotel. She didn't offer to buy back the painting but offered to accept it on consignment and resell it to another buyer. Le Grange was astounded that she would have the audacity to pass the "fake" Pollock off to another buyer. But that was Ann. Where money was concerned, she would do whatever it took to make it—and everything she could to not give it back.

Understandably, Le Grange went ballistic and threatened to ruin Ann. He knew what he knew because of the news breaking about the Motherwell fakes. He promptly hired Jamie Martin to look at his Pollock; Martin said it was a fake. Then Eugene Thaw, one of three authentication experts in the Pollock Foundation, confirmed Martin's findings.

Game. Set. Match. Le Grange sued—and Michael Hammer immediately closed the Knoedler Gallery after 152 years of continuous operation.

Now that the top was knocked off the proverbial hornet's nest, the hornets flew out, and they were screaming. Before Knoedler's closed, Domenico and Eleanore de Sole visited to buy a Sean Scully painting. Ann told them she did not have a Scully but offered a fabulous Mark Rothko instead. Domenico was about to retire as President and CEO of Gucci, and about to take the same role at Tom Ford. They talked to their consultant, Jim Kelly, who owned a gallery in Santa Fe, New Mexico, an art haven set within the oldest city in America, its Spanish architecture and purple mountain setting pleasing to the eyes and health. Jim Kelly happens to be the most honest direct dealer in the business. He went to Ann and asked questions. She told him any number of experts authenticated the painting—and then named names. Jim believed her, and approved the sale of the Rothko for $8.4 million.

After they got the painting home, Eleanore de Sole read the Motherwell and Le Grange lawsuits. She literally screamed. Dominick immediately hired art fraud layers, who demanded documentation. Within those documents, they immediately noticed Knoedler's profits from the deal. They brought in Jaime Martin, who looked at their Rothko and declared it a fake. By this point, Martin had access to 18 of the 41 works Glafira had sold Ann; all were fakes.

Jim Kelly told me that the de Sole did everything possible not to sue Knoedler. They offered to take other inventory, even to let

Knoedler reimburse them over time. Very nice people, aren't they? But Knoedler's counsel backed them into a corner and left them no choice.

In 2013, they sued Knoedler, Ann Freedman, Michael Hammer, Glafiria Rosales, and Glafiria's boyfriend, Carlos Bergantinos, The whole lot.

. . .

Of particular concern to me were the fake Pollocks. And, in particular, those in the David Herbert collection. Everyone knew fake Pollocks were exhibited as early as 1984-85 in the Knoedler Booth at the ADAA art fair, but no one would say anything because they knew they would get sued. And when IFAR came back with its conclusions that the works were fake, the experts felt they were right after all.

So many times, I'd go to Carter Radcliff and be offered a Pollock. He's a friend, but he would tell me, "I can't authenticate it at this time."

I looked at him incredulously. *Why the fuck would I work with a painting that wasn't authenticated?* He knew that.

"We're friends!" I fired back.

"I can't authenticate it," he said sheepishly. Like everyone else, he didn't want to get sued.

As for Ann, she was so possessed by the almighty buck that she actually bought a Pollock from Glafiria Rosale and the signature was spelled "Pollok." How could you buy a painting with the name spelled wrong? There were so many red flags.

. . .

Finally, the feds and New York law enforcement stepped in. Glafiria was arrested after making some $26 million off the scam. She was taken to jail. Her boyfriend, Carlos Bergantinos was in Spain, where he was able to avoid extradition because Spain and the United States did not have an extradition treaty for non-capital crimes. White-collar crimes like art fraud need not apply.

After several weeks in jail, Glafiria told the truth about the scam they perpetrated on Ann Freedman, Knoedler, and the art world—and what a story it was. Evidently, Carlos met a Greenwich Village street painter, Pei Shun Quong, in the mid-1990s and convinced him to make fakes. At first, Quon's works were not great, but Glafiria encouraged him to work on his craft until he could become a (near) masterful forger. So he did. In addition, they stained the canvases to make them look older, utilized old nails that were prevalent in the middle of the 20th century, and then Pei Shun Quong imitated the signatures of all of the artists on the bottom right-hand corner. They sold fakes and paid no taxes.

When the shit hit the fan, Peii Shun Quong fled to his native China, which most certainly doesn't have an extradition treaty with the United States. So both he and Bergantinos were out of harm's way, dumping the entire punishment to come onto Glafiria.

When the trial happened, Knoedler got its karmic comeuppance: no expert was willing to testify on their behalf. Why would they? You testify to the purported authenticity of fakes, and you, too, are out of the business. I watched art historian Irving Sandler, the expert of experts on Abstract Expressionism, and author of The Triumph of American Painting, testify. He told the court that when asked to review the paintings, he was given 30 seconds. If Ann had truly wanted authentication, he testified, he would have arrived with a magnifying glass to authenticate them and gotten IFAR involved.

The trial was falling apart for the culprits. The day before Ann was to testify, the defendants settled. Glafiria received credit for time served and then was ordered to pay the victims $81 million. Of course, had Bergantinos and Quong been arrested and sat as co-defendants, as they should have, then they would have split that

$81 million debt. Glafiria told authorities that every time she tried to quit the scam, Bergantinos would threaten to take her daughter to Spain and never see her again. He also beat her, according to Glafiria. I'm not surprised.

I'm not sure how you pay back $81 million with a waitress job in Queens, which is where Glafiria works and lives with her daughter today. But that's something she should've thought of before deciding to perpetrate a monstrous scam.

Once the dust settled, Ann Freedman opened a gallery on the Upper East Side. Who on earth would do business with her? She is shunned at art fairs and just walks around with her assistant, looking at work. That assistant happens to be Bill O'Reilly. It was as if working with the convicted Larry Salander, who did prison time, was not enough. Can you imagine? Now, he works for Ann Freedman.

. . .

What a terrible stain on the profession. An honest art dealer would never have believed the provenance and checked into it thoroughly. They would have had IFAR look at the work sooner. And the profits made? Unimaginable. Everyone knows that the more expensive things are, the less you make. I once sold a Rodin sculpture for $1.2 million, and only received a $40,000 commission.

This was a horrible lesson to learn.

In my world, it made my clients suspicious. That's why I tell anyone who will listen, "Just just check the provenance."

I once sold a Rockwell for the same woman who owned the Innis painting, which I mentioned before. The origin of the Rockwell is a great story. We're talking about the famous painting called "The Auctioneer." One time, when Norman Rockwell was in California, he had a toothache. Like most young (at the time) artists, he didn't have any money. He couldn't afford the dental work. So, he made the painting in exchange for the dentist's services. Well, as the circles of life would have it, the woman who owned the Innis was the daughter of the dentist! I also checked with the Rockwell Museum, and they were delighted the Auctioneer had resurfaced.

I sold the painting for $125,000. It's worth half a million now. I had all the authenticity and provenance I needed right there. And that's what you need—a clean, indisputable line of ownership and equally undisputed authenticity that the work in your hand was made by the artist himself or herself.

I made about ten percent on the Rockwell, and as I said earlier, only $40,000 on a $1.2 million Rodin. You don't make 600 to 800 percent profit like Ann Freedman did. As for GR, she was taking less money than market value because she knew the works she was reselling were fakes. She still walked away with $25 million. If that doesn't raise every red flag in the house, nothing will.

It made us all look like sleaze bags. Internationally, the story was well known. To this day, buyers who have never bought anything before ask where I obtained paintings. I immediately tell them the five steps to take that I outlined in the previous chapter. Lesson learned? Don't put your trust exclusively in the dealer.

CHAPTER 20

Art Table Redux: From 12 Members to 1,200

I'm a huge believer in networking, which is a good thing, since without strong contacts and networks, you don't last long in this business. Being an outgoing, social person who loves engaging with others on everything from culture, music, sports, movies, and life to art (of course), I also find networking a wonderful way to make and keep friendships and to meet people from all walks of life that might not otherwise touch mine. When you're in the art world, that means meeting people from all over the world, who have succeeded and/or achieved greatness in all sorts of ways.

In that spirit, I made my move to California a lot easier by reconnecting with the networking and business support group I'd co-founded in New York in 1979. By the time I rejoined ArtTable in 1990, it had grown to hundreds of members, with chapters all over the country. I became part of the Southern California chapter, which helped me immensely as I established a deeper network in the LA and California art world. Plus, I was delighted to be part of ArtTable again and to see how much it grew.

Now in its 44th year, ArtTable is without question one of the most important things to happen for women in the art business and for students, artists, and advocates of art in all public and private sectors making their way up the ladder. When I look back on my life and see decisions made that really made a difference, this is one of them. Despite our lofty visions and aspirations, I'm not sure any of the twelve of us who met at Peng's Restaurant in 1979 could imagine so many thousand women and students of art, art history, and art business throughout this country and world would directly and indirectly from our decision to form a networking organization. But that's what happened, and it feels great to know I was an integral part of it.

Obviously, in 1990, it was a different organization than what I co-founded. Because of that, I was able to work toward fulfilling some of the larger goals I had; I also went much further in the organization than I had before and put in another 13 years, which turned into quite a story in itself.

My second stint began with Ellie and I going to the monthly meetings. In 1991, we traveled to Palm Springs and met Mary Mac-Naughton and her husband, Sperry. Mary served as President of ArtTable from 1999 to 2000, a great and tireless advocate for our cause nationwide. She regularly arose at 5 a.m. to prepare for important meetings, which didn't happen until much later in the day. I quickly found her a delight to talk to and be around, and she became my best friend. We continue to get together whenever she's visiting from her home in Utah.

While President on the all-important 20th anniversary year, Mary oversaw the various chapter chairs, including an active crew in California. During her year at the top, ArtTable welcomed a couple of wonderful discussions and events to continue an increasingly impressive list of them. There was an important discussion led by Northern California Chapter Co-Chairs Josi Callan and Jacquelynn Bass on "Women Museum Directors: Successes/Challenges/Insight," and ArtTable also contributed to a campus conference at my alma mater, Rutgers University, on "Arts Transforming the Urban Environment." But even more importantly, Carol Covington, Louise Gregory, and Ruth Braunstein founded *The Oral History Project,* to tape stories of accomplished women in the arts. A few years later, it was substantially upgraded when the Archives of American Art at the Smithsonian Institution came in as a partner; now these tapes are historical documents, as they should be.

. . .

These are just a few things that happened in one year out of the first 20. I was so impressed.

Mary did another thing during her term: she hired future Executive Director Katie Hollander. Let's just say Katie and I didn't see eye-to-eye from the get-go, nor did she see eye-to-eye with a lot of other prominent members—especially if you were not based in New York. It didn't take too long for all of us to feel the receiving end of Katie's temper. When it flared, along with her defensiveness, watch out. And it flared whenever there was any pushback on initiatives she tried to run through, no matter how popular or unpopular to members. She had no problem doing things unilaterally, which didn't square with the collaborative nature of ArtTable, a part of our culture since we met at Peng's to get this whole thing started. Her disagreements and confrontations got so bad that, during her first year, ArtTable paid for her to attend anger management classes.

My contentious personal history with Katie began right away. After Mary hired Katie, she got to work on planning for the 20th anniversary luncheon gala. Then she did something unconscionable, when she got around to recognizing Founding Members: she failed to include me. Apparently, she'd gone off the rote and not exactly 100 percent memory of a long-term member (whose name I will not mention) in her 80s. I mean, how hard is it to know the names of the twelve people who started the organization you now serve as president? Or to look it up in ArtTable records if you don't know?

Consequently, for the gala, she would not allow Ali Anderson or myself to be recognized as Founding Members until Joyce Schwartz, Lowery Sims, and others vouched for us. "Wait a minute!" Lowery protested. "Patty Hamilton brought me in! She is a Founding Member."

Lowery's words carried major weight. Thankfully, it was straightened out.

A few years later, in 2003, I was in charge of the Southern California Program Committee. My peers loved the fact that a Founding Member was taking such a direct interest in the 21st century, and I loved my increased involvement in an area near and dear to me—creating programs for tomorrow's leaders in the art world and business of art. ArtTable President Kathleen McCumber called and asked if I'd become the Southern California Chapter Chair for 2004-2005, the 25th anniversary year. I thought, *how cool is that? A Founding Member chairing her home chapter on the silver anniversary?* I was all in.

When I took over as Southern California Chapter Chair a year later, I was able to advance a project they'd started before that I really liked, the summer internship programs. There were a number of active programs nationally. Every summer, we award internships for $3,000 per person in L.A. and New York, which also includes studying directly with an ArtTable member. One year, the award went to journalist and art critic Hunter Drohojowska-Philp, who was writing the book *Rebels in Paradise: The Los Angeles Art Scene and the 1960s.* Hunter later told me that she couldn't have written the book without our internship (a great book, too; it was published by Henry Holt in 2011). She's gone on to write several other books and has put in a highly respected 40-plus year career. These are the outcomes that made every bit of this project worthwhile to me.

But Hunter wasn't alone. Not by a long shot. The applications Mary, myself, and other committee members reviewed every year were unbelievable. These people were so ambitious! They started art programs at schools; they were Grade A students before that, and in every case, I would have been happy to go anywhere near them. They were really, really impressive. The internships were a great program.

The other support initiative I really liked was an AirBnB program. You could stay with an ArtTable member when you traveled to New York or other places, which saved a lot of money, to say the least, not to mention the tutelage and mentorship the recipient would receive through that quality one-on-one time with a mover and shaker in the art business. ArtTable later discontinued that program, but I saw it in action pretty directly. During the 1999 luncheon gala, my secretary wanted to go to New York, but she couldn't afford a hotel. So she stayed with an Art Table board member in Spanish Harlem, which made the whole experience complete for her.

Likewise, the ArtTable lunches in NY were amazing. There was great schmoozing, great speakers and discussions, and the *crème de la crème:* The Distinguished Service to the Visual Arts Award, which we started in 1993. One year, Paula Cooper got it. In another, Lowery Sims won. They also began the New Leadership Award. As for the speakers, they ranged from national icons like Hillary Rodham Clinton and Gloria Steinem to women who worked hard and became distinguished in our field, and then advanced their knowledge through schools, businesses, or community programs to touch hundreds or thousands of others.

At the 20th anniversary luncheon, the New Leadership Award went to Sarah Lewis, who was so impressive. A scholar, she wrote books and was incredibly smart. In her acceptance speech, she talked about unfortunate beginnings, once being ignored because of her skin color when she walked into a fancy shoe store. She was so elegant. Violet Davis is elegant. Later, she ended up living with the famed jazz musician Wynton Marsalis. I invited her to stay at my house whenever she visited the West Coast. I was very, very impressed with her.

Some programs came and went, like the AirBnB program, but ArtTable always looked for new initiatives. Years later, in 2019, they introduced the Career Roundtable Program, which gives college students mentorships with an ArtTable member. I could only smile with a great deal of personal fulfillment and gratification when I heard about this. A lot of programs had developed since the other 11 women and I founded ArtTable back in 1979. They were really positive and worthwhile. Our vision of imparting our experiences and knowledge to help the next generation become art business leaders and our overall theme of networking was really growing.

In fact, as I stepped into the Southern California Chapter chairmanship, ArtTable welcomed its 1,200th member—a hundred-fold increase from our dinner at Peng's. We had fantastic chapter chairs all over the country; I felt so privileged to be counted among them and also very proud as one of the godmothers of this whole organization. The chapter chairs would arrange visits before major openings, including select walkthroughs with the curators, and would also arrange garden visits. Plus host important discussions and seminars. They were terrific. Even the monthly board meetings I conducted were wonderful; I really liked a lot of the women. I met Maria Luisa de Herrera, who ended up taking over for me. She was classy and did a really good job, and we became friends. It's hard for me to count how many friends I made through both my stints at ArtTable.

. . .

However, not everything was perfect. In New York, an Executive Director took over when I became the Southern California Chapter Chair—Katie Hollander. The one and the same. *Shit.*

My established Founding Member status has long since been reaffirmed. Our 25th Anniversary event rolled around: "Looking Back-Moving Forward: 25 Years of Women's Leadership in the Visual Arts." I'd been honored to step up to the Southern California Chapter Chairmanship on this special year. And this time, I was duly recognized as a Founding Member, which of course meant the world to me.

Sadly, Katie and I weren't done. Before the event, we held an auction. While we were preparing for the April 2005 luncheon, Diane Frankel asked me to come up with an item to offer for the post-event auction, which would take place online six months later. I had an idea: The famed gardener and landscape architect Robert Dash designed my home garden, among many others. "How about a Robert Dash garden tour?" I suggested. "It will increase the value of the auction winner's house greatly." This is what Robert Dash garden tours do.

Diane loved the idea, and we placed the initial bid at $5,000—Robert's typical price. I thought we would easily exceed that figure, and the recipient would be thrilled to receive a Dash Garden tour. As it turned out, the winning bidder never got the tour. Here's what happened:

Six months later, when the online auction took place, a member of Art Table said she would pay $2,000 for a Dash garden tour at her home in the Hamptons. She knew exactly how much a Dash critique would positively impact the value of her property. Without bothering to see what she could get in the auction, our auctioneer for the day, Katie Hollander, *sold it! For three grand below the opening bid!* Without talking to me.

I went fucking ballistic. I called her on my cell phone. *"Call fucking me!* I am very upset."

She returned my call. "Well, we couldn't get $5,000, so I sold it for two," she said.

"You couldn't have sold it for two, because he makes his living giving garden tours for $5,000. You couldn't have done it without talking to me first."

"Well, where does it say that?" she asked.

"On every Sotheby's or Christie's record available," I said. "You've never run an auction, and you don't know what the fuck you're doing."

I promptly withdrew the Dash Garden tour from the Art Table President. Can you imagine how insulted Robert would have been? I also made sure someone besides me told the buyer, since the deal was between her and Katie.

Once that unpleasantry was finished, I got on the phone with Diane Frankel. "I'm not only withdrawing this from the auction, but I find Katie so incredibly offensive, the way she talks down to me. I'm a founding fucking member!" I said, my voice quite loud. "We have the catalogue and program for the 25th anniversary coming out. I was going to buy a full-page ad. Because of Katie, I will not be taking that ad any longer. So Katie has cost you $5,500 as of now."

A few days later, Katie apologized to me by postcard. *Un-unh. No way.*

Later, a major ArtTable event was held in San Francisco. Mary Kay Lyon, the ArtTable chair who headed up the San Francisco tour, informed me that Katie wanted to direct the bus traffic from New York. Among other things, she didn't know there were one-way streets in San Francisco. Who does that? Also, it was an expensive

$250 lunch, and she didn't want to serve dessert. Mercedes Mader was the guest entertainer and did an act from her Broadway show at the time, so her fee was considerable, but it didn't matter. *You serve dessert at a $250 lunch!*

Need I go on? Well, there was one more thing—During the 25th anniversary meetings, we voted for a $5,000 raise for the chapter chairs who worked near the home office in New York, plus Katie. We also voted a $2,000 raise for all the out-of-town chapter chairs who directly assisted in event preparation, which involved work in a lot of areas—event setup, securing speakers and entertainment, producing the catalogue, coordinating the schedule, the auction, and more. Katie unilaterally decided the $2,000 raise was irrelevant and refused to give another penny to the out-of-towners. Why? Because they weren't based in New York.

I called Diane Frankel. "You either give me that raise, or all of the chapter chairs are leaving, and you're going to end up with a New York chapter only," I said, my feet dug in like a high-rise cornerstone.

After we hung up, I decided, *that was it*. Three strikes. Make that four. Time to swing into action for the sake of the organization's future.

I organized all of the out-of-town chapter chairs, and we decided that we needed a mediator to try to get through to Katie. The mediator spoke to all sorts of people within the organization before arriving at the clear conclusion that Katie could not continue. We'd already sent her to anger management classes. She was never going to respect any out-of-towners. She had no problem making unilateral decisions, which is not how groups with boards, national chapters, and chairs typically operate. Or operate at all, for that matter. We held a video conference meeting and universally decided to fire her. Linda Sweet, who was then the Governance Chair and soon-to-be President, in the business of hiring people, was tasked with sensitively firing Katie. We directed her to offer a generous severance package and a glowing recommendation for her future endeavors, focusing on her achievements rather than her difficulties. Each of us rose above our personal anger and took this step with kindness in mind.

After we gave Linda the details, she went to Katie, who was sitting outside, waiting to hear the outcome of our meeting.

"How did I do?" Katie asked.

"You're fired," Linda said. She said it just like that. So much for sensitivity and kindness.

. . .

Katie grew hysterical, which is to be expected if that's the tone in which you learned your years of hard work were over. Linda Sweet handled it as badly as she could. At the next New York chapter meeting, Katie was still hysterical, and the members were understandably sympathetic to her. Unfortunately, they all directed their gaze toward Los Angeles—and blamed me. Prior to the meeting, Linda Sweet just so happened to leave for vacation. How convenient.

In response, I wrote an angry letter to all the people in the New York chapter. Thankfully, I showed it to Mary and Sperry MacNaughton, who calmed down the tone and some of the wording before I sent it. Several nights later, at about 9:30 p.m., while in the middle of watching a Dodger baseball game on TV with friends, Diane Frankel called, furious as hell. "I need to talk to you!" she screamed.

"Not right now. I have company. I'll talk to you tomorrow." Afterward, I thought, *what conversation starts out well with an angry beginning?* I never called her back.

I had about six months left in my term as the Southern California Chair. Linda Sweet, the new president, flew out to California and met with all the chapter chairs and the board of trustees. She made sure not to invite me. She shut me down and out. It was so awful. I thought, *this is a bitchy organization run by Type A-personality women, and I've got one of them. I can't stay in this.*

When my term ended later in 2005, so did my ArtTable membership. I will always be a fan of the great people in the organization, the programs and will always cheer on the young people who are served by them, but as for being an active member? No thanks. I've had my fill.

CHAPTER 21

Sam Simon Suit

The longer you do resale, and do it well, the easier it is to find good art deals. It's very much a "who you know" proposition, as well as what you know: Sellers know that you have clients and get results. This is why networking, reputation, and integrity go hand in hand in this business and why I've fiercely protected and nurtured all three in my 50-year career. Sometimes, in a way that leaves others scratching their heads, but that's life when you do business with me: Let's either do it right, or don't bother. I stick my neck on the line every time I make a deal.

Such was the case one Christmas when I received a call from Les Firestein, an old client. He introduced me to a friend looking for photorealism works, Sam Simon. Normally, when red flags go up for me, they start flying after I've met the person and realized they do things in a way far different from mine. However, I was warned about Sam by everyone I knew.

Sam Simon has a culturally important claim to fame in the way a groundbreaking television show format and content with a 30-plus year network run can open up a whole new genre of shows: Sam was one of the three creators of *The Simpsons*, which led to a host of adult-content animated series with impressive runs of their own, though 30 years is unprecedented. It has set records as the longest animated series, longest sitcom, and longest run of original episodes in television history; the only series that tops it in longevity is *60 Minutes.* However, Sam didn't play nice: after the first season, he was thrown off the show for being so mean and ended up in litigation for years.

Finally, all parties settled—and what Sam received was legendary. In order to make him go away, the remaining two partners gave Sam *lifetime residuals* on the show. Lifetime means lifetime. He was paid residuals until the day he died for each of the more than 730 original episodes broadcast to date (as of May 2022), every rerun and syndicated showing of *The Simpsons,* even though he hasn't worked on the show since 1990. After that smashing legal success, Sam felt that lawsuits were the only way to handle every difficult situation.

Like I said, I was warned about Sam by everyone I knew. I was told he was the biggest prick in Hollywood. That is saying something! I heard one bad story after another, all from people I thoroughly trusted. One of the worst tales came from the wife of a famous Hollywood attorney. Her husband sat next to Sam at a dinner party when Sam told the story of his parents' divorce. Apparently, Sam's father asked his son if he could stay in his guest house while he figured things out, which is not an easy thing for anyone going through a divorce. Sam told his father, "I'd rather burn it down."

The lawyer was so disgusted that he changed seats.

When I met with Sam, his first interest was in buying photorealism works. The first painting I sold him was a Mel Ramos, owned by Louis Meisel. Ramos was a figurative painter who blended realist and abstract art in his paintings, primarily of female nudes. Books on his work include *The Girls of Mel Ramos, Mel Ramos Pop Art Fantasies* (with his portrait of a '60s-era model sitting in a martini glass on the cover, done very stylishly), *Mel Ramos: Heroines, Goddesses,*

Beauty Queens, and *Mel Ramos: The Definitive Catalogue raisonné,* featuring another stylish cover of a blonde peeking out from a body-length Cohiba cigar. PG-13 level covers. You get the picture. I sold Sam several works from Meisel's collection.

Later, he bought a John Singer Sargent portrait of the mother of his lover. I love Sargent's work, and this work was glorious—a great buy. Then Sam called me and wanted to build a sculpture garden, so I sold him a Rodin, a Max Ernst, and a Robert Graham, among others.

So far, I was impressed with his interests and the works he bought through me. I deeply respect all of the artists, and it always gives me great fulfillment to watch these works go to new homes and be appreciated and adored for many more years for the gems they are.

However, I struggled with his personality and his legendary mean streak. His reputation in show business was as bad as it was everywhere else. If he were a director of a TV show, he would walk into the writer's room and consider it his mission to torture the newest, worst-paid writer on the show. On many occasions, the writer burst into tears and left the job, and one can only wonder how that trauma impacted their careers moving forward.

All of this was in my mind as I worked out my commission fees to charge him. I was emotionally done with men like this and didn't know how I could handle that type of treatment if it were directed at me. In the end, I rose above my trepidation and went with my typically optimistic viewpoint. If I was completely honest with him, made him fall in love with his purchases, and only charged him a minimal commission, what could go wrong?

Well, silly me.

Soon enough, something did go wrong—and we ended up in litigation. It began with a *60 Minutes* episode featuring Sam. He and the interviewer strolled around his sculpture garden, which included the Rodin, Max Ernst, and Robert Graham sculptures I had secured for him. Someone from the State Board of Equalization saw the show and wondered if he paid any taxes. In response, he told the State Board that I was responsible for his taxes. When a State Board representative told me of this, I literally laughed. I have never paid taxes for a client, ever.

. . .

So Sam sued me.

I learned from Les Firestein that nothing made Sam happier than destroying "little people." Despite my reputation as one of the top art businesswomen on both coasts, through all of my career iterations from curator and gallery owner to agent and reseller, he saw me as a little bug he could squash. Maybe it was my 5-foot-4 height; I don't know. It's very hard to do any business when one of the richest guys in L.A. is suing you. It seems no amount of money you paid to lawyers made any difference. He wanted to destroy me.

It was a completely malicious lawsuit that went on for three years, the worst three years of my life. He sued me for what is called a "use tax." This is applied when the buyer purchases something outside of California and then puts it to use in California. It is paid by the client, not the dealer. My attorney, Rafael Bernardino, assumed that the State of California nailed Sam for all sorts of "use tax," which is why he went after me so hard. Sam pummeled Raphael with motions daily, all designed for Raphael to get sick of fighting the suit.

I thought about a *Wall Street Journal* article I had read. It states that when you purchase a piece of art, you are paying not only for the stated sale price of the work itself but also for the additionals—framing, shipping, and tax. The full responsibility for all of the above sits with the person who purchases the work. When I worked with him, Sam would constantly ask me if the price was "all in." I assumed he meant, "Are you all in, Patty? And is the dealer you're buying it from all in?" Like the previous dealer and I are throwing ourselves and our wallets into the sale, too.

Well, "all in" is a poker term. I don't play poker. Sam assumed the price *included* framing, shipping, and tax. Now that would be silly. As I mentioned, I only made $40,000 on the Rodin I sold him for $1.25 million—just over a 3% commission. That's not much. If I had to pay sales tax on the $1.25 million? It would cost me more than twice the commission.

He didn't care. He was out for blood. After those three interminable years, I realized something: there was no way to fight such a lawsuit successfully with someone rich and vindictive. It was settled by my attorney, Rafael Bernardino.

From that, I learned an important lesson moving forward: never deal with people whose bad reputation precedes them.

Six months after my lawsuit was dismissed by the courts, I learned that Sam had Stage 4 colon cancer that had spread to all of his organs and brain. For years, he ruefully ignored all the symptoms his body sent him, which happens all too often. By the time he got to a doctor, it was too late. He died two years later while still in his 50s.

CHAPTER 22

How Art Fairs Transformed the Art World

Many people love attending art fairs, often events where dealers, buyers, collectors, and art enthusiasts from around the nation and world gather to admire and buy the works of artists they know, as well as check out breakthrough works by young artists.

I, too, enjoy really good art fairs and have gone to many, primarily to look for new work and to do business. My personal preferences have always been curating shows, dealing through galleries, and of course representing artists and works as a reseller. But still, even 40 years after I attended the early fairs, they can knock me off my feet, as the Frieze event in L.A. did early in 2022. Art fairs are a big part of the art world—even though they came perilously close to skidding to irrelevance in the face of the internet revolution in recent years.

. . .

Art fairs came into being in Europe while I owned the Hamilton Gallery, the fairs opening first in Cologne and then in Basel. I went to those in the 1980s, and loved the classiness and excitement of Art Fair Basel in particular. It wasn't long until New York caught on. I and others were more than delighted when the Art Dealers Association decided to hold a fair for members in 1988, during my first foray as an artist's agent. The ADAA fair quickly became a very classy affair, showing nothing but classy art, and it encouraged dealers to put on solo shows as well. It remains a great annual fair on Park and 60th. It is only open to ADAA members to exhibit every two years.

Then, in 1994, when I was working bi-coastally, four young dealers in New York—Matthew Marks, Paul Morris, Pat Hearn, and Colin de Land—organized a fair at the Gramercy Park Hotel as an effort to recover from the recession. It was a counterpart to the ADAA fair, focusing on younger galleries with less expensive art. They couldn't put nails in the walls; so much of the work leaned against walls and covered every inch of the rooms from the bathrooms to the kitchen. It was exciting, a huge success. The next year, they had 400 applicants and rented the Armory space. In the East 20s in Manhattan, Japanese art star Takashi Murakami flew a balloon over the newest fair, and it became packed and popular.

Then, the Armory rented both sides of the West Side Highway and held the Armory Fair in March, a day or two after the ADAA art fair. They held the fair in two massive tents and many galleries. Then COVID-19 happened. In September 2021, the Armory Fair decided to rent the Javits Center.

Art fairs were the first thing to fundamentally change the art world during my career. Prior to their arrival, nearly all business was conducted through galleries and auctions. With fairs coming aboard, though, artists and dealers realized they could sell to the larger world rather than only to individual galleries in the then-few

U.S. cities with substantial art presences, like New York, Chicago, San Francisco, LA, and Philadelphia. Chicago used to be a lively fair, and I twice exhibited there while owning Hamilton Gallery.

My timing was ideal: by the time the new art fairs launched in New York, I had closed the gallery and was deep into agenting, so having that worldwide market access was greatly beneficial to my artists and my ability to do business. It became even more so in the 1990s, when galleries were struggling mightily to maintain relevance, and I needed even more market reach since I was working with artists from both coasts. Timing is everything, right?

Yes, unless another sea change sweeps through that forces everyone to shift their perspective.

. . .

The next tidal wave broke in the years following the recession. Art fairs began losing their sweeping popularity, thanks to the 800-pound octopus, the internet. You can't replicate face-to-face human interaction online (sorry, Zoom fans), but you can reach a much broader audience. In particular, the search engine artnet.com, which had been created in the 1990s, was now ubiquitous. This website can trace the history of every painting that has been auctioned off, and the price paid for it. Previously, dealers would buy paintings at auction, double the price, then offer them to collectors. This was no longer possible.

Because of the internet, clients were instantly offered paintings and no longer had to go into galleries. Or fairs. A good client was offered 50 to 100 paintings a day, whether by email or Instagram.

Two years later, in 2008, the art world, like the world at large, was in the throes of the Great Recession. The stock market had crashed, many people had lost their jobs, and no one was buying art. Fairs were keeping galleries open, so that gallery owners could exhibit at booths and broaden their reach. However, the booths were tremendously expensive. A booth space would cost $10,000-$100,000. Then there was shipping, insurance, staff, and entertainment. By this time, art fairs had proliferated across the country; you could find a fair every month in one city after another. Buyers, collectors, and patrons literally were not going into galleries to see shows but choosing to attend art fairs instead. The deeper-pocketed dealers got into the act, doing up to ten fairs a year, while others didn't do any at all.

During that time, a Miami dealer was interviewed about Art Basel Miami Beach. He lives in Miami, so he doesn't have to worry about transportation or hotel costs—yet the fair costs him over $80,000. Granted, 90% of his business for the year was done at that fair, but $80,000 is an enormous investment to make in a very uncertain market.

Furthermore, dealers couldn't appreciably expand their clientele during the Great Recession. Not only did the fairs cost a fortune, but they were exhausting. They could really wear on you.

In 2012, Frieze New York opened during a particularly hot spell in May. Instead of turning on the air conditioning the night before to prepare for the heat of the next day, they chose to wait until morning. The tent grew hot as a greenhouse, which led to an expected outcome: overheated collectors left after a very short period of time. When Frieze offered exhibitors a 2.5% discount on their next Frieze fair, the exhibitors laughed. They upped the offer to 10%. Recently, Shane Campbell Gallery in Chicago sued Frieze for a full refund, saying the fair, whose average booth costs $125,000, was a disaster.

It looked like art fairs might be going the way of the dodo bird, affected by internet sales and the hot new/old game in town, the retooled auction houses. But it seems you can't keep a good thing down, and as I and others learned, our assessments of the decline of art fairs proved premature. In some ways, it took a new decade and a crippling pandemic—and its surprising aftermath.

· · ·

This led to the auction houses, which drove the final nail in the gallery's once-exalted position as the center of the art universe. In the same way, banks expanded to become financial institutions offering many brokerage services, swallowing up three types of business at once, auction houses expanded to add many things a gallery used to do. They engaged in private dealing in order to stay open year-round, not just on auction days. They also started holding solo exhibitions, and recently got into estate management for deceased artists. Why did well-known artists need a gallery, with Sotheby's and Christie's around?

In a nutshell, the art world became all about money. Did I ever twist in the wind about this? It flew against everything I believed and worked for. In its soul and essence, art is about great creative expression, not about who can make the most of it. But when investors buy art and hold it in warehouses to flip at an auction a year or two later, rather than hanging it prominently in their homes or offices and admiring it every time they pass by, then what is it but the latest commodity? It sickened me to watch more and more brokers reside in my beloved art world, one once almost entirely filled with art enthusiasts.

We saw this madness never before between 2015 and 2018, which not coincidentally is when the stock market flew through the roof and home sales also rocketed into the stratosphere. From 2000 to 2014, worldwide auction sales totaled $40 million. Over the next four years, they jumped to $850 million. To give you a quick snapshot of sales: in 2015, the *New York Times* reported that Christie's sold Modigliani's "Nu Couche" painted a century before, for $170.4 million. The same year, they sold Picasso's 1955 work "Le Femme d'Alger (Version O)" for $179.4 million—some $40 million more than its estimate. In 2013, Warhol's "Silver Car Crash (Double Disaster)" sold for $104.5 million. Sculpture also got into the act. Giacometti's "Pointing Man," a beautiful but razor-thin bronze piece, went for $141.3 million in 2015. He made it in 1947. What strikes me is that all of these works were made in the last century; we're not talking about Renaissance masters or the classic European art centuries (17th-18th-19th) here.

At the heart of these outrageous sales, and the countless others at lesser prices, was an ever growing stream of willing buyers. And the internet. People were buying lots of art on auction sites or through gallery websites. Things were going up for sale at internet auctions, and the sites took less commission than Sotheby's and Christie's. Many times, the collector bought pricey treasures sight unseen; all they needed to see was a high-quality, high-resolution JPEG. Not only that, but auctions used to stake their reputations on acquiring and selling treasures and masterpieces that had stood the test of time. Now, some take works that are only a year old. They're literally flipping pictures.

. . .

The art world is a mysterious and secretive business. It is the largest unregulated business in the world, other than prostitution, guns, or drugs. There are no rules or laws on how much profit a dealer can make. Generally, when an artist is represented by the gallery, the gallery pays all exhibition expenses and sometimes fabrication expenses, and the profits are split 50/50. Famous artists can demand a higher percentage: for example, Jasper Johns gave Leo Castelli only a ten percent commission at the end of his career. His multi-million dollar paintings were guaranteed to sell, so he was able to make that demand. And Castelli went along with it, because 10% of, say, $2 million definitely helps keep the gallery doors open.

Then we have resale, which is like a ride in the wild, wild west. Generally, when a client gives a painting to a dealer to resell, the gallery takes a 20% commission, which is equal to what I took at

Hamilton Gallery. Today, even if the buyer has it in writing, there is no guarantee that the gallery will honor the commission—and who knows? The dealer might have marked it up 100% on top of that! One of the things that infuriates me about all of this is how casually people act with the darkest intentions: dealers with dubious reputations will lie to your face. Nothing illustrates this more than the demise of the Knoedler Gallery after 160-plus years, which I laid out earlier. I mean, this was a gallery that once sold work to Cornelius Vanderbilt, JP Morgan, and Henry Frick, three juggernauts and creators of the Industrial Age.

After watching the breakdown of old-school gallery protocol, the new rules of doing business, internet-driven auctions and debacles like Knoedler, many people were getting sick of this new art world. More dominoes fell, and sadly, the people closing doors were some of the classiest acts in the business. Margot Leavin ran a first-rate gallery in West Hollywood for 40 years, and put on wonderful shows. She was also tremendously loyal to her artists. She chose to close in 2012, rather than go on the art-fair merry-go-round. She didn't become a dealer to do fairs. I couldn't help but admire her for that; I could not imagine myself ever having to buy booths for Hamilton Gallery. In 2015, David McKee, a distinguished New York dealer, closed for pretty much the same reason. Both of these dealers, their knowledge of the work, and their *love of art*, were irreplaceable losses. How do you replace 40-year commitments fueled by a deep, abiding love for the work?

Recently, another fine gallery owner, Lisa Cooley, closed her space in New York after eight years. A comment she made was quite poignant: "I have art-fair exhaustion and dealers have become roving merchants." As for the clients attending art fairs who were interested in buying? Exhibitors might be displaying in front of their faces, but they had plenty of invisible competition. As Lisa pointed out, these clients were also getting 30 to 40 JPEGS from dealers every day and being offered works on Instagram. She felt there was a glut on the market, and very little connoisseurship in the buying and selling art.

Consequently, all the middle galleries are being squeezed out of the market. By mid-2017, when CRG in New York and ACME Gallery in Los Angeles closed within a month, it was clear that things had changed. Both galleries had been in business for 25 years and were well-liked by everyone.

Galleries are no longer places buyers and collectors must visit to see great art or find their desired work. They can go online and to art fairs. No longer is a dealer willing to give an artist three shows before the selling starts, as Cy Twombly used to do at Leo Castelli. If a single show doesn't sell, the artist is out.

And yet, just as with art fairs, galleries found new ways to exist—with surprising results. It began with the rise of the "mega" gallery.

Larry Gagosian certainly led the way with this idea. Buoyed by a lot of money, Larry hosted exhibitions in his galleries, better described as "museum" shows. He even hired museum curators to produce the exhibitions. The first was the great Sir John Richardson, author of the eponymous five-volume Picasso biography series. Richardson, at age 90, curated one of the greatest shows ever, *Picasso and the Camera,* with the assistance of Castellani and Carey—one of several Picasso shows he did. At about the same time, Gagosian hired John Elderfield, the prominent curator-at-large at MoMA, to come on staff. In 2013, he organized his first show, a survey of early paintings by Helen Frankenthaler (Elderfield always had extraordinary taste). His Matisse show at the MoMA will never be equaled; it was a masterpiece. Gagosian also opened branch galleries all over the world, with 15 sparkling galleries in Europe, South America, and Asia.

Suddenly, the minute an artist was "hot," he was scooped up by one of the mega galleries and promoted worldwide. This is usually an artist's dream to be promoted globally. This is not the case with California artist Mike Kelley, a versatile artist who made drawings, paintings, installation art, sculpture, and performance videos for all the right reasons; he was a deep, sensitive, old-school creator of wonderful work. He also advocated for other artists. Kelley was highly influential; as Paul Schimmel, the chief curator for the Museum of Contemporary Art in Los Angeles, told the *Los Angeles Times*, "LA would not have become a great international capital of contemporary art without Mike Kelley. Of all the artists in the 1980s, he was the one who really broke out and established a new and complex identity for his generation." In particular, he greatly influenced the evolution and growth of installation art.

However, Kelley felt he had "sold out" going with Gagosian. He fell into a serious depression and didn't come out. Later, many friends and observers felt this decision contributed to his suicide in 2012 at the age of 57.

. . .

Along with the mega galleries came a generation of young dealers unlike anyone I had met in my career. These were 20- and 30-year-olds right out of college, many times with no art history background, opening galleries with Daddy's money, oftentimes unscrupulous, immoral, and untrustworthy.

One such dealer was a young man named Garth Greenan. Garth, a student of Mary MacNaughton's, befriended me over dinner. He wanted to know all about dealing. He was very bright and studied art history. In the summer after Garth's junior year of college, I found him a job working for my friend Mark Borghi in Mark's gallery in the Hamptons. Garth proved to be a terrific salesman but lacking in moral fiber. Frequently, he wouldn't tell the client a painting had not sold at auction, when in fact it did. Then he sold a painting out of the gallery—and didn't cut the gallery in on the deal! He did this at 20 years old. Already, he'd exhibited the sharkish demeanor of one who would do anything to make a sale, vis a vis Ann Freedman, and it drove Mark nuts. When Mark faced the prospect of hiring Garth back after he graduated, which he didn't really want to do, just two people warned him this was a bad idea—his wife and I. Still, Mark reluctantly hired him as a manager, owing to his ability to bring revenue to the gallery. It didn't take long before Mark found out he sold a painting to a client—and did not cut it in the gallery. *Again.* He was immediately fired for double-dealing. Later, Garth went to work for a dealer in Chelsea and squeezed the dealer out of his own gallery. Today, Garth owns another gallery in Chelsea, and I keep hearing one unethical story after another coming from that shop.

Garth reminds me of another young dealer, Vito Schnabel, the son of the artist Julian Schabel, and his work with one of my old artists, Ron Gorchov. I owned a painting by Ron and recently had it cleaned and restored. I told Vito I was interested in selling the piece and asked if he knew its worth. "$25,000 retail," he said. I noticed Vito was holding a show for Gorchov in London, so I did my due diligence and emailed to ask the price of a same-sized painting from the same year. Funny, the painting in London was $90,000. Who could be so stupid to think that the artist's former dealer wouldn't check the London price?

I went back to Vito. "When you're willing to make me a reasonable offer, I will consider selling the picture," I said. I wasn't going to play with this kid. He made a better offer and I sold him the picture, but I will never forget how sleazy he was.

In the 1970s through the first decade of this century, art dealers were friends or, at the very least, highly respectful of each other. We were comrades-in-arms in many ways, dining together, warning each other about difficult artists, and joining together to put on shows, since money didn't fly around the way it does today. A seemingly innocuous encounter I had at the Hamilton Gallery in

1979 shows how protective and concerned we were for each other's well-being, even if we were business competitors.

One day, Bill Cosby came into my gallery to buy a painting. Bill was at the height of his acting career, between his comedy act, TV specials, and *The Bill Cosby Show* early in the decade (with a mega-hit series to follow in the mid-1980s), the *Fat Albert* cartoons, his work on *Electric Company*, and so much more. He was the most beloved and successful actor-comedian in America, the only person crossing over between kids and adults. Since he and I were both from Philadelphia and attended Temple University, sharing the same English Literature professor, we spoke comfortably with each other and shared a few laughs.

After Bill committed to buying the painting, he left and next visited Jill Kornblee's gallery, where he told her how much he liked me. Flattering, right?

Later, Jill called me to pass the message along. As I began smiling on the other end of the phone, delighted that Bill enjoyed our conversation as much as I did, her tone grew serious. "If he invites you to his apartment or hotel suite, have a prepared excuse, and *do not go*. Even if it means picking up cash."

"Why?" I asked.

"He's a leach. Beware."

Sure enough, Bill invited me to his suite. "A museum curator is on their way for an appointment, so I can't come over," I said. "I will send Jay to pick up the cash and deliver the painting."

Bill declined. Given what we all know about Bill Cosby today, I'm very happy I listened. It is easy to imagine what would have happened. I dodged a bullet.

I don't think dealers today would express the care or concern that Jill showed me in that situation.

. . .

If anything aptly describes the sad state of the art world today, it would be collectors known as "bottom feeders." These are generally rich guys who offer starving artists nickels on the dollar for their work and buy it in bulk. However, there have always been bottom feeders. When I owned Hamilton Gallery, Sid Singer was the biggest bottom feeder around. He wanted to buy all the work for 50% of the retail value. At last count, he owns more than 1,000 works of art, many by artists that no one cares about anymore. Most dealers won't have anything to do with him, since he feels dealers should not make any money.

One time, Sid commissioned Peter Gourfain to fabricate bronzes and then wanted me to reproduce the bronze in color in the catalogue when I did a show for him at 112 Greene Street Gallery. "No," I said. So he made a black and white poster of the bronze and didn't have the phone number correct. Talk about penny-wise and pound-foolish!

Just five years ago, I told Sid to digitize his 1,000-plus piece collection. He won't spend the money to do it and never took JPEGS of the paintings. His family will be screwed when he dies.

Switching coasts, the biggest bottom feeder in L.A. was a private dealer and consultant nicknamed by the *New York Times* the "Patron Saint." He's also called the Donald Trump of the Art World, and sees no reason why our world can't just be reduced to numbers. Many galleries, like LA's prestigious gallery Blum & Poe, won't let him into their space. He came out of the film industry and ended up in the computer field with no art historical background. He sees nothing wrong with "flipping" pictures—buying the work of a "hot artist" and putting it up at auction a year or two later, strictly for the quick profit.

The Patron Saint of Art Dealers didn't stop there. He decided to specialize in promoting young artists—or should I say, exploit artists who are broke. Sometimes he provides studio space, pays them ten cents on the dollar and proceeds to own everything they make in the studio. It's kind of like most music producers and managers in the 1960s and 1970s. Then he turns around and sells the work to his group of collectors who are movie producers, poker players, professional athletes, and doctors. He calls this group his Club. They rely purely on his vision—no due diligence, provenance, establishment of authenticity, or nothing. What vision? He has promoted the work of a few artists who have hit it big. If the artist isn't painting the way he wants them to, he becomes abusive. If the collector does not do his bidding, he is abusive to that person as well. Once his "little bubble" of clients all buy paintings, he is done with them and the artist is sometimes ruined. Consequently, he has ended up in lawsuits with artists and clients.

With all these currents and crosscurrents ripping through the art world I once knew, and ridiculous amounts of money flying around at the cost of *art appreciation*, it took something entirely out of everyone's control to bring things to a skidding halt.

CHAPTER 23

COVID Hits—and A Big Surprise Follows

When the members of the Art Dealers Association assembled at The Armory for the Spring 2020 ADAA Fair, no one knew that the plague was coming. We'd heard of a flu-like illness spreading out of China and likely to reach America, but it didn't matter: the fair was packed with business moving in the busy exhibitor booths. Buyers, collectors, gawkers, and dealers alike carried on, maybe not hugging and kissing, but certainly showing their love with their wallets. Business was brisk.

After getting my fill of the ADAA Fair, I flew back to California on March 6. The plane was delayed. By now, the prospect of the flu-like illness with quite the regal name—Coronavirus—hitting our shores was more than the typical concern we have with any flu season. It was a full-blown fear. When I flew in winter, I had a standing habit of wearing a mask to avoid catching colds and the flu. Never did I realize the importance of wearing a mask more than after watching what happened after getting home.

New York was overwhelmed first, shuttering the city and, with it, thousands of art galleries and the art world. Then-Gov. Andrew Cuomo closed all businesses and urged people to stay inside. People across the country thought he overreacted or was overly paranoid, but many other cities quickly followed suit. In New York, they ran out of personal protective equipment and supplies for nurses and doctors, and hospitals were at capacity. At first, no one knew how to treat the illness, and no medicines were available; it was the HIV/AIDs disaster all over again, only this time, involving the entire population. New York officials set up The Javits center for emergency COVID-19 work and positioned refrigerator trucks in the parking lot of most hospitals to take on quickly dying patients, because morgues and funeral homes could not take anymore.

Then-President Donald Trump didn't help. He ignored scientists and said wearing a mask was unnecessary. He and his adviser and son-in-law, Jared Kushner, initially withheld funding and equipment assistance to New York and neighboring New Jersey, the two hardest-hit places in the world in Spring 2020, because *they were Democratic states.* How callous and uncaring can you get? I thought presidents were supposed to protect their citizens, not endanger them. Even after being infected months later and taken seriously ill, Trump advised that wearing a mask was optional, a personal choice—and turned it into a political statement that resulted in nearly half the country refusing to vaccinate or wear masks. And on the pandemic marched, variant after variant.

For the remainder of 2020, the whole world shut down.

Needless to say, museums and galleries were closed. All art fairs were called off. People left the city in droves. If they had a country house, they packed their bags, took the drive, and stayed. For months, even a year or two.

In Spring 2020, as COVID-19 wreaked its first wave of what became several waves of havoc, the Swiss art dealer and Levy Gorvy gallery co-owner Dominique Levy was interviewed on YouTube about sales. Every gallery that could do so was putting their art online, just like every other business able to function through the internet. She said expensive works did not sell online, and the online art fairs were a bust. She said her business was down 80%. Larry Gagosian admitted his business was down 30%, but everyone in the industry knew that was an understatement; it was probably closer to 50%. People were holding onto their money, uncertain when the shutdown would end, when society would return to normal, how badly the economy would suffer, and if the government had any plans to offer relief packages.

What did art dealers do? Those with means took their businesses to the places to which affluent city dwellers and art buyers escaped. They rented spaces in the Hamptons. COVID-19 or no COVID-19, the Hampton realtors stuck to their very tough guns, and rented spaces for on two-year leases. Not six months, nor a year. Two years. Then, once they'd collected from those able to afford it, the realtors laid down more laws. To enter a gallery, your temperature was first taken. Appointments had to be made in advance. Very few visitors were let into the gallery at the same time.

Neither history nor the new regulations were kind to the "expat" dealers. Art has never sold in the Hamptons, and sure enough, it didn't sell in the Summer of 2020.

Wealthy New Yorkers, those who buy the most art, are Hamptons or Catskill recreationists in the summer and snowbirds in the winter. To try to survive the ongoing lockdown in New York, several galleries took note of that and rented spaces to sell to the winter crowd in Palm Beach, Florida. Collector Beth de Woody has a home there, so the gallery openings featured Beth and her friends. Smart move. Also, the Acquavella family, which has run its gallery in New York since 1960, has a home in Palm Beach. Renting a winter space there seemed logical, but then New York dealers with no previous ties followed: Paula Cooper, Zwirner, Pace, Lehman Maupin, White Cube, and Steve Wynn, to name a few. It also did not turn out so well, I hear. Evidently, there are only six collectors in Palm Beach able to buy from these galleries. For the snowbirds who like real snow, a few New York dealers found temporary solace in gallery space in Aspen, Colorado.

During all of this, numerous galleries closed for good, including New York dealer Gavin Brown, who went into business with Barbara Gladstone, and Metro Pictures, which shut down at the end of 2021.

Museums were also hit particularly hard. Many small museums did not make it, and large museums took massive hits to revenue and bottom lines that will take years to recoup. More than a third of America closed temporarily, and 15% shuttered permanently—and it is not over yet, as new variants bring new waves, including the Winter 2021-22 wave. Fully 30% of a museum's income comes from admissions, gift shop sales, restaurants, and special tours—and it all fell by the wayside.

I'm a people person, and what pains me greatly is who this pandemic most deeply affected: the employees of galleries and museums. Large museums have had to lay off hundreds of staff. Smaller museums and galleries not only had to permanently lay off workers when they closed, but where would those employees find work? Even the old fallback for artistic types, working in restaurants, was out: the restaurants were closed, too. To date, art museums, galleries and nonprofit institutions have laid off masses of people.

One market remained remarkably unaffected by COVID-19—the auction market. For a change, Sotheby's is ahead of Christie's for the first time in years. They have reported that their market sales are down 15%, while Christie's market is down 20%. While not numbers you'd normally celebrate, in the 2020-2021 time period, that's a measure of success. They have found a great deal of luck with contemporary artists. Several hot young artists are getting six-figure sales, like Salmon Toor and Christine Quarles, and black artists at large are greatly boosting sales. However, private sales are through the roof. Christie's and Sotheby's have seen a remarkable upswing, with Sotheby's up by 50% and Christie's 57%. A lack of art fairs during the pandemic helped the auction private market, along with the surging Asian markets. Online sales are way up.

As for the emergence and popularity of black artists, the new surge has not gone unnoticed. David Zwirner Gallery has hired a black director and staff for a space that only shows black artists in Chelsea, New York. Gagosian has done the same.

. . .

We have largely emerged from the social and business shutdowns of the pandemic, though the pandemic is by no means over. Out of the COVID-19 fog also arises two huge surprises, certainly compared to what many of my friends and I saw in the crystal ball just a few years ago: the re-emergence of new and improved art fairs and galleries, tailor-made for a fickle 2020s crowd notoriously short on attention span and brand loyalty and ready to switch to the internet at a moment's notice.

I'll tell you how surprised (and delighted) I am: *very*. When I sketched out an early version of this memoir some time ago, here is what I wrote:

Needless to say, it is very hard to compete with mega galleries. The middle gallery, which promoted artists in mid-career like I did at Hamilton Gallery, is all but gone. I think going forward, galleries will either be huge, like Gagosian, Hauser & Wirth, or David Zwirner, or the small mom-and-pop varieties. There simply are not that many collectors to support 300 contemporary galleries in L.A. Some opened specifically to keep their major artists exclusive to themselves. I think L.A. will reduce all the way down to 50 galleries, the way it was when I moved here in 1990. New York will cut back as well. A smaller art world is coming, I predict.

Well, surprise, surprise! A new and electric momentum started rumbling like a low-grade earthquake pre-pandemic, and then came roaring out of it. I now sit right in the middle of the action in LA, in two different ways: the proliferation (rather than shrinking) of galleries and the booming Asian art market, which interacts deeply with LA and its large and culturally sophisticated Asian population. Sean Kelly, Zwirner, Sargent's Daughters, James Fuentes, and at least ten New York galleries are opening in L.A.

Today, more and more New York dealers think more than the weather makes it hot in L.A., and they're opening up. They use their L.A. space to offer works to the larger world, given L.A.'s portal-like location to the smoking hot Asian market. One dealer said that they would presell the shows to L.A., the artists would love the resulting exposure, and that it's cheaper to open in L.A. than in New York City.

Therefore, they are pouring into the Western District, which now houses the showpieces of more than 100 private galleries city-wide, plus annexes and branches. Only New York is more populated. Among the larger galleries, you are considered a nobody if you don't have branches in L.A. and elsewhere. For instance, Various Small Fires, opened by Esther Kim in L.A. in 2012, expanded to Seoul, Korea in 2019 and Dallas after that. The L.A. gallery shows Billy Al Bengston, Calida Rawles, Will Gabaldon, and other hot contemporary artists. And Anat Egbi now has two galleries in LA and soon to be opened a gallery in New York, with her flagship gallery sitting within Bentley's left-hand turn from Beverly Hills and its many buyers and collectors in the Wilshire District. Another is in the once-again-trendy Los Feliz District, on the northside of L.A. And the third is on the Lower East Side of New York.

They are not alone. I put together a list of galleries with branches all over the world. As of May 2022, Hauser and Worth had 17 galleries throughout the world, with Gagosian at 15 and growing. Following them are galleries like Pace (nine worldwide), Zwirner (eight), White Cube (six), Matthew Marks (five), and Miles McInerney, who has three based in New York. Plus those I just mentioned.

As for the industry-wide fear that many of New York's galleries would shutter en masse because of declining business, art fairs, and the knockout punch of COVID-19? At last count, more than 1,000 are thriving—a far higher number than I thought possible just a few years ago.

But there's a catch. When I opened Hamilton Gallery in 1978, I put together a couple hundred thousand dollars from my investors and managed to open the doors. Today, to open a mega-gallery or a gallery with branches, I estimate one needs a total of $1 billion at various points of the process.

The other massive revival comes from art fairs. Recently, I talked to a New York art dealer, and he said the 2000 ArtBasel Miami Fair, which *Bonfire of the Vanities* author Tom Wolfe used as his backdrop for his final novel *Back to Blood,* began the current resurgence. It brought new excitement, lavish and sometimes wild parties, private planes, and plenty of celebrities. No one had seen anything like it. Dealers saw a market opportunity before their eyes, and if their galleries weren't huge, they went to where the extra buyers were, some exhibiting in six to ten fairs per year.

In mid-February 2022, I grabbed my ticket to VIP Day, jumped in the car, and headed to the Frieze Los Angeles fair in Beverly Hills. The show was extraordinary. It was very active with celebrities galore and dealers selling out their booths. There were quality art dealers there, including a lot of Europeans. Amidst all the trade fair buzz, I heard something quite extraordinary: everyone but everyone was moving to L.A. from New York, Europe, and elsewhere. In a delayed way, that confirmed my earlier thoughts from 2015. I don't know, for instance, if Matthew Marks sells out his shows here, but I do know the fair offered more inventory for the hot sellers to sell.

What Frieze Los Angeles further confirmed to me was that art fairs are busier than ever—something I never imagined before the pandemic. Art fairs are held in major cities every month, sometimes five fairs in a single city over the course of a year, particularly in Miami and New York. The onsite buzz is contagious, and sales are brisk. I believe part of it comes from people finally released from up to two years of shutdown, growing tired of looking at JPEGs, socializing and doing business online, and just being *happy* to see each other again. The other part comes from the current fairs' appeal to the pocketbook and the eye, especially with the prevalence and timeliness of contemporary art from a diverse group of artists in all ways—style, subject, ethnic, and racial background. We've never before seen such diversity or bolder presentations on center stage by young artists. There have always been young breakthroughs, and we saw our share in the 1960s and 1970s—Andy Warhol and Julian Schnabel—but never as the center of an industry-wide marketing effort, from galleries to resales to auctions.

So much for my earlier theory of art fairs.

It leaves me very excited to keep my feet in the middle of the pool, which might sound odd for someone celebrating 50 years in the business—but I've got some very fun and ambitious plans of my own.

CHAPTER 24

I'll Never Stop Pushing the Envelope

I *love* curating shows, whether gallery exhibitions, pop-ups, or shows in other venues. Perhaps that's because I started doing it early on, when I curated for the Crispo Gallery in the early 1970s. Or, that curating requires a combined knowledge and appreciation of art history, the market, promoting and dealing with the media, how to present a room and a work, how to produce a highest-class catalogue, and how to work with artists and dealers to make the exhibition as great and memorable as possible. It requires creativity, a good eye, some ingenuity, strong people skills, and a level business mind—a 360-degree view of what I love about this business. Not to mention the thrill of discovering emerging artists or helping those in mid-career find new audiences and a new passion for their work.

Curating runs deep in my blood and might be the biggest reason I feel the fire for what I do. I love good art that is so edgy, intelligent, and evocative that it knocks me off my chair. When I look at it, I fall in love all over again with our capacity as human beings to create and originate, especially when it comes to female artists, which I love to promote in this industry that has woefully underpromoted them—a major objective of mine moving forward.

Some might say, "Patty, after 50 years in this business, you've done it all. Aren't you ready for a well-deserved rest and to reminisce about your experiences?" *Hell, no!* That would not be the Patricia Hamilton I see in the mirror every day. Simple as that.

I curated many shows in the first 15 years of my career, starting with other galleries, then as one of the nation's first independent traveling exhibition curators, and right through my years owning Hamilton Gallery. After that, I moved into the artist and representative phase for another 15 years—and found myself missing the action, which led me to begin guest curating shows.

In 2000, I was asked by my friend Dick Pollich of Tallix Foundry to curate Gold and Silver, a show of sculptors to work in gold and silver. These works would be made at the foundry and then circulated to galleries all over the country. I selected Frank Stella, Peter Shelton, Ursula von Rydingsvard, my old friend Isaac Witkin, Bill Harper, Bryan Hunt, Maya Linn, and Kiki Smith, among others. Only one artist, Maya Linn, worked in gold. We put together the show, a traveling exhibition, and opened that summer in the Baldwin Gallery in Aspen, Colorado. After that, we traveled to Boca Raton, New Orleans, and New York.

The show reignited my passion for creating—big time. My "day jobs" as an agent and then a reseller kept me busy, but I knew I wanted to curate again. I began looking for the right opportunities.

The first came in 2007 through an article I read in *The New York Times*. The article stated that Indian Art was the next big thing. It mentioned Peter Nagy, the owner of several galleries in India, who I knew from his East Village days. He was the perfect man to contact, a delightful, smart, personable guy who really knew the scene there. It would be hard to find someone who didn't like Peter. I emailed and then met him at the Miami Art Fair. While I was thinking about independent curating, Peter had something else in mind: he wanted me to open a branch of his gallery, Nature Morte, in Los Angeles. "No," I said, certainly appreciating his offer. "I think strange things are going on in business." This was true: the housing bubble and its disastrous subprime mortgage pipeline was beginning to burst, about to take the stock market and entire economy down with it.

However, Peter and I worked out a deal for what I really wanted: to curate two shows at Western Projects and Den, located in the West Los Angeles community of Culver City. These shows, which took place in the Summer of 2008, came with a special twist: they included 100% women artists. We featured mix-media sculpturist Anita Dube, fascinating conceptual artist Mithu Sen, women's rights activist and photographer Sheba Chhachhi, figurative and abstract painter and printmaker Shobha Broota, whose works have a meditative quality, and Chitra Ganesh, who works with everything from drawings to murals. This group captured many forms of art, and also many views of looking at the world. They also had a 32-year age range between them, from Chitra, the youngest, to Shooba.

The show "Contradictions and Complexities: Contemporary Art from India" was a huge hit. It landed three reviews in the Los Angeles *Times*—three!—and the openings were packed. It was one of the best-received shows I curated, a show I thoroughly enjoyed hanging out with. We divided this uber-talented pool of exhibiting artists between two galleries, showing the photography and edgier art at Den, and the paintings at Western Projects. The only factor separating the show from perfection was, sadly, a major factor: we didn't sell as much as we'd expected. We made some sales, but this was the summer all hell broke loose with the economy. Shortly afterward, Den ended up closing, and sadly, Western Projects followed two years later.

In the mid-2010s, I became friendly with Eva Chimento from Chimento Contemporary Art and suggested we do a show at her gallery, focused on the bustling scene in Bushwick, Brooklyn. An old artist I represented at Hamilton Gallery, Michael David, broke out a Facebook bullhorn to sing his praises about Bushwick, how it was like SoHo in the '70s, and all the artists living there. As with Williamsburg a decade ago, Bushwick was on the cultural rise, with young people flocking in, and lofts, catchy galleries, and other trendy living arrangements were available. They even have a very cool little art fair and, in 2017, no less than 15 very well-received exhibitions. The area hasn't seen such excitement since the Brooklyn Dodgers owned the place, but that was way back in 1958.

I got to work with Eva. In the Winter of 2017, I curated "Straight Outta Bushwick," a show that included the work of large-scale abstractionist C. Michael Norton (who painted on linen), painter Brenda Goodman, painter Farrell Brickhouse, who used color to illustrate archetypes and myths, Dana James, who does pouring and mark making exquisitely, and multi-material sculptor Daniel John Gadd, who works in everything from oil, plaster and copper to steel, mirrored glass and string. And more.

Behind the scenes, there was some drama. Michael David had teamed up with Keith Schweitzer and formed the Schweitzer/David Gallery, but that partnership quickly fell apart. Today, Keith owns SFA Projects, a gallery in New York, and is an artist representative, arts organizer, and curator himself. Unfortunately, Michael was not on medication and drove me and Eva nuts. Just like he'd driven me nuts in the final two years I owned the Hamilton Gallery. Eva told me that there would be no way she would show any of the artists if it meant dealing with Michael. I had to honor her request, which was sad, because Michael has a great eye for art and artists.

"Straight Outta Bushwick" received blurb reviews. The show was beautiful, and the talk of the town, and sales were brisk. One of the artists, all cutting-edge, was Daniel John Gadd. Also, Brenda Goodman, Farrel Brickhouse, and Michael Norton got exposure in L.A., and they are terrific painters.

The last show I curated was "Kick Ass Painting: Louise Fishman, Brenda Goodman, and Carrie Moyer," which took place at Anat Ebgi's gallery in the Wilshire District. Anat and I met on a plane on the way home from an art fair and really hit it off. I loved her gallery as well; in some ways, it felt like the atmosphere at the Hamilton Gallery, where everyone on staff knew their art, and dealers and collectors really enjoyed visiting and seeing the art she exhibited, all of which was good.

Shortly thereafter, Anat asked me to curate a show. "It must be women," I said. I really felt strongly about promoting women's works and knew the market was hot among collectors and buyers. I wanted the women artists I liked to have every advantage to further their careers and to be recognized for the creative geniuses they were. I had known Louise's work for many years in New York, as well as Brenda's work. Both seemed to be making the paintings of their career. I saw Carrie's work at the New York ADAA art fair in 2020, right before New York City was locked down. Her paintings knocked me out. They were fabulous.

"Kick Ass Painting" was originally scheduled to take place in the Spring of 2020, but Los Angeles was just as locked down as New York and the rest of the country due to the pandemic. We had to wait over a year to present the show, but when we did in June 2021, it was a huge success. I really enjoyed working with the gallery. I found each of Anat's employees terrific. Sadly, the Los Angeles *Times* has released all its part-time critics during COVID-19, so we did not get an Los Angeles *Times* review.

I survey the state-of-the-art world today, though I sometimes feel like I need to hit "pause." Especially when asked the question, "Would I do it again?" Honestly, with the current atmosphere and approach to how art is viewed and how it fits into people's lives, I lean toward, "No, I wouldn't."

Today's art world is so much different. The creation of art it-self is an eternal act: someone will always see and feel something profound and deep, and express it in whatever form suits them—painting, sculpture, drawing, canvas, bronze or gold, wall murals, steel, paper, oil, acrylic, you name it. We've been doing it for at least 40,000 years, as the prehistoric paintings in the Lascaux Caves of France indicate, and we will be doing it 40,000 years from now.

However, what really hurts to see is that, above all, art has become a commodity, more so than a creative expression to be admired and treasured. People buy and sell it and put it in warehouses, then turn around and sell it again. Sometimes, they never even see their work. They transact their business by viewing digital photos, known as JPGs. Just as disappointing, if not more so, fewer dealers appreciate the beauty and history of art. Very few have art history back-grounds; they focus purely on profits and what hot trend or style is selling this week. Consequently, a great deal of art has become pretty ugly, certainly when you compare it to any past period of time.

Back in the day, when galleries were the galaxies of the art uni-verse, there was an old expression: "How do you make a million dollars selling art?" "Well, you start with two million."

Dealers loved art. They loved the process, the creation, and the beauty of what they put in their galleries and sold. They invested in the works and made sure their galleries properly showcased them. Today, sadly, that is an extremely rare quality. So is the practice of dealers working together, exhibiting together, "battling in the trenches" in unison, and having each other's back. It's very dog-eat-dog now.

Art dealers like art that sells. Period. If a show doesn't sell, the artist is out. The galleries have 40 to 50 other artists lined up to take that spot—and they're out, too, if their work doesn't sell.

This leads to the question, *what to do next?* I would enjoy museum work because it ties together art history, educating guests, and putting together exhibitions of great artists, but there is no money in that. I know I will never own a gallery again, and my days of being an artist representative, agent, and consultant are over as well.

But when it comes to curating shows? How about putting together exhibitions of excellent artists for those rare gallery owners who do carry old-school values and sensibilities about what they hang on their walls?

You bet—and my eyes are focused on the same place as the art world at large: Asia. Everybody's opening there. It's red fucking hot. When I look at the New York or LA-based galleries branching out in the world, virtually all now have branches in Seoul or Hong Kong. However, since the Chinese took over Hong Kong in 2021, businesses have been deserting like a sinking ship. They're going to Seoul, where there are no taxes and no oppressive governments. The big Frieze art fair series is moving to Seoul. When I attended Frieze L.A. in late February 2022, the place was packed with Korean buyers, dealers, and others from that major hotspot.

I can describe the attraction of Seoul in three words: "Clients! No taxes!" It is full of clients that art dealers have never met. Most are under 45, and they're buying like crazy. Esther Kim Varet, the owner of Various Small Fires, tells me she has more clients from Seoul than she can count. But here's the thing: They primarily buy art that sells for under $25,000. Still, they are buying like crazy. Esther opened in Seoul years ago because she speaks Korean and has a whole Korean staff there. She was one of the first.

During a conversation I had with Esther's director, he told me that people call all the time and ask where to stay. They are coming to Seoul to buy. I saw Esther at the Billy Al Bengston opening, and to that point, very few things had sold. Two weeks later, the show was practically sold out.

· · ·

I have a new idea for a show called Meditation, which prominently promotes women artists. Just as I have been a feminist from day one. I've decided to curate more shows besides "Meditation," because, unbelievably, as we approach the mid-2020s, their works are still half the price of men. As a simple believer in equal pay for equal work, I find this ludicrous. But the popularity of women in the arts is through the roof. Look at the 2022 Venice Biennale. This entire show featured women artists. The United States showed a black woman for the first time, rightly featured on the front page of the Arts & Leisure section of *The New York Times*. While Cindy Sherman does well at auction, though, most women don't.

How can this be? Well, it comes down to the dealers: galleries continue to drag their feet to show women. When I was showing women more than half the time at the Hamilton Gallery in the late '70s, that was unheard of. And I took a heap of shit for it. *Whatever!* The fact Grace Hartigan had to show as George Hartigan in the Abstract Expressionist years? That Lila Hartnett had to write as a guy? That's what is shitty.

Moving forward, I'm going to push hard to undo this inequity, while keeping my eyes open for art that knocks me off my chair. I got into this world to bring together an artist, her or his work, and a happy buyer or collector to behold a piece that moves them in some way.

Next stop: Asia. Where the clients are ready, the art scene is hot, and the next 50 years begins for me. See you at the next show!

Acknowledgments

I would like to thank all of you who told me that I should write a book. I was such a good storyteller. But boy, is it hard. It took me ten years and many editors. So first of all, I would like to thank the editors: Charles Rappleye, Tulsa Kinney, and Robert Yehling.

The friends who encouraged me to keep writing: Christopher Ford, Paul Gardner, Terry McInerney, Mary MacNaughton, Lowery Sims, and my niece, Nancy Geer Hamilton who was beyond helpful.

I am grateful to all the artists and dealers who contributed to this project. I'm especially grateful to the artists: Peter Alexander, Fred Eversely, Jill Moser, John O'Brien, the head of the Deborah Remington Trust, Margaret Matthews Berensen, and Robert Wilhite. Among the dealers that encouraged me to keep writing were George Adams, Riva Blumenthal, Eva Chimento, Jim Kelly, and Ronald Sosinski.

I want to especially thank my lawyer, Jack Sherer.

About the Author

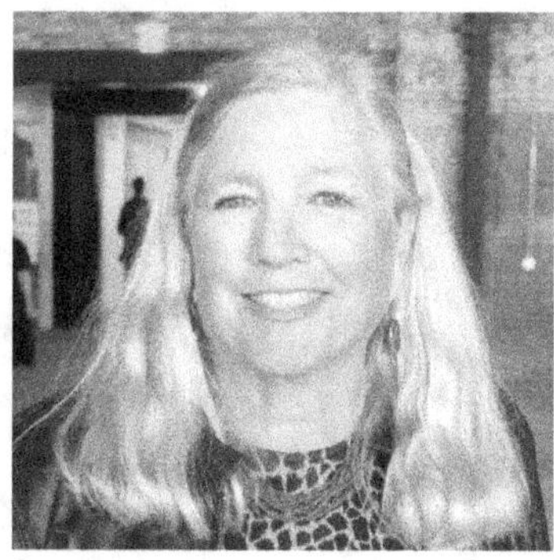

Patricia Hamilton has been involved in the art world for fifty years. First as assistant to Robert Doty at the Whitney Museum, then as Senior Editor of Art in America. Finally, she found her calling as a dealer and was Curator of Exhibitions at the Andrew Crispo Gallery. At the age of 26, she opened her own gallery on 57th Street, the Hamilton Gallery of Contemporary Art. This was 1977, and 10% of women were dealers, and most had family money. She raised all the money to open and showed 60-70% women. She wanted to show mid-career artists who had been ignored by the world. What better reason to show women? She showed Louise Bourgeois (for the first time in a commercial gallery in 15 years), Grace Hartigan, Deborah Remington, and Joan Snyder. Six of the artists have attained blue chip status. Aside from Louise, Deborah, and Joan, she would include Ron Gorchov, Sam Gilliam, and Robert Colescott. Then due to a family tragedy, she closed in 1984 and became an artist's agent. She rented pop-up spaces and showed artists in New York, Chicago, and Los Angeles.

In 1990, she moved to Los Angeles before it was fashionable. She became the first director of Salander-O'Reilly Gallery and then went off on her own, selling art to Hollywood collectors.

Today, she lives in Whitley Heights in Los Angeles with her two dogs and is peaceful and content.